ANCIENT GODS
and
HUMAN ORIGINS

A Sitchin Studies Book

Neil Freer

THE BOOK TREE
San Diego, California

© 2019 Ursula Freer

All rights reserved

No part of this publication may be used or transmitted in any way without the expressed written consent of the publisher, except for short excerpts for use in reviews.

ISBN 978-1-58509-155-3

Cover Art
© Andrey VP

Interior and cover layout
Paul Tice

Editor
Paul Tice

Published by
The Book Tree
San Diego, California

www.thebooktree.com

We provide fascinating and educational products to help awaken the public to new ideas and information that would not be available otherwise.
Call 1 (800) 700-8733 for our FREE BOOK TREE CATALOG.

CONTENTS

Foreword………………………………………………….............5

Introduction…………………………………………………........9

Chapter One
Mythology Unmasked……………....……………………………13

Chapter Two
Alien Contact in the Remote Past………………………..…….35

Chapter Three
Planet X and Geo-Catastrophes………………………………....49

Chapter Four
Ancient Aliens and Modern Astronomy………………………....61

Chapter Five
Hidden Truth of Human Origins……………………….......…....67

Chapter Six
Sitchin's Extensive Evidence….………................………………85

Chapter Seven
Return of the Red Sun……………………….…..………………..101

Chapter Eight
Human Evolution on Steroids: The DNA of the Gods……………111

Chapter Nine
Beyond the Illusion…………………………….…..………………137

Chapter Ten
The Vatican Connection..143

Chapter Eleven
The Oopart Dilemma.......................................…....................149

Chapter Twelve
Preparing for Nibiru.............................…..........................155

Chapter Thirteen
Approaching Godhood: What Happens Next..…....…................163

Appendix I
The Alien Question: An Expanded Perspective.....…..................171

Appendix II
Saving Sapiens: A White Paper to Leaders of the World
A Briefing for All Heads of State of Planet Earth:
The Essential Survival Operations Necessary to Preserve
Our Species' Existence...…..195

About the Author ...…...…......204

FOREWORD

This is the fourth book authored by Neil Freer, whose previous titles were based on the work of Zecharia Sitchin. That is the case with this one, but with a major difference. His earlier books cover the implications of Sitchin's work for us today, so require a basic familiarity. With this book one can skip the neccesity of Freer's other titles. It stands on its own as a great introduction to Sitchin's work, which leads directly into a course of serious study.

Who was Zecharia Sitchin and why was his work so important? Freer explains it better than anyone, but we will include some basic information here. Sitchin was one of about 200 people who could translate the oldest known form of writing on Earth, the Sumerian cuneiform texts from the ancient Middle East. It is here where the original creation stories and the flood story were found, both of which appeared in the bible in shorter and less detailed versions. Various other detailed stories of the gods have also been unearthed from this area. Sitchin came to the conclusion that many of these stories, long considered myth, were in fact real events and that the "gods" themselves were real. His research is fascinating and extensive. It includes information on their home planet called Nibiru, which is believed to orbit our own solar system in an elongated path, thereby allowing a periodic return of these gods. Nibiru is said to have an internal heat source similar to other planetary bodies, which conceivably supports their existence.

These ancients "gods" came here for the purpose of mining. They did so extensively, but became weary of the toil. A solution was needed. As detailed in ancient texts, they formed a new creation out of ancient man using "clay," quite likely by changing or manipulating human DNA. After a number of failed experiments, these visitors successfully infused ancient man, this new creation, with their own DNA, thereby providing them with proficient workers for these mines. This also resulted in a major jump in human evolution, which could explain the long-standing, evolutionary mystery of the "missing link."

This basic premise involving the gods and our creation is found in Sumerian cuneiform documents, which were translated and discussed by numerous scholars long before Sitchin came along. This is not some "crazy idea" that came out of the mouth of Sitchin. It is a clear and basic story detailing how mankind was "created" by these gods, found in these ancient documents which anyone can read. Later, Sitchin fills in more details based on his knowledge of cuneiform, archaeological evidence, and first-hand travels into ancient lands undertaken to examine related ruins. For three years, off and on, I accompanied Sitchin on many of these travels as his personal videographer, documenting the evidence, and can vouch for the fact that he left no stone unturned.

Although Sitchin passed on in 2010, the research to support his work has continued—with much of it assembled and examined in this book. Sitchin and Freer were close friends and shared a great deal of information. Sitchin wrote the Introduction to Freer's first book in 1987, *Breaking the Godspell*, because it was the first time he recognized another author's work as being important and worthy.

In Sitchin's later years and following his death, his work had come under attack from some sources. This book can, in large part, be an answer to the critics. It brings together information as to how and why some of the world's most brilliant people have backed Sitchin's research. It is best to leave it to Freer to explain this, and for the reader to examine it.

The critics have pointed to a somewhat newly published "dictionary" of ancient Sumerian to attempt to show how Sitchin either mistakenly or intentionally misinterpreted certain words or phrases in order to support his theories. A widely available Sumerian dictionary did not exist during the time Sitchin wrote his first few books. He translated much of his work directly, while conducting most of his research in the British Museum in London. Despite this criticism, one should keep in mind that the basic premise Sitchin stands on—the existence of the gods based on ancient texts—is rock solid. The stories of the Sumerian gods (with equivalents throughout the world) plainly and clearly remain, concerning the direct activity of gods in the great flood, the creation of mankind, and their existence in the ancient world in general. No dictionary, Sumerian or otherwise, can remove these gods from antiquity.

Cuneiform started out as a symbolic language that could allow different meanings for many words, depending on context. One must understand the context of usage before jamming in standard meanings from a dictionary that was created centuries later, by Akkadians (who had transformed the symbols into script), which some critics have blindly done. Many nuances can be and have been lost, unless one recognizes the context of usage—which Sitchin claimed to have done.

The dictionary still offers a more complete understanding of the language. Sitchin was not perfect and the dictionary now allows a better context, in some cases, that Sitchin did not see. We must be fair on all sides. He was a pioneer and pioneers, being the first into uncharted areas, cannot help but make mistakes. Despite the errors he may have made, he also made important breakthoughs.

Sitchin's work has been supported by highly educated, respected people the world over—none of whom are stupid. Do not be distracted by the naysayers, but examine the evidence found within this book first, and then decide for yourself. Neil Freer was an incredibly brilliant philosopher who chose to devote a large part of his life proving out Sitchin's work, getting the world to notice it, and exploring, better than anyone, the implications for us all. Dare I say, there was no better person to write this book, including Sitchin himself, because Freer understood clearly what this work means for mankind today—and into the future. His goal was to bring the work of Zecharia Sitchin to the next level and this book succeeds brilliantly in that endeavor.

It had always been Freer's intention to create a Sitchin Studies program to help with this process. A few of the chapters in this book were part of a Sitchin Studies on-line university class he taught for a few years before his passing in 2016. It has been our job, as his publisher, to assemble all other related information from his vast research and computer files to form the best collection of Sitchin Studies material available, brought together in this one book. It is far more extensive than his original class and the material he, Sitchin, and others presented at the First Sitchin Studies Day (found in the book *Of Heaven and Earth*). Not only does it cover Sitchin's main thesis, it powerfully presents the implications for us all in the modern world, which Sitchin never covered.

Although written by philosopher and futurist Neil Freer, this book began thousands of years ago, with the oldest recorded stories in the world—found, translated and interpreted by other scholars long before Neil Freer and Sitchin. These records speak of the gods having been here on Earth. Sitchin based his work on these solid documents, coupled by extensive first-hand research at archaeological sites, and was not trying to fool anyone. Both he and Freer were trying to go deeper—to bring the truth of who we are and where we came from out into the open. There can be no question for anyone reading the works of Freer and Sitchin—they were both exceptionally brilliant people, which is exemplified in this book.

Throughout the ancient world are scattered important clues that can reveal who we really are and where we came from. If these clues can be pieced together, this great puzzle can be solved once and for all. As these pieces are assembled, found largely throughout this work, everything starts to make sense. Explore it and see for yourself. This important book should be in the library of anyone interested in the origins of mankind.

Paul Tice

INTRODUCTION

We have reached a point in our development as a species where we can begin to re-examine our history. Is the current story true? Are we a product of evolution or creation? Or is an alternate story worthy of credible examination? Where did we come from and is it possible that our origins have an ET connection?

In this book, we will ask this question through the eyes of venerable Sumerian scholar Zecharia Sitchin, who presents a compelling argument as to our extraterrestrial beginnings. This revolutionary new worldview, already intruding on the common consciousness, finally answers the perennial questions about our beginnings and development as a species. The archaeological and historical evidence recovered over the past one hundred and fifty years demonstrates clearly that we are a hybrid (part alien) species created by the Anunnaki by genetic engineering two hundred thousand years ago. But this profound paradigm, with its transforming ramifications, is being generally resisted, even suppressed, by the religious, mainstream academic and scientific arenas for less than noble reasons. This book introduces and explores comprehensively Sitchin's Nobel Prize-worthy works, developed in his Earth Chronicles series of books.

Zecharia Sitchin

If his findings are true, how does it affect our worldview? What are the social, cultural, economic, and political implications? How does it change the very way in which we should view our world, both personally and collectively? What are the evolutionary implications for mankind itself?

Together, we will examine and address our current planetary situation against the broad context of exopolitics. Exopolitics is defined as "the sociopolitical relationship between human and alien species." It is intended to offer a new and exciting perspective from which to examine our current socio-economic-political arena. It affords us a perspective from the leading edge of our species' development from which to view and understand ourselves now, socially, culturally, and evolutionarily in terms of IQ, CQ and EQ (Intelligence, Consciousness, and Evolutionary Quotients).

This book will examine the ramifications of this radically new world view, apply this new paradigm to our current situation and plot a concrete path forward for the maximum benefit of each individual and species involved.

In any social, philosophical or scientific study, it is imperative that the serious student, scholar or investigator be thoroughly aware of the premises at basis of the work at focus. Premises comprise, variously, the sets of data, assumptions, dogmas, laws, rules… falsehoods, misinformation…. whatever the author being read or studied has *taken for granted* as basis for the work's logical or illogical arguments and conclusions.

The major premises at basis of this book are: We have reached a point in our species development at which we can begin to reexamine our history. We can understand that the mythologies and theologies that have formed and occluded our cultural perspectives can now be set aside for a cosmic view. We will also survey our human technological developments which enabled us to comprehend the advanced technology, from space flight to genetic engineering, attributed to the Anunnaki, our parent species. We will learn the astronomy that identifies the home planet of the Anunnaki, Planet X, Nibiru, tenth in our solar system. Alien species of many types have been visiting Earth for a long time and have made contact with humans over the planet. We have reached a point in our species development at which we can begin to reexamine our history. We can understand that the mythologies and theologies that have formed and occluded our cultural perspectives can now be set aside for a cosmic view.

The agenda and approach for this book is to examine the planetary situation, subsuming, correcting, discarding or integrating the partial scenarios being advanced as they apply to a survey of our species' alien contacts to establish the off-planet context for the basics of our part-alien beginnings, and our history as elucidated for us by the Nobel Prize quality work of the Sumerian scholar, Zecharia Sitchin. We shall develop the ramifications of this radically new world view/paradigm, and apply them to our current situation.

We shall also endeavor to develop a scenario of the most efficient, rapid and sapient means of bringing about our conscious evolutionary Transmutation to the maximum benefit of each individual and the species, which incorporates both long-term cosmic and short-term sociopolitical elements.

The practical goal is simple: implementation of this meta-scenario will effect a consensual, planet-wide, peaceful unification of our conflicted, divided species, beyond nation, religion, culture, civilization in terms of generic humanity, thereby breaking species standstill, enabling us to consensually self-transmute and meet the conditions for entrance into stellar society. This book is an invitation to you, as a thinker, seeker, concerned human, to learn—and contribute—the concepts needed to implement the expansion of species intelligence, consciousness and evolutionary development (from cosmic to practical) to define and refine the direction of the trajectory and accelerate our conscious evolutionary Transmutation.

How to Approach this Work

When I taught college introductory Philosophy courses I would assign one history chapter per week dealing with the philosophical work of one well-known philosopher. The summary of that particular philosopher's work would constitute her or his "version" of the nature of reality or some important part of it. I taught my students to understand best the work of any philosopher by determining her or his basic postulates. A postulate is defined as an unquestioned statement, principal, rule, law, an assumption, something assumed, taken as a starting truth from which to begin to reason and develop one's thoughts and convictions. If one can determine the starting assumption(s) of a philosopher's thought, it becomes rather easy to understand her or his reasoned world-view or personal point of view and to determine one's agreement or disagreement. It is obvious that, if a person begins with an erroneous or false assumption, the rest of her or his philosophy will most likely be flawed. I recommend this approach to study in general and, in this case, to study the Sitchin paradigm.

I have called Zecharia Sitchin "the Darwin of our Day." His contribution is pivotal to the dawning of the new human civilization already upon us. Sitchin makes the clear assumption that the transcultural "gods" were, and are, not mythological but real flesh and blood, three-dimensional humanoid individuals. I have always found Sitchin's scholarship impressive: he presents comprehensive sources and references to demonstrate and prove his claims in a carefully logical sequence. I have always had the greatest respect for his intellectual integrity: Sitchin was raised in a full Jewish context, attended

Biblical school in Israel, where the text was in the older Hebrew. Yet it was in that context that he—at 12 years old—had his first awakening to the possibility of deliberate textual mistranslation or warping. His intellectual acuity and bravery left him no choice but to eventually attempt to cause a revolution of thought within both his own culture and that of the world.

In order to give you a broader view of Sitchin's thesis, I will refer to the writing of the English scholar, Sir Laurence Gardner, who, writing some twenty years after Sitchin's earliest books, contributed profoundly to the filling out of fact and detail to Sitchin's work. And I will refer to my own writings as well. I released *Breaking the Godspell* in 1987, working on the modern ramifications of Sitchin's work. Sitchin published first in 1976, and Gardner, having done incredible research for many years, was able to continue, enhance, and expand the paradigm. My contribution has been to develop the ramifications and make known their profound significance to the general population. So it is accurate to say that the current status of the topic may be understood as the Sitchin-Gardner-Freer paradigm. This book will educate you in all three phases of this topic because it is the most salient and revolutionary subject contributing to intellectual and sociopolitical change currently.

Sitchin and Gardner are both deceased: Sitchin at 90, in 2010; Gardner at 67 in 2010. Both gentlemen should have received more attention for their remarkable contributions. I consider myself privileged to have been associated with them both. So this book will have a threefold aspect: primarily Sitchin's basic thesis, with major elements expanded on by Gardner's penetrating scholarship, including the addition of his Grail expose, and my sparing commentary about current ramifications.

Chapter 1

MYTHOLOGY UNMASKED

This first chapter presents an overview of the Sitchin paradigm and of the current academic attitude regarding it in the modern context.

Our planet, this agonizingly beautiful little planet, is on hold. Seeking relief and release, in a perverse ecology, we recycle outmoded, primitive paradigms. In a time when we are required to deal with the politics of alien realities, we are not able to resolve the separations caused by our intra-species realities. It has rendered us theologically inane, philosophically naive, scientifically cramped, socially isolated, ecologically damaged, politically challenged, and intellectually bewildered.

Yet, whether we chose to acknowledge it or not, we are already well into one of "…those Grand Moments when the whole scale of being is reevaluated," as futurist John Petersen of the Arlington Institute has characterized it. Evolutionarily, we are already into a profound transmutation of our species, which will characterize this 21st Century, and it is no longer feasible to think in partial terms of national, cultural, religious, or civilizational adjustments and solutions.

The crises we face planetarily today cannot be resolved within the context of our current socio-political-economic paradigm. It's all over. Not only must we address our future from outside the box, but the box itself must be reevaluated and redefined. We now have the keys to integrate our past with our present and future in the concept of generic humanity, the critical factor for achieving planetary peace, unity—and matriculation into stellar society— planetary peaceful unity being the only adequate benchmark in these times of profound transition to a new human society and cosmic citizenship.

The most comprehensive, overarching paradigm of the current planetary human situation has four major components: 1) The general alien contact situation. 2) Our true history and development as a part alien, genetically engineered species. 3) The existence, nature and potential threat to Earth and us as a species by the Anunnaki home planet, Planet X, Nibiru. And 4) How to most consciously experience, facilitate and bring about the profound Transmutation of ourselves as a species.

The first three major components are the subjects of separate suppression and cover-ups in the United States, although inextricably interrelated. The acknowledgement or disclosure of any one of these first three topics would immediately raise serious questions about the other. The powers that be do not want that.

Concerning the first component, the general alien situation: We are being observed, monitored, abducted, examined, contacted, and to some degree instructed by a large variety of alien civilizations, many of whom have been here or visited here for thousands of years. We are being invited into stellar society by some of the more advanced species and have been given the rules for matriculation: you get admitted when you reach a species wide, planetary state of unity and peacefulness and you don't take weapons into space—or you don't get admitted. These essential conditions will not be met until we move beyond the Babel-factoring of religious absolutes, at root of most wars and our primitive conflicts, through the restoration of our true history as generic humans. We do not agree about who and what we are and kill each other over those innocent questions.

We cannot continue to try to force our way into space, backing into it as if no one else was there. We need to move from a terracentric focus and become an exosocial species, and soon. We are indeed rising—but in a halting and confused mode, uncertain even about what our preferred future really is. To truly envision our future we must know our past. We must restore our true history and, as a result, deeply understand our real nature, history and potential. Do we have the means to do these things currently? Unequivocally, yes.

Von Daniken asked questions we could not answer about the ooparts (out of place artifacts—tools, toys, technology, architecture, devices—in time) and evidence of advanced civilization recovered in archaeological digs and ruins. We now have the answers. The Nobel Prize quality scholarship of Zecharia Sitchin, through the archaeological, historical, anthropological, astronomical information and artifacts recovered and translated over the last 150 years primarily from the Middle East has afforded us the opportunity to totally reinterpret and understand our beginnings and history.

Zecharia Sitchin, who was my good friend, was one of only 200 scholars of his day able to read and understand Sumerian. The biographical note on Sitchin on his book jackets is quite concise. "Zecharia Sitchin was raised in Palestine, where he acquired profound knowledge of modern and ancient, Hebrew, other Semitic and European languages, the Old Testament, and the history and archeology of the Near East. He attended the London School of Economics and Political Science and graduated from the University of London, majoring in economic history. A leading journalist and editor in Israel for many years, he lived and wrote in New York City. One of the few scholars who could read a cuneiform clay tablet like you and I can read a newspaper, Sitchin based *The Earth Chronicles*, his series of books dealing with Earth's and man's histories and prehistories, on the information and texts written down on clay tablets by the ancient civilizations of the Near East. His books have been widely translated, reprinted in paperback editions, converted to braille for the blind, and featured on radio and television programs."

Sumerian clay tablet with cuneiform writing, the earliest form of writing on Earth.

There are other important facts about Sitchin that will help you gain insight into the details of his thesis. I can draw on my personal experience to explain these nuances because I knew Sitchin quite well—he wrote the introductions to my two first books. He also invited me to do a major presentation at a conference on his work (the first and only Sitchin Studies Day) that he personally organized and resulted in the 1996 book, *Of Heaven and Earth,* of which he and I were both contributors. Two of the other six contributors were university professors with Ph.D.s, who stepped forward with important research, showing that Sitchin's work must be seriously studied. The purpose of this current book is to give people the means to do that, and to understand the ramifications.

Working from 40 years of research, study and translation, Sitchin provided a detailed reinterpretation of that history which had come to be considered mythological: the transcultural "gods" known to all the ancient civilizations were not mythological but flesh and blood humanoid aliens from the tenth planet in our solar system who colonized Earth and created our species by genetic engineering. Based on his research, this large elliptical-orbiting planet has a self-heating core, which would provide warmth and support life.

A brief synopsis is as follows:

Working from the same archaeological discoveries, artifacts, and recovered records as archaeologists and linguists have for two hundred years, Sitchin propounds—proves, in the opinion of this author—that the Anunnaki (Sumerian word meaning "those who came down from the heavens"), an advanced civilization from the tenth planet in our solar system, splashed down in the Persian gulf area around 450,000 years ago and colonized the planet, with the purpose of obtaining large quantities of gold. The word for them is also found in Old Testament Hebrew as Anakeim, Nefilim, Elohim; and Egyptian as Neter or Neters.

Some 250,000 years ago, the recovered documents tell us that their lower echelon miners rebelled against the conditions in the mines and the Anunnaki directorate decided to create a creature to take their place. Enki, their chief scientist and Ninhursag their chief medical officer, after getting no satisfactory results splicing animal and *Homo erectus* genes, merged their Anunnaki genes with that of *Homo erectus* and produced us, *Homo sapiens*, a genetically bicameral species, for their purposes as slaves. Because we were a hybrid, we could not procreate. The demand for us as workers became greater so we were genetically manipulated to reproduce.

Eventually, we became so numerous that some of us were expelled from the Anunnaki city centers, gradually spreading over the planet. Having become a stable genetic stock and developing more precociously than, perhaps, the Anunnaki had anticipated, the Anunnaki began to be attracted to humans as sexual partners and, being genetically similar, children were born of these unions. This was unacceptable to the majority of the Anunnaki high council and it was decided to allow the human population to be wiped out through a flood that was predictably coming. Nibiru, the tenth in our solar system and the Anunnaki home planet, came through the inner solar system again (around 12,500 years ago) on one of its periodic 3600-year returns and brought this destruction. Some humans were saved by the action of the Anunnaki official, Enki, who was sympathetic to the humans he had originally genetically created.

For thousands of years, we were their slaves, their workers, their servants, and their soldiers in their political battles among themselves. The Anunnaki used us in the construction of their palaces (we retroproject the religious notion of temple on these now), their cities, their mining and refining complexes and their astronomical installations on all the continents. They expanded from Mesopotamia to Egypt to India to South and Central America and the stamp of their presence can be found in the farthest reaches of the planet.

Around 6000 years ago, the Anunnaki, probably realizing that they were going to phase off the planet, began, gradually, to bring humans to independence. Sumer, a human civilization, amazing in its "sudden," mature, and highly advanced character, was set up under their tutelage in Mesopotamia.

Sir Laurence Gardner is the author of a series of works that elucidates the history of the Grail Bloodline of human genetically-enhanced kings initiated by the Anunnaki/Enki to take the place of the Anunnaki rulers when they phased off the planet. Gardner's work picks up where Sitchin's leaves off, in this respect.

Human kings were inaugurated as go-betweens, foremen of the human populations answering to the Anunnaki. They were a strain of humans, genetically enhanced with more Anunnaki genes (passed down through direct, procreative genetic transmission), a bloodline of rulers operating in a tradition of "servants of the people." These designated humans were taught technology, mathematics, astronomy, advanced crafts and the ways of advanced civilized society (in schools, now called now "mystery schools," but back then, there was no mystery about them).

Sir Laurence Gardner has brought to light the fact that there exists a robust, highly documented, genealogical, genetic history carrying all the way back to the Anunnaki, possessed by the heterodox tradition of Christianity, which is only now coming forward, no longer gun shy of the Inquisition. This tradition, preserving the bloodline, is the one branded "heretical" and murderously persecuted by the Roman Church. There were no Dark Ages for this tradition, only for those whom the Church wanted to keep in the dark about the real nature of human history and destroy the bloodline, a direct threat to the power of the Bishops. Gardner's extensive historical documentation includes the restoration of the real nature and history of alchemy: the manufacture and use of monatomic gold, a single atom form of gold, a fine white powder with extraordinary characteristics (superconductor at body temperature; antigravitic; capable of correcting DNA abnormalities) ingested for extreme longevity and fed to the graal kings for wisdom enhancement.

The most profound revelation produced by Gardner's meticulous scholarship is that the two Anunnaki brothers who oversaw the colony here, Enlil, who was/is Jehovah/Yahweh and Enki, who was/is Adonai/the Lord, i.e. together were/are the monotheistic god(s), God, of the Old and New Testaments, of Abraham, and were gradually cosmified, infinitized, by theologians and the Roman Church. The reason why Elohim, a plural noun, was used for the "one" God of the Hebrews is obvious.

Sitchin posing with statue of Enlil, the main god said to have exploited mankind.

The reason why this major fact is ignored and suppressed is also obvious: the major god-fearing religions would be history (not to make a bad pun). There could be disruption in society as predicted in the 1950s by the Brookings Institute study. The powers that be do not like contemplating that we could no longer be herded into conflicting factions and goaded into combat for easy crowd control.

Enki, who was partial to humans, depicted on ancient cylinder seal.

The constant internecine warfare in which we slaughter each other is due largely to religious absolutes concerning who and what we are and because the "our god is better than your god and we will have to kill you if you do not subscribe" syndrome keeps us close to destroying ourselves and the planet. The only way we are going to meet the essential conditions of peace and unity is to restore our true history to ourselves as a genetically engineered species by the Anunnaki; see that the creationists and the evolutionists are both half right and half wrong (there was a creation but in a genetic engineering lab and we are evolving, but not according to the principles or pace of Darwinian evolution); and arrive at planetary unity as generic humans, beyond religion(s) as we know them (sublimations, extensions of the ancient master slave relationship for which we were invented).

This is not atheism, does not even address the question as to whether there is some metatranscendental Being who is responsible for all that is, multiple universes, beyond the beyond and infinity—which should remain the focus of human inquiry—it just rectifies some very significant politics, takes us beyond the "my god is better than your god" insanity that Babel-factors us and opens up the potential for world peace and unity, the essential conditions for matriculation into stellar society.

The Tenth Planet of our solar system, known in the Sumerian as Nibiru (Planet of the Crossing) rediscovered by the IRAS (NASA-Dutch Infrared Imaging Satellite) orbited to look for it in 1983, constitutes a planetary wide, species threat to Earth through cataclysmic gravitational upheavaling of the Earth and it's existence is being covered up and denied the public. Tombaugh, looking for a tenth planet, discovered Pluto in 1930 in the solar ecliptic plane in which he was searching but did not find a tenth planet. Subsequently, "residuals," wavelike, up and down movements in the solar ecliptic plane orbits of Uranus and Neptune indicated the existence of a tenth planet. Sitchin published his first book in 1976, *The Twelfth Planet* (the ancients had been taught and knew all the planets of our system and counted traditionally all ten plus the Sun and our Moon as twelve solar system bodies, as depicted on a 4500 year-old cylinder seal, known as VA/243, and described on clay tablets.

As Allan and Delair (authors of *Cataclysm!*, the excellent study of the "Flood" event of the Bible) and the Sumerian records have shown, The Old Testament is simply a rewrite of much more precise histories from the Sumerian, Babylonian, Hittite, Akadian. The almost children's' story version of the Flood in the Old Testament would make the Flood seem as if it was just a tsunami that swept up through the middle east—but it was actually a cataclysmic upheavaling of the entire planet Earth, leaving only a few surviving pockets of humans over the entire planet. It was caused by the passing of Nibiru/Planet X (they used the Greek name, Phaeton) around 9500 B.C., by their calculation.

Planet X/Nibiru is called, depending on the tribal or cultural tradition, the Purifier, the Destroyer, the Frightener, the Doomdragon, Phaeton (Greek), the "Red Sun" of the Hopi, and the Wormwood of the New Testament Book of Revelations, among many other historical references. Its return is a cyclical event as evidenced from historical records. This Uranus, perhaps Neptune-sized planet is both an overriding, horrendous threat to species survival and a main point of leverage to unite the people of our planet for survival. The exact date of its return will be covered a bit later but for now, the simple fact of its return is a matter of grave import.

The IRAS infrared telescope was run by a Dutch-NASA effort in 1983 and their findings and conclusions were announced six times—the last one being by Ray Reynolds of the Ames Research Center, astronomer member of the team, in the *New York Times*, January 30th, 1983. He said, "Astronomers are so sure of the tenth planet that they think there is nothing left but to name it." A number of web sources have developed concern over Planet X/Nibiru, with some promulgating the theory that X/Nibiru is not a planet but a brown dwarf star. However, Dr. John Andersen of NASA confirmed in 1987 that, having received the data from the twin Pioneer spacecraft sent out in opposite directions in the plane of the solar system ecliptic, X/Nibiru was definitively not "a brown dwarf" or "a failed star," or that our Sun had a twin star. Some theorize that the highly elongated orbit of X/Nibiru suggests that our sun has a twin star around which it also orbits, but this twin would have long ago been identified. It's elongated, 3600-year orbit is due to it's being captured into the solar system and colliding with a planet in orbit now known as the Asteroid belt, as given in detail in the ancient records taught to us by the Anunnaki.

In the early 1990s, Dr. Robert Harrington, Chief of the Naval Observatory, having read Zecharia Sitchin's book, *The Twelfth Planet*, invited Sitchin to his office at the Naval Observatory for an interview/conference. For more info (as of this writing), go to http://xfacts.com/x1.htm, and click on "See the Video." Harrington and Sitchin correlated the ancient information with that which Harrington had accumulated from the Pioneer and other probes, Andersen's information, computer studies, clues from other planets, and the IRAS information. Harrington acknowledged the total correspondence between the two sets of information, even adding to it and said that he, by then, was quite certain that X was "a nice, good planet with an atmosphere in which we could be comfortable"(!). Soon after his meeting with Sitchin, he sent a scope and team to the southern hemisphere for a visual (since this planet is known to travel on a 40-degree pitch "below" the ecliptic). He subsequently traveled there for a visual himself, but died shortly afterward, before publishing. Some feel that, because he was going public so openly on the topic, he was killed.

The Twelfth Planet, first book from Sitchin's Earth Chronicles series.

Not all passings of Nibiru at perigee between Mars and Jupiter cause cataclysmic effects, apparently depending on whether the Earth is on the same side or the opposite side of the Sun and, therefore, shielded to a degree.

This information should be released to the public over the entire planet, since Nibiru is on the way back into the solar system. Our increasing climate and Earth changes could well be caused by, or at least affected by, the beginning approach of this Uranus to Neptune-sized tenth planet toward the inner solar system and the people are so far not being warned or instructed. Intelligent measures should be taken now in anticipation of stronger effects, building slowly in the coming years, that will ultimately cause huge population movements and redistribution, the need to secure pure water, food, safe housing and fundamental services transnationally.

Our transmutation to the new human should not have to be endured without understanding—with many lost in a ridiculous kind of Darwinian thinning of an unconscious herd. It should instead be a planetary triumph and transformation of the entire species through conscious participation, cooperation and contribution beyond anything known previously. We have identified the fourth major component of our current human planetary situation as the challenge of how to most consciously understand, experience, facilitate and bring about this profound Transmutation of ourselves as a species. We now possess the intellectually transformative information concerning alien species in general—meaning our own unique, part-alien nature and history. We also have transformative technologies on the material level: free energy; nanotechnology, the ultimate advantage of which is the ability on the molecular level to change almost anything into anything else, and rapidly developing artificial intelligence to manage it all, soon, better than we currently can. This could well qualify us to "graduate" to another level, if we prepare ourselves to step into it properly and be recognized for our true potential.

This is the end time of our species' bewildered adolescence and our transformation into a mature stellar species, which has already begun. Let us reclaim our planetary identity, our own cosmic credentials and genetic wisdom, and prepare as a united planet, in the only adequate, truly planetary, "right" new World Order, to matriculate into the heavens, into space, into stellar society as, finally, *Sapiens sapiens*, the truly doubly wise. I stand to speak for, and to, all of us—to urge all to make it so for our children and ourselves.

I believe that this overview should be quite adequate for you to grasp the general picture of Sitchin's basic thesis and its ramifications as well as the academic, scientific and religious reactions to it currently. Beyond *The Twelfth Planet*, Sitchin published six other books in his Earth Chronicles series, which develop particular topics of his thesis in depth. Though complementing each other and serving to bring the saga of gods and humans on Earth ever closer to our time, each book of the series looks at the tale from a different perspective. It would be well to read them to fill out your expertise even more.

The Twelfth Planet

We've just given a general overview of this book here so, given in sequence, the other Earth Chronicles books are as follows.

The Stairway to Heaven

This book traces man's unending search for immortality (which the Anunnaki intentionally did not give us) to a spaceport in the Sinai Peninsula and to the Giza pyramids, which had served as landing beacons—refuting the notion that these pyramids were built for use by human pharaohs. Recently, records by an eyewitness to seeing a forged inscription by the pharaoh Khufu inside the Great Pyramid corroborated the book's conclusions. Mythic memory has long held that somewhere on Earth there is a place where we can join the gods and transcend death. This book deepens Sitchin's fascinating explorations into Earth's history by looking at this longing for a return to the divine. It examines the legends of human attempts to ascend like gods to heaven in search of immortality, and delves into the lives of the pharaohs of Egypt, who taught how to travel the Route of the Gods to the "eternal Afterlife." It also covers the Sumerian king Gilgamesh, who journeyed to distant lands in his quest to "scale heaven" and ward off his mortal fate. There is additional information on Alexander the Great, who believed he was actually the son of a god; and Ponce de Leon, who explored Florida in search of the legendary Fountain of Youth. The legendary Sphinx, the "Sacred Guide," is revealed as a symbol for eternal life. Its mysterious gaze seems to look forward into the future while crossing into centuries past. Who built it and why?

The Wars of Gods and Men

Reveals startling evidence that the "gods" who inhabited the Earth tens of thousands of years ago were actually real, that they came down from their home planet, Nibiru, tenth in our solar system, and battled for supremacy. Sitchin relies on a careful study of ancient records—Sumerian clay tablets to Hindu mythology to the Old Testament—to prove his theories of how humankind began upon our planet. He also shows how modern sources—such as NASA photographs of Earth taken from space—reveal evidence of a huge nuclear blast in the Sinai peninsula that took place 4000 thousand years ago in a conflict between factions of the primordial "gods." Photographs of the Earth from space clearly show evidence of such an explosion. The Great Flood, the Trojan War, the destruction of Sodom and Gomorrah—these and many more cataclysmic events in human history are explained in this unique revelation of ancient mysteries.

The Lost Realms

Such gratifying corroboration of audacious conclusions has been even swifter for *The Lost Realms*, which transports the reader to the Americas, to the pre-Columbian civilizations and ancient empires that preceded them, revealing hitherto unrecognized links between the Old and New Worlds. When the Spanish conquistadors came to the New World in search of El Dorado, the fabled city of gold, they instead found stone edifices of massive proportions mysteriously constructed in inaccessible regions—huge monuments built with a skill level and tools yet unknown to the indigenous cultures of that part of the world. In the years since publication, new scientific discoveries have provided mounting corroboration of the scientific conclusions, unorthodox and incredible as they were. In the relatively short interval between the completion of the manuscript and its publication, archaeologists, linguists, and other scientists have offered a "coastal theory" in lieu of the "frozen trekking" across the ice of the Bering straits theory to account for man's arrival in the Americas—in ships, both across the Pacific and the Atlantic, as this volume has concluded. They have "suddenly discovered 2000 years of missing civilization," in the words of a Yale University scholar—confirming this book's conclusion. We are now linking the beginnings of such civilizations to those of the Old World, as Sumerian texts and biblical verses suggest.

When Time Began

The fifth book of his Earth Chronicles series is also based on the premise that mythology is the depository of ancient recollections, that the Bible should be read literally as an historic scientific document, and that the ancient civilizations were the product of knowledge brought to Earth by the Anunnaki—"Those Who From Heaven To Earth Came." Night and day, month after month, year after year, our ancestors dutifully recorded the passage of time on clay tablets, watching the heavens from stage towers and pyramids and from megalithic monuments whose incredible size and precise architecture boggle the mind.... Who were the builders of these mysterious structures? What was their purpose? Whose signature is indelibly written on these timeless stones? Why were Stonehenge and its likes built by ancient civilizations at the very  same time, 4100 years ago? What is their message for our time? With these questions in mind, Sitchin, renowned researcher of past ages, takes us on his latest journey through the records of time. Drawing deeply on Sumerian and Egyptian writings, millennia-old-artifacts, and sacred architecture, ranging from ancient Mesopotamia to pre-Columbian civilizations in the Americas, this bestselling scholar provides astounding insights into the origins of the calendar and of astronomy and astrology. This all leads the reader to a climax, circa 2100 B.C., when Marduk, the Babylonian national "god," triumphed over Thoth, the Divine Architect, to proclaim the New Age of Aries, after which society, religion, science and the status of women were never the same.

The Cosmic Code

Many thousands of years ago, a group of extraterrestrials from another planet guided the evolution of life on Earth—determining the existence and nature of humankind as we know it today. How did the master builders from the stars construct the miracle called man? Is the DNA that is at the core of all life in the universe a "cosmic code" that links Earth to heaven and man to God? In this sixth volume of The Earth Chronicles, Sitchin unveils writings from the past to decipher prophesies, and reveals how the DNA-matched Hebrew alphabet and the numerical values of its letters serve as a code that bares the secrets of mortal  man's fate and mankind's celestial destiny. Sitchin explains how the rankings of the gods reveal secret meanings in their divine names and what we know of the highly sophisticated genetic knowledge that was passed on to us. He also explains how Enoch could know the secrets of Creation and the cycles of important events on Earth—and how he could write down prophecies of future events as explained in *The Book of Jubilees*.

The End of Days

Why is it that our current twenty-first century A.D. is so similar to the twenty-first century B.C.? At a time when religious fanaticism and a clash of civilizations raise the specter of a nuclear Armageddon, many ask: Is history destined to repeat itself? What does the future hold? Will biblical prophecies come true, and if so, when? Are the ancient gods still here, or did they leave? Will they return? What will happen then? Will there be another Deluge or Apocalypse when Nibiru passes the Earth? What about the Messianic tradition and Jesus? In this remarkable and relevant conclusion to his Earth Chronicles series, Sitchin shatters perceptions and uses history to reveal what is to come at the "End of Days."

Genesis Revisited

This is a standalone work, a master summary outside of the Earth Chronicles Series. As Sitchin says, "...if...The Sumerians were correct in what they were recording—the discovery of Nibiru would mean not only that there is one more planet out there but that there is Life out there. Moreover, it would confirm that there are intelligent being out there—people who were so advanced that, almost half a million years ago they could travel in space; people who were coming and going between their planet and Earth every 3600 years. It is who is out there on Nibiru, and not just its existence, that is bound to shake existing political, religious, social, economic (and we might add scientific), and military orders on Earth."

And in 1983, it happened: the IRAS telescope team *found* Nibiru and made six major announcements in the mainstream press... and then the cover-up began.

The Cosmic Code and *The End of Days* are fascinating reading but are perhaps more "far out" and speculative than necessary to grasp Sitchin's master thesis relative to this book, but they certainly are valuable in the grand picture. And there are some disagreements with the research of Laurence Gardner that will be profitable to investigate. The works of Gardner are pertinent and generally supportive, so I list them here and briefly summarize his entire body of work as it relates to this book.

Bloodline of the Holy Grail
Genesis of the Grail Kings
Lost Secrets of the Sacred Ark
Realm Of The Ringlords
The Magdalene Legacy
The Shadow of Solomon
The Origin of God

It is important to know Gardner's background in order to appreciate his work and its significance. Sir Laurence was Prior of the Celtic Church's Sacred Kindred of Saint Columba, was an internationally known sovereign and chivalric genealogist. Distinguished as the Chevalier Labhran de Saint Germain, he was Presidential Attaché to the European Council of Princes—a constitutional advisory body established in 1946. He was formally attached to the noble household guard of the Royal House of Stewart, founded at St. Germain-en-Laye in 1692, and was the Jacobite Historiographer Royal.

Laurence explained to me personally how he came to write this series of books. He was hired by thirty royal families in Europe as a historiographer and geneaologist to adjust and bring up to date their family genealogies. That gave him unique access to their private archives. He began to find repeated references in their genealogies to a puzzling line of kings that he could trace back to very ancient times. At first, when he would ask about the nature of this kingly line, the families would slough his questions off. But finally, when they realized they could trust him, they told him that this bloodline of kings was the "Holy Grail." He quickly learned that the Grail was not a golden chalice, or a cup and spoon or any kind of object, as the traditional legends would have it. Subsequent research and probing into the families' histories brought to light the amazing facts: when Enki, the Anunnaki, realizing that soon—in their time frames—they would be pulling back or phasing off Earth, he determined to create a line of kings as Anunnaki surrogates to take their place to shepherd and take care of the people. To initiate this line of enhanced humans, Enki fathered a male child by a selected human female—the Eve of the second story of Adam and Eve in the Book of Genesis. The child's name was Cain, the individual that the Bible (in Genesis) claimed murdered his own brother, Abel. But Laurence found that, researching all the way back to the early Hebrew, the original Hebrew didn't say that Cain slew Abel, but said that Cain was superior to Abel. The Sumerian GR AL (meaning special bloodline) is the source for the gradually transmuted Cainship, Kingship, Kinship, Graal, Grail, or Holy Grail. Enki trained these Grail kings to be "servants of the people," prepared for high status. The followers of Enlil, Enki's jealous and harsh brother, knew they did not have the Bloodline and opposed it.

Eventually, the opposition evolved into outright persecution and killing. The Inquisition by the Roman Catholic Church was an extraordinarily cruel attempt to wipe out the Bloodline entirely. The Enlilites knew that the Bloodline was transmitted by the women of the line and that Jesus was a king in the Line and that he and Mary Magdalene were married, both Essenes, and had children. Mary Magdalene was royalty, but the Enlilites who wrote the New Testament, knowing she was Bloodline, made her out to be a whore. The Bloodline has been in retreat, in the woodwork to protect itself for centuries, but Gardner has allowed it to become public without too much fear of persecution again... even though the Vatican still maintains an Office of the Inquisition.

Gardner begins where Sitchin stops with regard to the Grail. Gardner references Sitchin in his work, but Sitchin only goes so far as to portray the Grail as a physical, symbolic piece of hardware although he does reference the "Blood Royal."

Briefly: *Bloodline of the Holy Grail* is an extraordinary and controversial book, packed with intrigue, begins were others have ended. Laurence Gardner was granted privileged access to European Sovereign and Noble archives, along with special insight into Chivalric and Church repositories. He proves for the first time that there is a royal heritage of the Messiah in the West, and documents the systematic and continuing suppression of records tracing the descent of the sacred lineage by regimes down theough the centuries. This unique book give a detailed genealogical account of the authentic line of succession—initiated with Cain, through Sumer, Egypt, the Middle East and Europe—of the Blood Royal through the sons of Jesus and his brother James, down to the present day. It casts penetrating new light on the Bible story and onto the enigmatic figures of Joseph of Arimathea and Mary Magdalene, and on the real truth behind the Arthurian legends and the Holy Grail. There is a fascinating history of the Knights Templars of Jerusalem, which also plays into this story and can be found in Gardner's research. In general, those are the most important points of Garbner's research, and well worth further study.

Going back to Sitchin, however, let's address the high points in his *The Twelfth Planet* and *Genesis Revisited* books.

300,000 years ago the Anunnaki miners mutiny and Enki and Ninhursag create *Homo sapiens* who begin to multiply, having acquired "knowing."

200,000 years ago *Homo sapiens* were upgraded, resulting in the mitochrondrial DNA of Eve.

75,000 years ago a new Ice Age begins, regressive types of Man roam the Earth, Cro-Magnon man survives during this time.

7400 years ago the Anunnaki grant man new advances, including the first city, Eridu, founded around 5400 B.C.

5800 years ago urban civilization blossoms in Sumer, centering around the largest city in the world at the time, Uruk. Large, temple-centered cities spring up, run by priest-kings that facilitate trade throughout the region, fueled by slave labor.

Sitchin began his work with an overall history of Man, rather than starting at the point in time of our species' creation/genetic tampering by the Anunnaki. This was done in order to compare and contrast our painstakingly slow rate of evolution with the incredible jump in brainpower and technology that occurred almost overnight after the Anunnaki appeared on the scene and made contact with us.

The disciplines of anthropology and archaeology are still developing a full history of the beginnings and evolution of the various types of anthropoid precursors to hominids and the earlier forms of humans. The science of genetics, which is valuable in the forensic determination of the age of species, the possible interrelationships between species, etc., is rather new and maturing even now. The scientists who are involved in these disciplines base their studies and conclusions on the postulate of Darwinian evolution. A variation is called Phyletic Gradualism: a species would gradually go through a transition over an extremely long period of time, exhibiting new traits and characteristics incompletely developed until finally a distinct new species emerges. An opposite theory, Punctuated Equilibrium, postulates relatively rapid periods of modification, separated by long periods in which the species remains unchanged. Anatomical change would be complete in ten or a hundred generations.

These are the two theories: a slow population-wide transition between one species and the next, or a brief evolutionary spurt separated by a long period without change. In view of the gradually accumulating evidence furnished by astrophysics concerning the collision of comets, fireballs, and meteorites with the Earth over the entire history of the planet, some of which are of such size as to cause hemispheric devastation and the extinction of species, the most comprehensive picture of evolution must also include this variable.

The gradually accumulated evidence from the Leakeys' and others' work in South Africa, the finds made in Java, Sumatra, China, the Middle East and Siberia, point to the same type of linear development in the evolution of the pre-hominid and hominid species. Once a species appeared on the scene the time spans for the development of that species, from inception to the fullest exploitation of its potential, are measured in millions of years. A striking characteristic of all species preceding us, including *Homo erectus*, is the extremely modest progress made in cultural and other developments even over those millions of years. Compared to our progress it seems as if, even for *Homo erectus*, there was almost none. The stone toolkit for *Homo erectus*, Acheulen tool technology, remained the same for at least 1,300,000 years.

It took millions of years for mankind to progress through each evolutionary phase—except for the last leap, to modern man. Why?

It is startling enough, as Sitchin and various experts have noted, that Man, if the normal time pattern seen in the sequence of succession of previous hominid species held, should not have appeared for another two or three million years instead of some 300,000 years ago. Working with only the information we have from paleoarchaeological finds, as has been pointed by Dobhansky, there is not even a real progenitor for us in the fossil records. But the nature of the evolutionary development that Man has exhibited since our sudden and too early advent is even more startling.

The historical evidence clearly states that, although there is solid evidence that the natural progression did, in fact, eventually bring about *Homo erectus*, the Anunnaki directly interfered with evolution at that point and used *Homo erectus* genes to combine with their own in order to create us as slave—animals that would be both sufficiently intelligent and docile to serve their purposes for menial tasks.

From the point when the Anunnaki decided to allow us to exist after they had decided and attempted to destroy us as species through the mechanism of the Flood, to the time when they gave us "crash" courses in civilization, to the advent of the flight of the space shuttle, is only a matter of some thirteen thousand years... it bears repeating: only thirteen thousand years. A comparison of the progress we have made in that relatively brief period with the millions of years it has taken other species of hominids to stabilize and progress relatively far less is startling, to say the least.

It is necessary to digress here to recognize the potential objection that any comparison between technologies as such can be very misleading. It is certainly true that one has only to examine the culture of, say, the hunter-gatherer groups of the Kalahari to recognize that a people using only the simplest of technologies and tools may have a rich cultural life and a profound knowledge of their environment because of their actual physical needs. But what is involved here is the radical dimension of innovation and exploration due to mental capacity and development and expansion over relatively very short periods. We do not see evidence for that in the culture of *Homo erectus* or any other hominid species known to us. We do see it dramatically in ourselves.

The speed, indeed the acceleration, of our progress can only be seen (against that background of known hominid development) as absurd. Measured by either the norms of a continuous *or* discontinuous type of evolutionary process, causes a serious question to be raised as to whether our kind of progress should be classified as being an evolutionary process, in the usual sense, at all. Certainly it does not resemble the slow, adaptive, selective molding of a species over millions of years, once it has appeared on the scene and as we can otherwise read in the paleoarchaeological records. Neither does it match the gradual process of emergence of a species filling a vacated ecological niche after a catastrophically destructive event. It *does* have the character of full-blown suddenness. And it does resemble the learning process of the maturing child who is rapidly retracing neurological processes. It certainly resembles the process of metamorphosis beyond the point of metaphor. I propose that the key to the phenomenon is our bicameral genetic heritage. What we are witnessing, indeed experiencing, is certainly an adaptive and selective process at base, but the greater part of the human experience, by far, *can only be understood as the effect of the rapid ascendancy of our Anunnaki gene components.*

It is obvious that genes code for intelligence. That the genetic code builds more and more complex brains, with greater scope and synthesizing power, is taken for granted. But once a new model (species) has appeared, however, the records show little evidence that there is any obvious or inevitable radical upgrading of intelligence within that species. Cultural evolution is the working out of the potential created by a neurological revolution (like plugging a new chip into a computer adding a function that it did not have), the advent of a new species with a new capability for intelligence. The manifestation of that new level of intelligence over time is too often interpreted as a cause rather than a result of the advent of a new neurological capability. For *Homo erectus* to change, in some geographical areas, from a non-symmetrical shaping of hand axes to a symmetrical shaping of hand axes has been the basis for theorizing about even the language capabilities *Homo erectus* might have possessed. Unequivocal evidence for the refinement of a tool-making technique needs no other explanation than the fact that the species under study possessed the potential to achieve it in the first place. These remarks are not intended as an argument for the punctuated equilibrium theory of evolution; the objective here is to point out a pervasive mind-set that causes a misinterpretation of the evolutionary process.

The result of our current thinking is that we tend to ignore the radical anomaly of our unique, created beginning and project our experience backward in our evaluation of the evidence concerning the development of previous hominid species. Our attempt to map our developmental patterns into the overall picture of hominid evolution simply warps our perception of the entire pattern. We should separate ourselves from the progression of hominid species up to and including *Homo erectus*.

One of the agendas we have set for ourselves to promote in the think tank that I'm involved with is to convince scientists and academics in these disciplines to at least consider the Sitchin thesis. The puzzling breaks and sudden beginnings that do not fit the expected evolutionary patterns with regard to our species cause those who do not, or will not, allow for our genetic creation, are beset by obstacles. This, in the case of the beginning of the human species, is a serious handicap. The primary reason for the resistance on the part of scientists and academics is not scientific but the usual funding fright, tenure tetanus, peer pressure: who-will-go-first and break the old pattern. The religionists, whose entire lives have centered around the Bible as the will of God, also resist because the simple recognition that the Old Testament and Book of Genesis is not divine revelation, but a condensed and skewed three-thousand-year-older Sumerian history redefines their religion as *godspell slavery*. But it's time: the decipherment of the writing on the clay tablets discovered in the ruins of ancient Mesopotamia more than a century ago led to the realization that texts existed that related biblical creation tales millennia before the Old Testament was compiled.

It is over only the last few years that the investigators have been able to read out the entire Neanderthal gene code and sort out the relationship of Neanderthal and early humans and determine whether Neanderthals went extinct or were adsorbed into human kind by interbreeding. The latest the geneticists have been able to determine is that we modern humans, *Sapiens sapiens*, retain from 1% to 3 ½% of Neanderthal genes and about the same percentage of Dinosian genes. How long those conclusions will hold remains to be seen. It is fascinating, although frustrating, to watch the scientists keep moving the various species around on the genetic tree and determine their interrelationships—and coming closer and closer to having to acknowledge our sudden beginning by genetic engineering and the anomalies of our partially alien gene code. There are only a tiny handful of scientists who have acknowledged and risked public announcement that we mysteriously seem to have alien gene components—none mentioning specifically the Anunnaki—but for the most part, these scientists are ignored.

But even the resisting scientists have to recognize Sumer as a "sudden" civilization—in fact, it was mainstream archaeologists who coined the term. The evidence shows that sometime around 3800 B.C. an advanced civilization was simply and deliberately put in place. Just about every institution, form of government, domestic convenience, record keeping system, and most things we consider "modern," appeared as a possible working prototype for modern society. The information needed for the sciences, the handicrafts and the arts was voluminous. Numbering more than a hundred, the ME's, perhaps a kind of computer disk/body of information given by Enki, included such diverse subjects as writing, music, metalworking, construction, transportation, anatomy, medical treatments, flood control and urban decay as well as astronomy, mathematics, and the calendar. The ancient records show that this donation of "wisdom" by the Anunnaki was by their choice and it was, as a rule, transmitted to select individuals who had a relatively high office serving the Anunnaki. This fact is a source of puzzlement to those who are reluctant or refuse to admit that it could only have been done by an advanced entity, obviously the Anunnaki.

Sitchin uses, as primary sources for the ancient information, The Bible and the recovered Sumerian, Mesopotamian documents and records. A focal tale in the Bible about our beginning is the Garden of Eden story, where its variety of vegetation is mentioned, and where still-unnamed animals were shown to Adam.

Modern science teaches that the crops and animals we husband were domesticated soon after 10,000 B.C. Wheat and barley, dogs and sheep (to cite some examples) in their domesticated and cultivable forms appeared, then, within no more than two thousand years. This, it is admitted, is a fraction of the time that natural selection alone would require.

Sumerian texts offer an explanation. When the Anunnaki landed on Earth, they state, there were none of such "domesticated" crops and animals; it was the Anunnaki who brought them forth, in the "Creation Chamber." Together with *Lahar* ("wooly cattle") and *Anshan* ("grains"), they also brought forth "vegetation that luxuriates and multiplies." It was all done in the *Edin*; and after The Adam was created, he was brought there to tend it all.

The amazing Garden of Eden was thus the biogenetic farm or enclave where "domesticated" crops, fruits, and animals were brought forth.

After the Deluge (about thirteen-thousand years ago), the Anunnaki provided Mankind with the crop and animal seeds, which they had preserved, to get started again. But this time, Man himself had to be the husbandman. The Bible confirms this and attributes to Noah the honor of having been the first husbandman. It also states that the first cultivated food after the Deluge was the grape. Modern science confirms the grape's antiquity; science has also discovered that besides being a nourishing food, the grape's wine is a strong gastrointestinal medicine. So, when Noah drank the wine (in excess), he was, in a manner of speaking, taking his medicine.

From the beginning of my exposure to Sitchin's work in 1976 there was always background questions about our early ancestors being able to speak, read and write. We will cover more on these topics later, but it is well to know that the evidence points to our ability to exercise all these functions, or at least have the capacity to do so, from our very beginning. There is evidence for there having been an ancient Mother Tongue… 100,000 years ago. Brain centers for speech existed in our early ancestors according to the anatomy of fossil finds. An intact hyoid lingual bone, which, associated with the tongue, makes human speech possible, was discovered as part of a Neanderthal skeleton. Writing began with symbols, progressed to syllables, then words. Cave paintings and symbols attest to our ancestors' capacity for art and the recording of items of importance to them.

This chapter presented an overview of the Sitchin paradigm as a context into which further and even more exciting material will fit.

Chapter 2

ALIEN CONTACT IN THE REMOTE PAST

This chapter, and subsequent chapters, will look at Sitchin's work in greater depth and will begin to explore the immense ramifications.

It is always well to keep in mind as background context for your studies the profound influence and control "religion" has had on Western culture particularly. Here is a quote from Gardner in *Genesis of the Grail Kings*: "…we now have to hand the Sumerian and Akkadian documentation which enabled the Captivity Jews to compile their ancestral story. What we now know is their biblical account was not an accurate transcript of ancient records, but a strategically compiled set of documents which distorted the annals of the original scribes in order to establish a new cultural and religious doctrine. This was the doctrine of the One God, Jehovah (NF Enlil)—a doctrine born out of fear, that was contrary to all tradition and historical record in the contemporary and preceding environments."

If any religion has truly corrupted the original concept of Jehovah and the pantheon, then that religion is materialist Christianity. This is not the honest first-century Nazarene faith of Jesus, Manes and the Celtic Church, but the State religion contrived by Roman imperialists in the fourth century, from which there are now many competitive offshoots. As discussed in *Bloodline The Holy Grail*, "…this hybrid cult (a mixture of Pauline doctrine and pagan beliefs) not only brought a new awesome, omnipotent, omnipresent God to the fore, but it gave him self-styled personal representatives on Earth—first the Emperors and then the Popes—who thrived on being the ultimate bridges to individual salvation. In practice, this repressive cult, which threatens a future divine intervention against humankind, has evolved not as any faith that would have been recognized by Jesus, but as a form of medieval 'churchianity' based on the subjugating dogma of the bishops." (p.120)

So, with that background information in mind, let us get directly to the material. With the first chapter of *The Twelfth Planet*, Sitchin sets the deep historical background. The second chapter brings to life the amazing suddenness and advanced sophistication of the Sumerian civilization. Later studies will show that the intent of the Anunnaki in bringing about this advanced culture with nearly every major institution and public service we now have in modern society, was partly for their own service but also as a model to make humans independent for when the Anunnaki knew they were going to phase off the planet. The third chapter focuses on the Anunnaki themselves, their nature, achievements and imperfections—in a sense, their level of evolution. Perhaps, a good comparison to their development six thousand years ago is ours of today.

We can begin to develop the advantage of historical perspective as we move into the fourth chapter of *The Twelfth Planet* and beyond. The recognition by secular scholars that the historical events—the accounts of wars, king lists, and the records of the "gods" from Mesopotamia and Sumer correlated with the Old Testament writings, was a turning point. This new question being (inescapably) posed was a difficulty for theologians: Was "the word of God" actual history written down by dictate of the Anunnaki, or by human historians three thousand years earlier?

It was 1876 when the scholarly and religious worlds were shaken by the publication of George Smith's *The Chaldean Account of Genesis*, followed by L.W. King's *The Seven Tablets of Creation*. Since then, scholars and theologians alike have come to recognize that the Creation tales of the Bible are condensed and edited versions of texts that were first written on clay tablets in Sumer, where Man's first known (post-Diluvial) civilization began some 6,000 years ago.

It should be emphasized that this is not a discovery but a re-discovery. The ancient authors of the documents that were recovered from the archeological digs recorded the facts accurately; any misunderstanding or misinterpretation or distortion has been the result of the actions of subsequent generations over time.

Most of us are well aware that opinions and theories of this nature have been extant for quite some time. In the recent past we have been able to view the television documentation of the sites and wonders of the ancient world that have moved von Dainiken and others to speculate along these lines with a great deal of conviction. It is to be noted, however, that the scholarship and information in this area has evolved to a whole new dimension through the work of a long progression of scholars and researchers, culminating in the recent work of Zecharia Sitchin. Through their efforts and Sitchin's master synthesis, we have at hand the information needed to define our origin as an historical event in its true nature, as well as the scientific knowledge to comprehend and verify that what we are examining is possible. The rejection of the flat earth theory or the geocentric theory of the universe, or the most profound discoveries of science, pales in the light of this realization. The simple fact is that there is no facet, no detail of human existence as we know it, that is not affected by the revelation of the nature of our true beginning.

As with most new ideas, we have gone through several phases of discovery and reactive attitudes. The early signs of modern questioning are well exemplified in the writings of Erich von Daniken, who brought to popular awareness the enigmatic artifacts and strange sites around the world that were the basis for his conjectures about the possibility of "extraterrestrial visitors," "astronaut gods" and UFOs.

The second stage is personified by the various scientists, especially in NASA, such as Maurice Chatelain, former head of the Apollo communications division, who began to recognize the possibility of a technological explanation for some of the more mystifying and even bizarre events recounted in the Old Testament of the Bible. A major advantage for arriving at the definitive resolutions concerning the reality of the Anunnaki and our beginnings as a species is our own modern scientific advancements. For centuries scholars and theologians could claim that the "gods" must have been mythical because of the amazing, seemingly magical things attributed to them: hurling laser-like "thunderbolts," causing atomic bomb type explosions, flying through the air and space, doing genetic engineering. But we now have the ability to do all of those things and it is no longer magic or mythical, but history.

The third general stage has come through the work of Sitchin, who fulfills and synthesizes the accurate parts of both the mainstream evidence and the dissenting points of view, regarding the real nature of the "gods" and our true origins.

The ramifications of such knowledge produces an immediate illumination of both the present and the future. Our institutions, social forms, political modes, customs, traditions, philosophy, religion, are all, when reexamined, shown to be influenced profoundly by our concept of ourselves as a result of that redefinition. The essence of the synthesis put forth is that, almost without notice, the last piece of the puzzle of the human condition has fallen into place and the revelation is the impetus for the unfolding of the next stage of the maturation of our species. And what an excitingly magnificent potential we have for that transition!

Consider the advances we have made in that direction. The ability to do genetic engineering enables us, literally, to create a new human race. The possibility of longevity and relative immortality is real and immanent. Travel to the stars is only a matter of space-time (questionable pun) and interplanetary travel taken for granted. Quantum physics has provided the real possibility of a grand unified field theory and what has been described as "the language of the universe," as well as the most adequate vocabulary to describe the most evolved human psychology. The intelligent use of psychopharmaceuticals like LSD has furnished us the keys to the doors of perception through which we may pass to explore the interior universe at will. The rapid development of computers may well bring the advent of aspects of an artificial intelligence superior in some respects to the humans that created it. The communication of information, which has been growing exponentially, has become extremely fast, impressing the fact of the unity of the global village. The national budgets of some of the major nations of the world allocate taxpayers' money to build space colonies. We are ready.

It is obvious that a view of human nature as a genetically engineered creation has risk involved with it. The problem of criteria is involved directly here. Our time is oriented to the scientific method as a criterion of certainty. The techniques of archeology can be methodical, scrupulously meticulous, and performed by persons of the highest integrity, ethical standards and mature judgment. But there is no way that rigorously controlled, repeatable experiments can be used here; in a court of law the evidence would be called circumstantial. It is not a matter of simply accepting a curious, previously unknown scientific bit of information that is only of incidental effect. It profoundly affects every aspect of human existence. I am well aware that there is always the possibility of misinterpretation, wishful projection or premature conclusions. I can only say simply that, in view of the direct evidence from the recovered records, reinforced by the questions that are unanswerable unless the evidence is accepted, I am as firmly convinced that we have arrived at the correct solution, as I am aware of the risk.

In view of the known pace at which we collectively accommodate to major change, it may take generations to assimilate and restructure—but is there any more vitally exciting, challenging, constructive enterprise in which to immerse ourselves and initiate our children?

Intensive archeological work in the Mideast, Egypt, and the Indus Valley has produced huge quantities of artifacts and, even more importantly, such a tremendous number of documents that some of them have not even been translated yet. The position of the honest archeologist becomes increasingly uncomfortable in that the traditional interpretation of any reference to the "gods" as "myth" becomes more and more untenable. One can only be amused by the bitter resentment exhibited by one scholar who, upon reading the actual accounts contained in recovered documents of the life and deeds of one of the gods, Ishtar (aka Inanna, Astarte, Anat, Anthat, Athena: an aviatrix, politically powerful among her peers, famed as manipulative and sexually promiscuous, a skilled warrior), complained bitterly that the facts did not befit someone who was of "mythological" stature! It would have been a bit easier to accept if her humanoid status had been recognized for what it was. The evidence has been at hand for some time, waiting only for our technological development to show us that indeed it could be so, needing only the keys for interpretation. The game has changed; the truth is beyond our expectations, the ramifications are inescapable. If we keep our sense of humor, we may evolve to racial adulthood rather gracefully.

Western written history shows a definite pattern of continual sophistication and maturation, while at the same time going through various stages of radical change of interpretive premises. As a result, the history of Western culture's historiography (that body of information which has been interpreted and written by those authorities who mold the academic textbooks and influence the opinions of other experts) may be summarized by describing how the historians have *interpreted* their material in any given age. Historiography in the West has passed through three major phases and is now entering a fourth. Since the Christian era in Europe and America is a central and dominant influence, we may understand these phases as the pre-Christian, the Christian, the post-Christian, and resolution phases. These divisions are generalized and only excusable as a means of simplifying the explanation.

To survey the changes in attitude toward history and its interpretation in Western culture we must start at the beginnings of historiography as manifest in the work of the Sumerian archivists. We have the writing of the Greeks and the Romans, closer to us by two to three thousand years, but only in a few handfuls of fragments of documents, predominantly through second and third-hand sources. By comparison, we have the Sumerians and their successors in one half *million* documents on resilient clay tablets, many not even translated yet because of the sheer volume. Roughly eighty percent of that documentation consists of contracts, records of legal matters, inventories, lexicons and texts on many subjects, while twenty percent is made up of historical and official literature. We can paint a far better picture of the details of the daily lives of the Sumerians than we can of the Romans. We do not have to depend on the excavation of an isolated disaster such as Pompeii; we have the 25,000 odd pieces of the seventh century B.C. bilingual library collected by Assurbanipal at Nineveh.

Although the Sumerian era had been all but lost to the Western world for centuries, it was recognized as the "cradle of civilization" soon after its rediscovery in the late 1800s when interest was once again shown in the ancient past, first through a faddish and fashionable collecting spree and then by a few pioneer amateur archeologists who began digging in ruins guided by descriptions and clues in the fragments of ancient literature. The successes were immediate, interpretations many times doubtful; the languages were mysterious, while the work was hard and too often a treasure hunt, rather than a methodical quest. The success of the driven amateur could not be ignored for long and soon, professional scholars became involved. Methodical techniques of meticulous digging, identification by strata, and preservation were developed. What was gradually uncovered and deciphered proved to be mind-boggling in its sophistication, immensity and grandeur. The complex picture of huge cities of great wealth, teeming with commercial enterprise, specialized technology and industry, provided us with an understanding of an all-encompassing social structure covering all the basic institutions we know in our world today. Record keeping wove the fabric of society.

From the beginning of Sumer, the "sudden civilization," there are a succession of rulers, a form of government by assembly, and an unquestioned understanding that the local "god" owned and controlled literally everything. The king was only a foreman of that "god," who could and would be removed or banished if he did not do exactly what he was told to do. The theme of historical change caused by "theological" offense is prevalent throughout Mesopotamian history. On the other hand, there is a strong sense of continuity and uniformity in the Sumerian view of history because everything could be anticipated since it was all a matter of either doing what the local "god" ordered or not. I include them in the Western framework since they are the earliest source in that context, representing the attitude and orientation of the Middle East and the West until the time of the Greeks.

The high culture, civilization and record keeping of the Egyptians were centered on the deeds of their kings rather than on the events of the past, and history as written. Careful records of commonplace things was not a priority with them, although they referred to the past accurately in terms of the events centering around the "gods." Yet, from the time their civilization arose, there have been records—no more or no less accurate than modern records. Carefully kept lists of rulers were recovered that stretch back very far in time, recording accurately the succession of human kings and queens preceded by, in the case of the Egyptians, a list of demigods, then preceded by a list of gods. Western historians often state that the Egyptians were not really interested in history. It is much more accurate to say that they were not interested in history in the same way as the Greeks and modern Western historians were, so we should take that as a clue toward understanding what they were really interested in—the gods, demi-gods (being half gods, half human), and kings.

The Greek culture, relatively young compared with the Egyptian and the Sumerian, had yet another orientation. They recorded and recounted the events and deeds of the heroes and gods of the past, yet their approach was characterized by a spirit of free inquiry; a tendency toward the analytical and the critical. It is generally agreed that the current concept of history as "knowing by inquiry," investigation, was invented by the Greeks although they freely admitted that their sources were usually Mesopotamian. From a slightly different point of view, their orientation to an investigative mode was the result of a removal in time and an obfuscation of events that forced them to pursue information in a way not necessary for those who were familiar with it in earlier times, "when the living past was an abiding reality." The Greeks were a relatively new cultural force and they were awed by, and respected and learned from, the much older Egyptian culture and history, as well as that of their Mesopotamian sources. Both the Greeks and the Romans have been criticized by modern scholars as deficient as historians because they saw politics as the prime moving force underlying historical change and did not take into account the interplay of material, economic forces. From another perspective, however, the social-political control over the economic arena may have been much stronger than modern historians project. By the time of the Greeks and Romans the view of man and history had moved away from the "god"-centered view of remote antiquity.

With the coming of Christianity, however, the orientation and attitude of the West toward history changed radically. If it is the Greek window through which we view the past, it is the graffiti of the subsequent times' religious gang wars scrawled thereon that obscures our view and turns it into a clouded mirror. Over the centuries, with the Western mind nurtured in the Judeo-Christian cultural context, history was considered to have begun where the Bible began—therefore the concept of pre-history, the era of the pre-historical, was a contradiction and the reality of a previous high civilization either preposterous or blasphemous. In Christianity, the story of nations, of politics, economics, art, war, law—in short, of civilization—had ceased in many ways, but had clearly culminated! For a thousand years and more, this religious view was the unquestioned interpretation of the meaning of history. It has been more influential than scientific history, at least until recent times. Religion has supplied the framework of our thought and the picture of our evolution, despite its crippling approach.

To set a perspective, it comes as a surprise to most modern minds to learn that in 1654, the same period in which Harvard University was granted a charter, modern musical harmony and modulation had flowered, and Japan was already beginning its modern development. Yet, at the same time, people could seriously accept the setting of the date of the Creation of the world by the Irish Protestant bishop, James Ussher (*Annales Veteri et Novi Testamenti*), with which the Bible opens, at 4004 B.C. (on October 26th at 9 A.M.). This was determined by working with calculations originally done by Martin Luther on the exact time of the crucifixion of Jesus, and corrected by Johannes Kepler the astronomer. That was "state-of-the-art scholarship" in the Western world less than four ago.

Less than a century ago the curriculum at Cambridge still equated ancient history with that of classical Greece; that of the Middle Ages with the rise of Christianity; modern history with that of Europe. It was only the efforts of Spengler and Toynbee that finally began to cure the myopia of a cultural-centric perspective.

Although dissent and philosophic and theological opposition to established Christianity sprung up from time to time and gradually became established in Europe and the Middle East, the critical break with the Christian interpretation of history came with the development of scientific geology. The time required for geologic events to occur began to reset our concept of the age of the earth and then of the solar system, and brought into serious question the traditional teaching on the accepted time of the beginning of the world. The weight of this geological evidence, written in the rocks and mountains and ancient sea beds, was too substantial to be ignored. Reinforcement gradually came from the science of biology, which contributed a wealth of details concerning the life of extinct flora and fauna. The disciplines of anthropology and paleontology also began to identify and trace the ancestry of animals and man back into remote times and the refinement of dating methods could be applied to artifacts and bone.

And so a curious thing happened about a hundred years ago. At the same time that the approach to history in Western culture settled into its familiar form and the interpretations of the politics, the economics, the conflicts and the leading personalities and trends of the modern world began to proliferate, our interpretation of the ancient past was radically challenged. The archeological evidence included detailed recordings of events described only synoptically in the Bible and written three thousand years before it existed. The Old Testament, including Genesis, came to be seen as an accurate recording of history and was further reinforced by discoveries related to details that it contained, but which were obscure or puzzling. Part of breaking the Godspell involves correcting the belief that the Bible is the revealed word of God: it has been shown to be a condensed historical accounting, not theology.

Over time, the Old Testament was put into a finer and finer historical perspective and the relationship between the Hebrew tribe and the preceding cultures in the Middle East clarified. At the same time, the panorama of much earlier civilizations unfolded through the work of shovel and pen. One could assume that this would be sufficient to free the vision of the scholars of the West to approach the information from the past with an attitude conducive to objective evaluation. Unfortunately, it took the experts only far enough to remove the domination of the Christian ethos, leaving a great deal of virtual influence and bias that exists to this day. Although historiography moved into what I have called the post-Christian era, a cluster of factors developed or remained that have hampered the impending resolution to this longstanding puzzle unearthed in the Middle East.

Although the material reality and the history of the ancient civilizations could no longer be doubted or denied, the categorizing of the traditions derived from them as myth had become so ingrained in the Western mind and vocabulary, that any change in that area came very slowly indeed. It took nearly forty years since Sitchin's first book was published to arrive at the point where Sitchin Studies is being introduced at the University level—not only through the courses taught by me at International Metaphysical University, but also through other professors bold enough to share Sitchin's work within their own standard classes, including Critical Thinking, History, Archaeology, and Mythology.

It has been hard for mankind to accept the fact that the gods were real on many different levels. For example, our legends and stories say their life spans were impossibly long, at least from our own perspective. As humans accustomed to a 24-hour day, 365-day year, the time frames familiar to the Anunnaki seem almost unbelievably long. As a single example: It took the lower echelon Anunnaki gold mining crews numerous centuries to finally get fed up with their working conditions and rebel. Extended life spans into the thousands of years seem not only incredible to us, but utterly fantastic. Yet that was usual for the Anunnaki. Sitchin indicates that their usual time frames and relatively long life spans were the result of having evolved on their planet, which has a year—one revolution around the Sun—equivalent to 3600 of our years. They noticed and became seriously concerned about the fact that, if they remained on Earth for a long period of time, their life spans were affected, apparently becoming noticeably shortened.

A very important topic, immortality, needs to be clarified within the context of the ancient records. When one first begins to learn that the Pharaohs somehow earned immortality when they died, the tendency is to think metaphorically and symbolically. The journey that the Pharaoh embarked on in a very ceremonious manner seems to be a celebration—after all, he is dead, is he not?—more than literally a journey to an immortal life. But Sitchin's careful analysis of the rituals and details of the process makes it quite clear that the Pharaoh, though dead, was embarking on a real journey by various means of transportation, with the anticipation of being revived on arrival at the off-planet destination. There is enough information about the Anunnaki's indefinite life spans and their possession of the technology to revive one of their kind (or a human), to confirm that they had conquered death as we know it. We know of one of the Anunnaki who, having been dismembered by another Anunnaki, was literally reassembled and revived. A small number of humans, mostly favorites of the Anunnaki, were granted immortality. So when we read of the process by which a Pharaoh was guided through a journey and, at the end of which, would be greeted by Anunnaki and apparently revived to live on Nibiru with them, we can assume that we are reading literal fact. But the journey, geographically, that the Pharaoh made to where immortality awaited him, has taken scholars some time to figure out.

It is now the consensus that the initial destination was the Sinai spaceport. Reflection on the purpose of the journey shows the logic of going to the Sinai peninsula because that was where a major Anunnaki space port was located.

It would have been the obvious place to get a ride to Nibiru if that was where one was to be granted immortality. It is logical also that, as Gilgamesh did, one might try to be granted immortality by an Anunnaki official by going to Baalbek. Baalbek was a major rocket launch and landing platform and Anunnaki vehicles traveled from there to Nibiru and back all the time. The platforms at Baalbek contain the largest cut stones in the world, some weighing well over 1000 tons. The largest cranes in the world today would have trouble lifting them, much less trying to move them into place.

The "Stone of the Pregnant Woman" in quarry at Baalbek, 64 ft. long, 19.6 ft. wide, x 18 ft. high, with estimated weight of 1000 tons. Was considered the largest cut stone in the world until "The Stone of the South" was found nearby in the 1990s, with an estimated weight of 1242 tons. The nearby temple contains blocks nearly as large, baffling experts as to how they were moved and lifted into place.

The Great Temple, also known as The Temple of Jupiter to the Romans, contains three huge stones in this wall. Each stone is 63 feet long, 13 feet wide and 13 feet high, with an estimated weight of between 800 and 1000 tons. They had to be lifted 20 feet off the ground to be put into place after having been moved over 800 meters from the quarry to get them here. No clear answer exists as to how this was done, and accomplishing this today borders on the impossible.

Another matter that bears clarification is the nature and type of advanced transportation used by the Anunnaki. The descriptions of rocket ships are quite clear. But they used smaller craft such as airplanes and helicopters also, as are depicted unmistakably on a frieze on a roof beam in the temple of Seti I at Abydos, Egypt. To the right of the image of the helicopter is what appears to be a medium-sized yacht, with an image of an airplane or similar type of aircraft below it, and perhaps a second one underneath it, with a large tail fin and cockpit.

It seems clear that the Anunnaki transportation technology 6000 years ago was at least equal to ours today, with what they used to get here of course being better. Although they likely have antigravity technology today, there doesn't seem to be any indication of it at that time. Which prompts the question: Do the Anunnaki still exist now? The answer is unequivocally yes. There is record of a time when some of the Anunnaki, apparently distressed that staying on Earth was affecting their life spans, decided to go back to Nibiru. But another group, it is said, was determined to stay. There is rumor that this group is living here in the background, perhaps in the vastness of the Tibetan mountains, concealed somewhere deep within the ocean or in an underground base, but there is no way to vet those claims. There are rumors and claims that there is a contingent coming back from Nibiru and there is conflict between that group and the one that stayed. Of course, there is no way to determine the truth or accuracy of any of those statements, as interesting as they may sound. The main point concerning this is that should the day come when the Anunnaki do in fact return, we would do well to watch out for our own best interests.

Is there a way to determine what the Anunnaki attitude is towards us as humans? Do they want to return here? Under what circumstances? Are they covertly already in contact with governments? If so, what kind of influence or control or direction do they exert if any? Do we really want to be in contact and interaction with them again? Should we poll our species on any of these questions? What could we expect concerning their donation of advanced technology or information as they have done in the past? Sitchin devotes an entire book, *The End Of Days* to the explication and analysis of the chronology of the comings and goings of the Anunnaki and the prophecies and predictions of the time of the possible end of the Earth and what the "end" might really mean. As an integral part of this book, you should be aware that Sitchin interprets the collective prophecies, predictions and information in the ancient records concerning the "end of days" as clear indication of a time when the Anunnaki will return.

Chapter 3

PLANET X AND GEO-CATASTROPHES

Zecharia Sitchin, Sumerian scholar and author of the Earth Chronicle Series of books, re-revealed the existence, size, orbit, and detailed characteristics of the tenth planet in our solar system through his interpretive translation of the *Enuma Elish (When in the Heights),* a major document unearthed at the archaeological digs at Nineveh by Layard. Its existence, size, peculiar orbit, and serious-to-catastrophic effects on the earth as recorded in the past, have profound implications for geology. It's potential for periodic havoc on Earth (and other planets of our system) ranks it with an enormous asteroid impact, oxygen depletion (anoxia), carbon dioxide poisoning of the oceans, or the effects from tremendous volcanic eruptions. All these candidate causes for Earthly havoc are not negated by this tenth planet's potential. All or some may have been responsible in the past for catastrophic effects on earth. The author is strongly suggesting that a probable key factor to be added to the theorized causes of global catastrophes is an element of periodicity, which otherwise leaves out certain kinds of identifiable and/or expected effects. It's gravitational influence, while periodically within the inner solar system, to cause a rollover or tip of the earth, pole shifts and reversals, disturbances of the Earth's internal dynamics, earthquake and volcanic activity, may make it a meta-causal agent for any or all of the theoretical causes now being entertained.

Sitchin definitively answers the question, "How could our earliest civilizations know of this planet?" with the thoroughly substantiated thesis that the transcultural "gods," known to all the ancient civilizations, were not mythological but flesh and blood alien humanoids. Their home planet was, is, indeed, this tenth planet. They came here 432,000 years ago, created our species as a slave race for their gold mines by crossing their genes with those of *Homo erectus*, moved us up to limited partnership, subsequently, and taught us civilization, science and astronomy. They eventually phased off the planet and left us on our own, to find our own species identity. They were known in the Sumerian as Anunnaki, "those who came down from the heavens." (Egyptian: Neter, the "Watchers;" Old Testament Hebrew: Anakeim, Nefilim, Elohim—all plural, same meaning.)

Before one rejects this thesis out of hand, it is well to understand that it is backed up by highly coherent, well-researched, well-developed archaeological data, documents, history, and some two million items of recovered artifacts. A key factor is our having reached a level of technological advancement which allows us to understand high science and technologies present in the past which, until only very recently, could only seem fantastic—particularly genetic engineering. As is the case with scientists in general, archaeologists can adjust to internal and incidental shifts in their consensual context but, when the paradigm itself is threatened with replacement, there inevitably occurs a great deal of unscientific chest drumming and incisor display. Obviously, the obstacle here is the word "alien." Consider that the cardinal reason why the alien topic has been considered the fringe "belief" of unbalanced personalities for so long, has been the relentless promotion of that idea by the government for half a century. The Brookings Institution (think tank) study (early 1950's, commissioned by the government) concluded that revelation of the alien presence would cause serious disruption in the fundamentalist religions and society, and recommended against. But extra-solar system aliens are not our focus here.

The Anunnaki, as depicted in hundreds of carvings, reliefs, drawings and descriptions in the recovered documents, are quite like us, male and female, and generally taller and huskier than humans in those times. They are from within our own solar system, are at home in our atmosphere, and radically different from the alien types allegedly from other solar systems. If we are half Anunnaki, that should not be so surprising. At the time they were on the planet, they apparently possessed only ballistic rocketry for interplanetary travel—no anti-gravitic technology had yet been developed.

King Hammurabi, left, issued the Code of Hammurabi, laws he claimed to have received from the Sun God, Shamash, right, circa 1760 BC. If Shamash should stand, note how much taller he is than the king (even without the step).

Objections To This Thesis

Those trained in the sciences, accustomed to carefully crafted protocols and rigorous proof will, no doubt, question this paradigm in several ways.

Quite reasonably, it may be asked why the Sitchin paradigm has not been embraced by the geneticists' academic counterparts in archaeology, anthropology and paleontology if the evidence is as voluminous and robust as claimed. It may also be asked, "Why has this not been the known and taught history of our kind through all the millennium?" and "Why should there have been suppression and perversion of this knowledge?" These questions are best answered in historical context and perspective.

There was literally no such thing as the discipline known as Archaeology in Western culture until the 1800s. The Roman Church controlled and determined the view of the past. The scholastic world, dominated by the Church, followed docilely. It was not until paleontological findings of millions of years forced that view to be reevaluated and Heinrich Schliemann, a wealthy German merchant, refusing to believe that the ancient cities and peoples were legend, dug up several stages of the "mythical" city of Troy. A new window into the past had opened and the mythic view of everything questioned. Scientific Archaeology, as we know it, came into existence only when academics reluctantly had to acknowledge the past being dug up and collected by amateurs in the Middle East. Archaeologists promptly came to be mistrusted and hated by the religious institutions that feared solid, scientific revelations would contradict their teachings and history as related in the Old Testament and other religious books.

A small part of the "mythical" city of Troy. The gods Apollo and Poseidon were said to have built the walls and fought on opposite sides of the Trojan War (as did other deities). Despite the extremely mythological-sounding tale, the amateur Schliemann believed the city was real and went out and found it.

Most in the scientific world are familiar with the scientist, Galileo, having to capitulate to the Inquisition to save his own life, dying while under house arrest for holding to a heliocentric view of the solar system, claiming to see planets through his telescope. Fewer are aware of the fact that the monk, Giordano Bruno, was burnt at the stake in Rome, through the solicitousness of the Roman Church, only thirty-six years before the founding of Harvard University, for holding to the Copernican view and claiming that there had to be other planets and other civilizations in the cosmos.

Literally no one in America had a Doctorate degree at the time of the founding of Harvard University in 1636 by John Harvard. Increase Mather, a president of Harvard, as a Dissenter, was ineligible for a Doctorate from any English university because all of them were controlled by the Church. Fourteen years *after* the founding of Harvard, Bishop James Ussher published his *Annales Vertis et Novi Testamenti*, dating the beginning of the world to 4004 B.C. One could be condemned as a heretic for contraverting this doctrine by decree of the Church in 1654, and the stricture was not removed until 1952(!) by Pope Pius XII. The arithmetical wonder of this fact is that it lasted virtually three centuries—part of which was from ignorance, followed by the refusal to admit it. Consider that almost everything written in this book would have been branded as "heresy." It is common knowledge that early geological findings are from ages far older than the quaint 4004 B.C. Bishop Ussher date, but could not be published until a rather short time ago.

As late as 1906, the Egyptian Exploration Fund, whose charter stated it was set up to promote archaeologists whose work would reinforce the Old and New Testament, refused to publish the discovery of an Anunnaki gold processing plant on Mount Horeb in the Sinai by Sir Flinders Petrie, the most distinguished in his field at the time. When he published news of this privately they pulled his funding, had the book expunged from the publisher's records and the British Library never cataloged the work—yet it was clearly one of the most important discoveries in archaeology ever made. (Sir Laurence Gardner: *Bloodline Of The Holy Grail, Genesis Of the Grail Kings*)

The mythic interpretation has been promulgated by religions because to recognize the Anunnaki as real would be to open the door to a radical reinterpretation of the entire phenomenon of religion and put into question the real identity of the very deity at center of their belief system. To relegate all the Anunnaki "gods" and their deeds—except of course Enlil/Jehovah/Yahweh, the God of the Judeo-Christian religions, who was sublimated out of that category—to fictional, mythic, unreal status, was supremely effective to this end. It is through this millenniums-old tradition of suppression, mythicization and manipulative control that the character, content and interpretation in the academic arena has been set and remains, largely, even to this day. Very few are going to make a complete reversal and negate their entire Ph.D. thesis in Mythology. In Archaeology, Anthropology, and Paleontology, tenure tetanus prevents most from "going first"—to admit they have been wrong in an area that is otherwise significant and profoundly revolutionary, perhaps even more so, than the Darwinian shock. Collegiate colitis is all too frequent—just from contemplating having to contradict oneself in front of students. Peer pressure finishes off all but the isolated, courageous academic or scientist, here and there. Thomas Kuhn (*The Structure of Scientific Revolutions*) is proven correct again. If you want that Ph.D. diploma you will repeat what you know you are supposed to believe and say. If you want that job, that funding... then follow the party line. The reason becomes apparent why the academic arena has attempted to ignore this forbidden archaeology and anthropology, and why a few of the more ruthless of the academic power elite have tried to address Sitchin with quick and nasty *ad hominem* attacks, just outside the factual forum.

The *Enuma Elish* gives a complete account of the formation of our solar system, including the gravitational capture into the system of this tenth planet (known to the Sumerians as Nibiru and the Babylonians as Marduk), its subsequent collision with a large planet, Tiamat, orbiting then between Mars and Jupiter, which resulted in the formation of the asteroid belt. It also covers the formation of comets and meteorites from the impact, with the movement of the larger part of the impacted planet arriving in our orbit, to become Earth. The *Enuma Elish* says that the intruder planet settled into a huge elliptical orbit of 3600 years around our sun in the "wrong" direction, counter to the orbital direction of the other planets, and that it returns to the inner solar system through the asteroid belt area periodically. It gives the details of the path that it can be observed taking through the constellations as it approaches and even mentions the disruptive events its close passing causes on Earth.

Tombaugh, searching for the tenth Planet X, discovered Pluto in 1930. Christie, of the U.S. Naval Observatory, discovered Charon, Pluto's moon, in 1978. The characteristics of Pluto derivable from the nature of Charon through the two Pioneer spacecrafts' data, demonstrated that there must still be a large planet undiscovered—mainly because Pluto could not be the cause of the residuals, the "wobbles" in the orbital paths of Uranus and Neptune, which had to be caused by a large planet. The IRAS (Infrared Astronomical Satellite), during 1983-84, produced observations of a tenth planet so robust that one of the astronomers on the project, Ray Ames, said, in a *New York Times* interview, that "all that remains is to name it"—from which point the information has become curiously guarded. In 1992 Harrington and Van Flandern of the U.S. Naval Observatory, working from two separate and different computer analyses and with all the information they had at hand, published their opinion that there was, at least, an 85% possibility of a tenth planet, even calling it an "intruder" planet. Andersen of JPL shortly thereafter publicly expressed his belief that it could possibly be verified any time. Harrington invited Zecharia Sitchin (having read his book and translations of the *Enuma Elish*), to a meeting at his office where they correlated the current findings with the ancient records that Sitchin has translated some 17 years previously. Harrington acknowledged the detail of the ancient records while confidently narrowing its current location to below the ecliptic in the southern skies, even acknowledging the possibility of a retrograde orbit. Harrington acknowledged that his information agreed with all these details and the maps they each had drawn of the orbits were almost indistinguishable. The current probable location of Nibiru (Planet X, our tenth) estimated by both *was the same*.

It is the opinion of this author and others, in light of the evidence already obtained through the use of the Pioneer 10 and 11, two Voyager space craft, the Infrared Imaging Satellite (IRAS, 1983-84) findings, and all other data available to Harrington when consulting with Sitchin, that the search has already been accomplished—in fact, that the planet has already been found. It is interesting that Harrington dispatched an appropriate telescope to Black Birch, New Zealand to get a visual confirmation, based on the data leading to the expectation that it would be below the ecliptic in the southern skies at this point in its orbit. Because the evidence is strong enough, Harrington designated an observatory in New Zealand to search for this tenth and last planet in our system using a twin 8-inch astrograph telescope on loan from the Naval Observatory in Washington, D.C. It reported back to NASA where the observational information is analyzed. For reasons given that were a bit confusing, to say the least, immediately upon Harrington's untimely death, the scope was removed and the search transferred to an observatory in Chile. As one observer noted rather cynically, this happened "almost before he was cold."

To acknowledge a tenth planet is to open up the possibility of the Anunnaki's existence, to rethink the entire history of the planet and to reevaluate "religion" as we have known it. Because of the power and influence of religions, and the status quo in academia, this will not happen easily or quickly. In the meantime, however, the sciences, geology in this case, are hindered, even obstructed. Not to mention the species in general. One must face the clear and simple fact—as Harrington was enough of a real scientist to do—that the information about this tenth planet, and all the others in our system, is there in the ancient documents and is continually being verified in finer and finer detail. *The obstacle to Sitchin's thesis is not scientific. It is the very unscholarly, traditional, pervasive, preclusive mindset, of academicians and scientists, long fostered by the religious absolutism that put Galileo under house arrest and burnt Bruno at the stake, which continues to demand that this history and information be disregarded as mythological.*

The work of Harrington, Van Flandern, Ritchie, the IRAS project, and now that of Murray and Matese, continue to reinforce and refine the details already known to humans for thousands of years—details lost and then recovered—in large part uncovered and revealed again by Sitchin starting in 1976 with the publication of his first book, *The Twelfth Planet*. As to officially naming the planet, Sitchin already has written years ago to the Planetary Society, charged with naming planets, to formally notify them of the fact that it already has been named *Nibiru* for thousands of years. Although too modest a scholar to put himself forward in this case, I personally think that Sitchin should receive a Nobel Prize for his research and master thesis. Let proper credit be given in due measure where it clearly should.

This is not to denigrate the impressive and astute work of any of these pioneering astronomers or to detract from their findings. Credit, however, should be given to whomever it is due in proper measure. The recognition of the information that Sitchin has published on the tenth planet (ten planets being recognized by astronomers at the time of this writing) and its utilization would save the astronomers great time and effort. It is precise and robust enough to provide all data necessary for a computer modeling of our solar system from its beginnings. A computer modeling would furnish an advanced mathematical prediction of the time and path of Nibiru's return to the inner solar system, highly significant because the *Enuma Elish* details the disruptive physical effects it causes on Earth by its close passing.

A summary of the astronomical information gathered from the recovered text, *Enuma Elish* ("*When in the Heights*"), now called by many, *The Epic of Creation*, is presented by Sitchin as follows:

Nibiru, apparently a wandering planet, was captured into the solar system very early in the existence of the system and was not a "native" planet. When Nibiru was gravitationally captured into the solar system there were nine native planets. Earth, as such was not in place but there was a large planet in orbit between Mars and Jupiter, called Tiamat. Nibiru is described as belching eruptions and emitting vast amounts of radiation at that time. The relative gravitational forces of its passing the outer planets caused its path to be bent inward first by Neptune which caused the side of Nibiru to bulge, then Uranus, which forced Nibiru to emit four satellites (see for modern correlation the article *Uranus*, by Andrew P. Ingersoll, Scientific American, Jan. 1987). Saturn then was forced to release its moon Pluto while, together with Jupiter, drew three more satellites from Nibiru, and then Tiamat. With Nibiru on a collision course for Tiamat, the perturbations of the fields caused Tiamat to produce from itself a total of eleven satellites, ten small ones and a large one known as Kingu. But the two planets did not collide at this first meeting. The satellites of Nibiru, produced in the awesome gravitational interactions during its introjection into the solar system, however, did collide with Tiamat and created some sort of physical cleavage of Tiamat. This created a huge "field discharge" between the two planets that left Tiamat neutralized, scattering Tiamat's ten tiny satellites, which might be still be members of the asteroid belt as a result of gravitational extraction. This may never be verified because the full asteroid belt was formed mostly from pieces of Tiamat after the collision (and possibly some from Nibiru and/or her moons). It might be of great interest to attempt to identify asteroids that have different composition, even spectrally, on the assumption that one type would be pieces of Tiamat and the others pieces of Nibiru. The pieces of Tiamat should have the same composition as the Earth, since the Earth is a congealed remainder of Tiamat. On a subsequent orbital pass, Nibiru itself struck Tiamat, splitting it into two parts. The result was the formation of the asteroid belt from debris and the congealing of the remains of the large proto planet into our Earth, dislocating it into current Earth orbit. The huge Pacific basin is testimony to the collisional event, as is the tectonic plate cycle.

Tiamat's large moon, Kingu, remained with the orbital exchange, becoming the Earth's moon. This catastrophic collisional event and subsequent reforming and congealing of the part of the proto planet Tiamat to become the present Earth could well be the ultimate cause of our Earth's colossal plate tectonics. Current information says that the plates move apart and then come back together into a large, single mass in a rhythmic cycle. It's as if the Earth is still ringing like a bell from the ancient collisional event. This information gives us a possible answer as to why less gross material is found in the asteroid belt, taken as a whole, than would otherwise be expected if a full-sized planet, meeting the criteria of Bode's Law, had actually broken up.

A comparison of the information contained in the ancient records with the facts and theories advanced about our solar system by modern astronomers obviously shows some startling similarities. The old records say Planet X is about 5 masses of the earth, while modern astronomy deduces two to five masses. The old records speak of an orbit highly elliptical and inclined up sharply, 30-40 plus degrees to the ecliptic, with modern findings showing the same but with a lesser inclination.

Two very striking dissimilarities also exist, being the orbital periodicities and the disagreement as to whether Pluto was originally a moon of Neptune or Saturn, which are, perhaps, the most significant clues to the reality of the matter. The modern astronomer works under the assumption that Planet X orbits, however eccentrically and elliptically, in the same direction as all the other planets. It is on this basis that orbital periodicity (the time once around the sun) is worked out and mass is deduced through the effect on other planets. But the ancient records claim unequivocally, however, that Nibiru, Planet X, orbits in the opposite direction of the other planets. This fact alone, if taken into consideration, should account for the disagreement on periodicity, resolve the enigmas of residuals that still do not allow a long term ephemeris (a chart that predicts the precise location of a planet in the near future) to be constructed for Uranus and Neptune. Since the original capture entry of Planet X was in this opposite direction, it might explain why the old records say that Pluto was originally a moon of Saturn rather than of Neptune, as the modern astronomers hypothesize.

It is clear that there is enough factual material in Sitchin's translations that a model of the orbital configuration and path is apparent even without computerized modeling, keeping in mind that the relative observational location was the Middle East about 30 degrees north. Computer modeling would, however, provide an added dimension by running our solar system backwards and forwards in time rapidly to study the details of the past and to anticipate the future. This model running backwards, if sufficiently precise, should eventually arrive at a point close to the time of collisional impact. Further modeling of the proto solar system before impact (from the information preserved in the ancient texts) should give us the details of that dramatic history.

Elaborating the collisional details should provide us with an accurate 3-dimensional model of the direction and trajectory of the ejecta from the impacts and their interaction with and effect on the various planets and satellites. The model, run forward, should indicate within a reasonable time-frame when Nibiru will return to the inner solar system the next time around, its orbital path, and whether its passing will constitute any special danger to the inner planets during its next approach.

As Nibiru travels in its 3600-year, cometary-like orbit it is recorded in ancient documents to be visually observable, at least as it approaches the inner solar system, as it passes through the Great Bear, Orion, and the vicinity of Sirius and the constellations of the south. It moves from Taurus to Sagittarius at some point in its incoming progress, coming in from the south in a clockwise direction, apparently making Venus "brighter" by a merging of the two images at one point. "…upon its appearance: Mercury; rising thirty degrees of the celestial arc Jupiter." [at an angle of 30 degrees to the imaginary axis of Sun-Earth perigee?] (*Enuma Elish*) It increases in brilliance as it passes from the location of Jupiter toward the west; when at its closest point to the Sun, passes through the point of the original collisional location, the Asteroid Belt "in the Zodiac of Cancer." The effect of the passing, the return of Nibiru through the region of the inner solar system and asteroid belt, is described as causing (on Earth) earthquakes, flooding, torrential rains and storms, volcanic eruptions, an actual sonic effect, the Sun going down at noon, for one day no light ("neither day nor night"), uncommon freezing, the Moon "as red as blood," these being the effects experienced on Earth, at least in times past.

When Nibiru is within the inner solar system there is a period when, from Earth, it is visible at sunrise and disappears from view at sunset. There is clearly enough information here for a computer modeling of the orbital path of Nibiru and its interaction with the other planets. It is fascinating to watch the information gradually being gathered by our astronomers concerning our solar system, coming more and more in line with the ancient records in finer and finer detail. Nibiru is described in the ancient records as a radiant planet, probably indicating a high degree of internally generated heat, somewhat ruddy in color (dark red when first visible to the naked eye) and five magnitudes of the size of the earth. When visible from earth it can be seen at sunrise and disappears from view at sunset (presumably from the typical Sumerian location of 30 degrees north latitude in the area of present day Iraq). The radiant nature of Nibiru emphasized in the ancient records may be a product of high geologic stresses. Astrophysics tells us that a body with an elliptical orbit—Nibiru's is very elongated and comet-like—is constantly tending to resolve to a circular orbit. This causes heat-generating stresses more or less proportionate to the degree of ellipticality. This relatively high degree of heat may be a reason why humanoid types very similar to us can survive on that planet even though it moves so far from the heat of the sun in its orbit.

Other effects in the solar system that were likely caused by a past Nibiru return includes the atmosphere being ripped away from Mars, the formation of the Oort cloud, Uranus becoming tipped over at a 90-degree angle, and more.

There is need for serious and immediate in-depth analysis of the ancient information and correlation with what has been gathered in modern time to determine when it will come back through again, where it probably will pass (a cardinal point), whether it shows a pattern of fluctuation in its orbit, if it will come closer to Mars or Jupiter—or maybe it could perhaps come through in between Mars and Earth. It would serve us well to determine potential collisional events with other planets under certain configuration of the planets at different times and, of course, a prediction of what effects it will have on the Earth and other planets when it does come through at any given time. This would allow us to determine if any catastrophic events would occur. To do so will require having all data available, including the current estimated location, which is, in all likelihood, being withheld from the public at this time.

Chapter 4

ANCIENT ALIENS AND MODERN ASTRONOMY

Going beyond the ancient records, it is time to move to the present and examine any modern astronomical evidence we have encountered. Let us start, as usual, with the work of Sitchin—who found a relatively recent space event to signify an "intent to return" on the part of the Anunnaki.

In his 1990 book *Genesis Revisited* he publicly revealed a hushed up event—the "Phobos Incident." It concerned the loss, in 1989, of a Soviet spacecraft sent to explore Mars and its possibly hollow moonlet called Phobos.

In fact, not one but two Soviet spacecraft were lost. Named Phobos 1 and Phobos 2 to indicate their purpose—to probe Mars' moonlet Phobos—they were launched in 1988 to reach Mars in 1989. Though a Soviet project, it was supported by NASA and European agencies. Phobos 1 just vanished—no details or explanation were ever publicly given. Phobos 2 did make it to Mars, and started to send back photographs taken by two cameras—a regular one and an infrared one.

Amazingly or alarmingly, they included pictures of the shadow of a cigar-shaped object flying in the planet's skies between the Soviet craft and the surface of Mars. The Soviet mission chiefs described the object that cast the shadow as "something which some may call a flying saucer." Immediately, the spacecraft was directed to shift from a Mars orbit to approach the moonlet and, from a distance of 50 yards (that's 150 feet!) bombard it with laser beams. The last picture Phobos 2 sent showed a missile coming at it from the moonlet. Immediately after that, the spacecraft went into a spin and stopped transmitting—destroyed by the mysterious missile.

The strange,, cigar-shaped shadow that was photographed during the Phobos mission.

61

The "Phobos Incident" remains, officially, an "unexplained accident." In fact, immediately thereafter, a secret commission on which all the leading space nations were represented, sprang into action. The commission (and the document it formulated) merits more scrutiny than they received, for they hold the key to understanding what the world's leading nations really know about Nibiru and the Anunnaki.

The geopolitical events that resulted in the secret group's formation began with the discovery, in 1983, of a "Neptune-sized planet" by IRAS—NASA's Infra-Red Astronomical Satellite—which scanned the edges of the solar system, not visually, but by detecting heat-emitting celestial bodies. The search for a tenth planet was one of its stated objectives, and indeed it found one—determining that it was a planet because it was detected once and then again six months later, shown clearly to be moving in our direction. The news of the discovery made headlines but was retracted the next day as a "misunderstanding." In fact, the discovery was so shocking that it led to a sudden change in U.S.-Soviet relations, a meeting and agreement for space cooperation between President Reagan and Chairman Gorbachev, and public statements by President Reagan at the United Nations and other forums that included the following words (pointing heavenwards with his finger as he said to them):

"Just think how easy his talks and mine might be in these meeting that we held if suddenly there was a threat to this world from some other species from another planet outside in the universe.... I occasionally think how quickly our differences would vanish if we were facing an alien threat from outside this world."

The Working Committee that was formed as a result of these concerns conducted several meetings and leisurely consultation—until the aforementioned March, 1989 Phobos incident. Working feverishly, it formulated, in April 1989, a set of guidelines known as the Declaration of Principles Concerning Activities Following the Detection of Extraterrestrial Intelligence, by which the procedures to be followed after receiving "a signal of other evidence of extraterrestrial intelligence" were agreed upon. The "signal," the group revealed, "might not be simply one that indicates its intelligent origin but could be an actual message that may need decoding." The agreed procedures included undertakings to delay disclosure of the contact for at least twenty-four hours before response was made. This was surely ridiculous if the message had come from a planet light years away.... No, the preparations were for a nearby encounter!

To Sitchin, all these events since 1983, plus all the evidence from Mars, and the missile shot out from the moonlet Phobos, indicate that the Anunnaki still have a presence—possibly a robotic presence—on Mars, their olden Way Station. That could indicate forethought, a plan to have a facility ready if there was need again for a way station for transfer of personnel or materials from or to Nibiru, or a general plan for a future revisit. Put together, it suggests intent for a Return. Based on his research, Sitchin suggests that what had taken place in a previous Age of Pisces long ago, could well be repeated again in the Age of Pisces now. If the prophecies are to come true, if the First Things shall be the Last Things, if the Past is the Future, cyclically—then the Return, the signs say, will happen before the end of our current Age.

Let us assume that the Return will be soon and that we are ready to greet and interact with whatever Anunnaki contingent arrives. Because they could have maintained control over the entire planet from the beginning or any time since, and could probably take control of Earth again with their advanced technology, it is probably safe to assume that it will be a peaceful Return. Having studied the history intensely for nearly forty years, I submit that the topic we need to discuss with them first is genetic: "You told us, as recorded in the ancient archives, that you had purposely given us only short life spans, so what other limitations did you set on us? What improvements and elimination of genetic defects and diseases can you show us how to make?"

It would be well if they were to give us the keys to the literally thousands of potential known genetic diseases and defects our DNA holds. Our medicine and science and health practices are all geared to providing us with better and better health and more and more extended life spans. The logical outcome, if possible to achieve, is immortality. The reciprocal interaction of the ancient information and our technological capabilities is well illustrated in the case of longevity and relative immortality. If we had not achieved an understanding of the basics of genetics and some proficiency in the mechanics of genetic engineering, we would not be able to understand what the ancient texts are saying. When the information does become clear, it aids us in being able to see the overall picture and find significant information that may serve as guideposts for us in our pursuit of the goal of immortality. That information takes the form of the history of the Anunnaki race while they were here, who lived exceedingly long lives because of the nature of the environment on their home planet. The information available shows that they were able to grant a human immortality, were quite certainly able to restore a dead Anunnaki (or human) to life, and that those abilities were not mysterious, but simply a function of their technological expertise, both in genetic engineering and possibly advanced botanics.

It is essential to establish a perspective on immortality from the beginning. The recognition of immortality as the next profound step in the realization of the fullness of human potential should include a clear awareness of that step, as profound as it certainly is, being one more step in our conscious evolutionary progress. It is not just that we will need very long life spans to move into space, interact with alien species, or time to assimilate the enormous volume of information we have already available to us in ever-increasing amounts: rather, it is a matter of simple human potential and dignity.

Currently the concept of human immortality, with its inevitable forcing of the development of a level of technology to restore, even under extremely difficult circumstances, someone unfortunate enough to be killed accidentally or deliberately, or an individual choosing to be placed in cryogenic suspension on death with the intent to be revivified when the technology is developed, meets with a number of deep-seated negative reactions. The most frequently heard criticism takes the generic form of a theological rejection that it is contrary "to the will of God." What is interesting, however, is that "God," first mentioned in the book of Genesis, translates into what we now know to have been Enlil, of the Anunnaki—called "Yahweh" when the book of Genesis was written. It is proven from the Sumerian records that the stories in Genesis originated in more complete form on clay tablets in ancient Mesopotamia. This was the home of the Anunnaki, the original "Gods," with *elohim*, also mentioned in Genesis and taken from these texts, being the plural word for god, despite it being used as a singular in Genesis, as scholars will consistently agree.

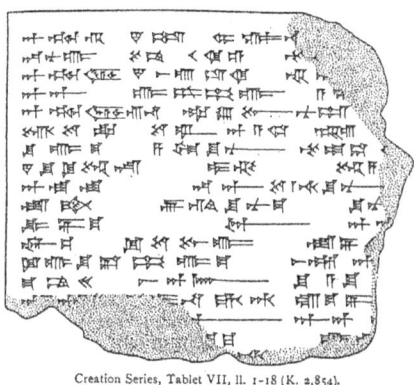

Creation Series, Tablet VII, ll. 1-18 (K. 2,854).

Part of Tabet VII from the *Enuma Elish*, which literally translates to "When on High," or "When Above." Also called *The Epic of Creation*, it was considered passed down from the gods and told from their perspective. It is the original, complete source for what we find in Genesis.

This makes it clear that we are dealing with an ancient and deeply ingrained fear. To seek what was the gods' or to violate a taboo (eating food reserved for the gods; entering territory that was their exclusive preserve, etc.)

could bring punishment. If we have lost sight of the real nature of the gods, we have not lost our sense of taboo. But immunity to death is only different from immunity to smallpox, by degree. It is only reasonable that we enjoy that which our Anunnaki forbearers enjoyed through the efforts of our own minds and hands—or by donation by the Anunnaki. The recognition of ourselves as more than we have ever thought ourselves to be, setting our own evolution in perspective by detaching it from the linear sequences preceding it, provides us with a touchstone for integrating the developing approaches and disciplines centered on the study of Man. We may never feel completely and easily at home on this planet until we achieve relative immortality and remove the shadow of death's inevitability that can mar our most conscious moments. In light of the Anunnaki example and our own tendencies, it is easy to say that it is simply "natural" for any advanced species to control their lifespan, to achieve relative immortality. I personally am completely convinced of that as fact. I am signed up for cryogenic suspension personally. But the concept will be the subject of philosophical debate from the cocktail tray to the faculty room to the laboratory for some time. And the laboratory will be where the answers are mostly determined. What we must carefully examine is how much of our unique bicameral genetic makeup determines not only our biological level of evolution, but what we may call our consciously determined evolution. We may be looking at a complex of imperatives; a tremendous potential and an exciting challenge.

Poets and scientists, visionaries and philosophers, explorers and scholars have sensed it, glimpsed it, suggested it, but we, thanks to the labors of many scholars and the definitive synthesis of Sitchin, can say it simply and without equivocation: we are an unique product of genetic engineering, a mutant species which has reached a relative state of development, both psychologically and technologically, where we can reflexively appreciate that concept of ourselves and act on it. The mutant slave-animal awakens from an ancient amnesia caused by taboo; sapiens unbound and rising. We become truly sapient on recognition of the full import of that simple genetic fact.

Chapter 5

HIDDEN TRUTH OF HUMAN ORIGINS

It is important in understanding the general context of this work, as Sitchin points out, "that all this material is not a new discovery, but a re-discovery." It may more accurately be called a recovery. The human population six thousand years ago knew all this information directly because they were in contact with the Anunnaki, who were present. They were here, and functioned as gods. Over the ensuing thousands of years, the Anunnaki having withdrawn, the knowledge simply faded.

The discovery and understanding of the ancient civilizations had been a process of continuous astonishment, of incredible realizations. The monuments of antiquity—pyramids, ziggurats, vast platforms, columned ruins, carved stones—would have remained enigmas, mute evidence to bygone events, were it not for the Written Word. Were it not for that, the ancient monuments would have remained puzzles; their age uncertain; their creators obscure; their purpose unclear.

We owe what we know to the ancient scribes—a prolific and meticulous lot, who used monuments, artifacts, foundation stones, bricks, utensils, weapons of any conceivable material, and slate, on which to write down names and record events. Above all, there were the clay tablets: flattened pieces of wet clay, some small enough to be held in the palm of the hand, on which the scribe deftly embossed with a stylus the symbols that formed syllables, words, and sentences.

The Deluge Stone from The Epic of Gilgamesh, providing a written record of the Great Flood.

Then the tablet would be left to dry or be kiln-dried, and a permanent record had been created—a record that has survived millennia of natural erosion and human destructiveness.

In place after place—in centers of commerce or of administration, in temples and palaces, in all parts of the ancient Near East—there were both state and private archives full of such tablets; and there were also actual libraries where the tablets, tens of thousands of them, were neatly arranged by subject, their contents entitled, their scribe named, their sequel numbered. Invariably, whenever they dealt with history or science or the gods, they were identified as copies of earlier tablets, tablets in the "olden language." (Sumerian)

One of the greatest discoveries in Mesopotamia was the library of Ashurbanipal in Nineveh, which contained more than 25,000 tablets arranged by subject. A king of great culture, Ashurbanipal, collected every text he could lay his hands on, and in addition set his scribes to copy and translate texts otherwise unavailable. Many tablets were identified by the scribes as "copies of olden texts." A group of twenty-three tablets, for example, ended with the postscript: "twenty-third tablet: language of *Shumer* not changed."

Ashurbanipal himself stated in an inscription: "The god of scribes has bestowed on me the gift of the knowledge of his art. I have been initiated into the secrets of writing. I can even read the intricate tablets in *Shumerian*. I understand the enigmatic words in the stone carvings from the days before the Deluge."

In 1853, Henry Rawlinson suggested to the Royal Asiatic Society that there possibly was an unknown language that preceded Akkadian, pointing out that the Assyrian and Babylonian texts often used words borrowed from that unknown language, especially in scientific or religious texts. In 1869, Jules Oppert proposed, at a meeting of the French Society of Numismatics and Archaeology, that recognition be given to the existence of such an early language and of the people who spoke and wrote it. He showed that Akkadians called their predecessors *Shumerians*, and spoke of the Land of *Shumer*. It was, in fact, the biblical Land of *Shin'ar*. It was the land whose name—*Shumer*—literally meant, "Land of the Watchers." It was indeed the Egyptian *Ta Neter*, Land of the Watchers, the land from which the gods had come to Egypt. As difficult as it was at the time, scholars have accepted, after the grandeur and antiquity of Egypt had been unearthed, that civilization, as we know it in the West, did not begin in Rome and Greece. Could it now be, as the Egyptians themselves had suggested, that civilization and religion began not in Egypt, but in southern Mesopotamia?

In the century that followed the first Mesopotamian discoveries, it has become evident beyond doubt that it was indeed in Sumer that modern Civilization began. It was there, soon after 4000 B.C.—nearly 6000 years ago—that all the essential elements of high civilization suddenly blossomed out, as though from nowhere and for no apparent reason. There is hardly any aspect of our present culture and civilization whose roots and precursors cannot be found in Sumer.

Astounded as the archaeologists were to uncover the grandeur of Assyria and Babylonia, they were even more puzzled to read in their inscriptions of "olden cities." And what was the meaning of the title "king of Sumer and Akkad" that the kings of these empires coveted so much?

It was only with the discovery of the records concerning Sargon of Agade that modern scholars were able to convince themselves that a great kingdom, the Kingdom of Akkad, had indeed arisen in Mesopotamia half a millennium before Assyria and Babylonia were to flourish. It was with the greatest amazement that scholars read in these records that Sargon "defeated Uruk and tore down its wall.... Sargon, King of Agade, was victorious over the inhabitants of Ur.... He defeated E-Nimmar and tore down its wall and defeated its territory from Lagash as far as the sea. His weapons he washed in the sea. In the battle with the inhabitants of Unna he was victorious...."

The scholars were incredulous: Could there have been urban centers, walled cities, even before Sargon of Agade, even before 2500 B.C.?

As is now known, the answer is Yes, indeed there were. These were the cities and urban centers of Sumer, the "Sumer" in the title "King of Sumer and Akkad." It was, as a century of archaeological discoveries and scholarly research has established, the land where Civilization began nearly six thousand years ago; where suddenly and inexplicably, as though out of nowhere, there appeared a written language and literature; kings and priests; schools and temples; doctors and astronomers; high-rise buildings, canals, docks and ships; an intensive agriculture; an advanced metallurgy; a textile industry; trade and agriculture; laws and concepts of justice and morality; cosmological theories; and tales and records of history and prehistory.

In all these writings, be it long epic tales or two-line proverbs, in inscriptions mundane or divine, the same facts emerge as an unshakable tenet of the Sumerians and the peoples that followed: in bygone days, the DIN.GIR—"The Righteous Ones of the Rocket ships," the beings the Greeks began to call "gods'—had come to Earth from their own planet. They chose southern Mesopotamia to be their home away from home. They call the land KI.EN.GIR—"Land of the Lord of the Rockets." The Akkadian name *Shumer* meant,

"Land of the Guardians," and they established there the first settlements on Earth. Sitchin says that an important statement made by the Sumerians was not made lightly, which said that the first to establish settlements on Earth were people who came down from another planet. In text after text, whenever the starting point was recalled, it was always this: 432,000 years before the Deluge, the DIN.GIR, "Righteous Ones of the Rocket ships," came down to Earth from their own planet. The Sumerians considered it a twelfth member of our Solar System—a system made up of the Sun in the center, the Moon, all the nine planets we know of today, and one more large planet whose full orbit lasts a *Sar* or *Shar,* 3600 Earth-years. This orbit, they wrote, takes the planet to a "station" in the distant heavens, then brings it back to Earth's vicinity, crossing between Mars and Jupiter. It was in that positioning that the planet obtained its name NIBIRU, Crossing, its symbol being the Cross.

Reflection on the volume of historical information from the ancient times of the Anunnaki's presence, now available in translation from literally multiple thousands of documents either dictated to scribes by the Anunnaki themselves or written by humans, shows us that knowledge of the planets of our system, their orbits and names, was common factual knowledge for humans of those ancient times, primarily because the Anunnaki were physically present and in control. Once the Anunnaki phased back or off planet, the knowledge became corrupted or faded. Retrogressive primitive concepts gradually took over, like the flat Earth theory or the notion that the Sun orbited around the Earth, which was considered the center of the universe, etc. When one comprehends the degree of retrogression, it can be mind-boggling.

The final phase of understanding the real physical nature of the "gods" and realizing that the fantastic deeds they were capable of were not myth but real, has come about through our science reaching a critical point at which we could understand the science of their deeds. The pressure of knowledge about alien species visiting Earth, the force of Sitchin's Nobel Prize-quality work on the Anunnaki and our half-alien gene code, the astronomy that has dated our solar system back billions of years, are all elements forcing the Church, the major controlling entity for centuries, to reformulate its position with regard to advanced alien species and the nature of reality in general, as we can see in the recent statements of Church astronomers, particularly. Advances in science, in general, have also caused—indeed forced—many of the changes in our thinking.

Let it be clarified here that neither the Akkadians nor the Sumerians had called these visitors, colonizers, to Earth "gods." It is through later paganism that the notion of divine beings or gods has filtered into our language and thinking. When we employ the term here, it is only because of its general acceptance and usage that we do so. The Akkadians called them *Ilu*—Lofty Ones—from which the Hebrew, biblical *El* stems. The Canaanites and Phoenicians called them Ba'al—Lord. But at the very beginning of all these religions the Sumerians called them DIN GIR, "The Righteous Ones of the Rocketships." In ancient Mesopotamia these visitors were said to be "worshipped," which is what people have done ever since, with their gods. However, the word "worship" in Sumerian actually means, "to work for." This is what we were created for (meaning the *second* creation story found in Genesis, not the first, where our DNA was "adjusted" or tampered with)—so we could work for them in the mines.

The sophistication in celestial knowledge—attributed by the Sumerians to the astronauts who had come from Nibiru—was not limited to familiarity with the Solar System. There was the endless universe, full of stars. It was first-ever known in Sumer—not centuries later in Greece, as has been thought and taught—that the stars were identified, grouped together into constellations, given names, and located in the heavens. All the constellations we now recognize in the northern skies, and most of the constellation of the southern skies, are listed in Sumerian astronomical tablets—in their correct order and by names which we have been using to this very day!

As Sitchin points out, geology was the science—and, we might add, astronomy—which brought about a critical turning point, allowing for a final understanding of the ancient records.

In historical perspective, although written in a matter of fact style, the seventh chapter of the *Twelfth Planet* is a mind-boggling and paradigm-breaking piece for the Western mind. We are given, through the translation of the *Enuma Elish*, The Epic of Creation, the complete story of the formation of our solar system. The latest modern versions of its formation are either reinforced or corrected in a definitive fashion. We are even furnished a physical mapping in a printout of cylinder seal VA/243 of the Sun, with all the planets surrounding it in relative size and position. The seal, remember, is 4500 years old. This is hard factual evidence that is difficult if not impossible to deny or refute. The depiction

Cylinder seal VA 243, planets depicted on left side.

includes our tenth planet, Planet X, home of the Anunnaki, known to the Sumerians as Nibiru (the planet of the crossing).

Although clearly discovered by the IRAS, Infrared Satellite Telescope, as astronomers in 1983 had announced six times in the mainstream media, it is being ignored or covered up by the powers-that-be. In a *New York Times* interview, Ray Reynolds, team astronomer, said, "astronomers are so sure of it that all that remains is to name it." Then the shades came down. Crucial points of consideration likely included the academic arena, where doctoral theses could be contradicted; the Vatican—that would have to recognize that their "God" was/is Enlil the Anunnaki rather than Jehovah/Yahweh of the Book of Genesis. Also, don't forget the other god-fearing religions, Hebrew, Moslem, Christian, all are threatened by this final knowledge and clearly do not want it out. On the other hand, breaking this godspell (our god is better than your god and we will probably have to kill you if you don't subscribe) is the key to reaching beyond conflict, becoming a generically human, peaceful species—the critical state to attain in order to be allowed to matriculate into stellar society, as we have been coached toward and even warned by advanced alien species for some time.

The Epic of Creation, still apparently seen as a philosophical work by most scholars, taken by them as an early version of the eternal struggle between the light and dark forces or the alterations of winter and summer, or death and resurrection, should be taken at face value, as Sitchin points out—as a clear statement of cosmological facts, as the formation of our solar system as told to humans by the Anunnaki. Because Genesis represents not just religion but also science, one also must recognize the role of the Anunnaki and accept that the Sumerian texts are not "myth" but factual reports. Scholars have made much progress in this respect, but they have not yet arrived at a total recognition of the factual nature of the texts. This is no doubt because of the religious nature of the Bible as traditionally taught. Although both scientist and theologians are by now well aware of the Mesopotamian origin of Genesis, they remain stubborn in brushing off the scientific value of these ancient texts. It cannot be science, they hold, because "it should be obvious by the nature of things that none of these stories can possibly be the product of human memory." (to quote N.M. Sarna of the Jewish Theological Seminary in *Understanding Genesis*) Such a statement can be challenged only by explaining that the information of how things began—including how Man himself was created—indeed did not come from the memory of the Assyrians or Babylonians or Sumerians, but from the knowledge and science of the Anunnaki. They too, of course, could not "remember" how the Solar System was created or how Nibiru invaded the Solar System because they themselves were not yet created on their planet. But just as our scientists have a good notion of how the Solar System came about and even how the whole universe came into being (the favorite current theory is that of the Big Bang), the Anunnaki, capable of space travel 450,000 years ago, surely had the capacity to arrive at sensible scenarios of creation; much more so since their planet, acting as a spacecraft that sailed past all the outer planets, gave them a chance at repeated close looks that were undoubtedly more extensive than our Voyager brief "peeks."

In passing, it is interesting to note that, although given short mention, Sitchin's brother, Amnon, is a professional astronomer and has contributed important information. It is also interesting to note, as Sitchin has stated publicly on George Noory's Coast to Coast interview program: when he attended meetings of professional societies of which he was a member, academic and scientific members would confide in him confidentially, secretly, that they agreed and approved of his thesis and work, reinforced him, but would not publicly recognize it. Again, we see peer pressure, funding fright and tenure tetanus hindering progress and handicapping coming generations. By contrast, it is known that the Chinese were already doing archaeological digging and studies in 200 B.C.—a time which Western culture considered ancient up until recently!

A meeting between Sitchin and Dr. Robert Harrington of the Naval Observatory can be searched for and viewed online (a link was provided earlier in the book but if it is no longer active, one could find it through Google). I sent Harrington a copy of *The Twelfth Planet* many years ago and apparently Sitchin sent him a copy also. Harrington was impressed by Sitchin's thesis and invited him to visit for a one-on-one conference. When I first saw the video of the conference and heard Harrington acknowledge the existence of Nibiru and then say that he knew enough about it to be quite sure it was, quote, "a good, nice planet with an atmosphere that we could be comfortable in," I was blown away. Here was an official astronomer of the U.S. Naval Observatory disclosing information that the powers-that-be were holding back. Subsequently, Harrington sent a team of observers with a scope to Black Birch, New Zealand, to get visuals of Nibiru because he knew—as recorded in the ancient Sumerian documents—that it could only be seen from the Southern Hemisphere at that time, the early nineties. Once he had apparently received confirming reports from the team, he went down there to see for himself. He is said to have taken a small, 8-inch, personal scope with him because he calculated where this planet would be and knew where to look. Unfortunately, before he could publish his findings and reports, he suddenly died from a fast-acting form of esophageal cancer in January, 1993. Some believe he was "taken out" because of his plans to disclose, although no proof for this exists.

In the very last two pages of my previous book, *Sapiens Rising*, I included a two-page Appendix document, different from the two Appendixes found in this book. It is called The Disclosure Proclamation, which demands of the government that the three major cover-ups—the general alien presence, our genetic creation by the Anunnaki and the existence and potential effects of Nibiru on its passing through the inner solar system, be disclosed and the people made aware of the mind-boggling ramifications of the first two as well as the potential physical consequences of Nibiru's passing. These concerns were also brought up at the very beginning of this book, and are referenced in the Appendixes in the back.

Why should there be so much attention given to cover-ups? Cover-ups are most often the last desperate defensive moves on the part of the various powers-that-be, the officials and leaders, of the institutions who know that they and their institutions are passé. It is the major institutions of the world that are uniquely affected. Godspell religions; social norms and practices such as the suppression of women or various forms of slavery; dictatorial forms of male chauvinistic government; military institutions, to name a few examples of the status quo. And "status quo" is the key word here: All these major institutions fight desperately to maintain their status quo. They sometimes give reasons that seem noble, such as keeping information about alien contact secret so as not to cause social panic. That was the reasoning behind the cover-up of the Roswell crash in 1947. For a short time after that, covering up the UFO presence was perhaps the proper thing to continue doing until officialdom could get their act together. But it has been perpetuated ever since, and it is clear that the intention was not for the common good, but to preserve the perception of power and control of the powers-that-be.

It is obvious that, if the godspell were totally broken and our real history restored to us as a species, the social, political and even economic revolutionary changes would be profound enough to constitute the most significant event in our entire history. However, before sweeping social change, the ideological revolution must come first. It is, to a good degree, with us already. But we must contribute to its positive growth and determine how best to more fully bring it about—to awaken others with proven facts delivered by bold and trusted authorities, for the maximum benefit of all.

But note that revolution of thought and restoration of our real history is yet only one cover-up among the three major ones. In a later chapter we mention the potential danger of species extinction at certain passings of Nibiru. The people should be educated about those facts, which are being covered up, even by NASA. We face a potential catastrophe—so the cover-up, in this case, is criminal.

The book by Allan and Delair, *Cataclysm!*, which I recommend, is a unique work if you wish to expand the scope of your knowledge. The author team traveled the world over, searching for geological evidence of the Flood, mentioned in the Old Testament and described in great detail in the Sumerian records. What they found and describe is horrendous: the Flood was not just a large tsunami that swept through the Middle East and then gradually subsided. It was a worldwide effect of the passing of Nibiru—they use the Russian term, Phaeton—that caused the cataclysmic pushing up and leveling of mountain chains, emptied seas and created others—a total, devastating upheaveling of the entire Earth. The evidence shows itself as caves, fissures and trenches crammed tight with the remains of plants, animals, humans, debris—often from other places on the Earth—jammed in by the water and geologic pressures. They estimate that only 1000-plus humans survived over the entire planet. All evidence points to Nibiru nearing our solar system right now, on one of its 3600-year periodic return orbits. Should not the people of the planet be warned of potential catastrophic effects—effects which are starting to cause the increasingly pronounced Earth changes and climate changes that we are experiencing (and should expect from such an encounter)?

In Chapter 8 of *The Twelfth Planet* Sitchin exercises in-depth scholarship, systematically clearing up the misinterpretations by previous scholars of the *Enuma Elish* as mythology and elucidating the astronomical reality as taught to humans by the Anunnaki of the formation of our solar system. This includes the capture of the planet Nibiru, its resulting alteration of the planetary system, and the formation of the Earth. This is another example of how the maturation of our human science—astronomy and astrophysics in this case—has allowed us to arrive, in our modern times, at a definitive understanding of the ancient records. As our development of genetic science afforded us the ability to understand our creation by the Anunnaki scientists, Enki and Ninhursag, so astrophysics and astronomy gave us the facts to understand the *Enuma Elish* as the detailed account of the formation of our solar system. But it should always be remembered that the historiography shows three phases: six-thousand years ago when the Anunnaki were among us and taught us, it was known generally that there were such things as planets and they numbered ten, including awareness of Nibiru, tenth and home planet of the Anunnaki. As the Anunnaki became remote and the competing cultures mythologized, followed by the Roman Church taking over a great deal of human society and denying and dictatorially concealing the true history, the intervening phases manifested a degeneration of the history and true facts to the point where academia was perverted to complicity. Sitchin's work borders on the heroic in these matters. It is a shame that he passed on before his work could be fully acknowledged and he would see the paradigm implemented, and the world literally profoundly changed.

The traditional approach to myth and legend that considers those phenomena as the science fiction of the primitive mind is simply no longer a viable or tangible explanation.

The *Enuma Elish* is giving us not only a complete picture of the state of our solar system and all its members in our time but a detailed recounting of the drama of its formation, evolution and stabilization. As I became aware of this, my personal reaction was one of amazement and awe. Here were the detailed answers to the questions that astronomers and geologists and scientists had conjectured and argued about for centuries upon centuries. The Earth could seem different under one's feet. We were given the sighting lines and orbital characteristics that would enable us to spot and track Nibiru, incoming to apogee, through the asteroid belt once every 3600 years—and coming again, quite certainly, soon in this orbit. This has been and will be a Uranus-sized planet, red in color, whizzing through the inner solar system, way too close to Earth for comfort and sometimes bringing great danger—but it is also indication of a new era, of contact with the Anunnaki, bringing a potential cultural and scientific upgrade, on the horizon.

Sitchin points out in chapter 8 that it can be seen that "Mankind's march to civilization—through the intervention of the Anunnaki—passed through three stages which were separated by periods of 3600 years: the Neolithic period (circa 11,000 BC), the pottery phase (circa 7400 BC), and the sudden Sumerian civilization (circa 3800 BC)." The 3800 number should stand out in one's awareness because subtracting 3600 years (a shar, a passing of Nibiru), from it, puts the return of Nibiru to the vicinity of Earth in the close, proximate future. There a number of opinions based on various calculations out there. Some say Sitchin's best estimate was 2078; others who knew him will strongly assert that he refused to give an exact date because he did not claim to be a scientist. He explained that such an elongated orbit can and has caused a slight variance of time at each passing, so if Nibiru should fail to appear on an exact date, critics would insist that all of his theories should be thrown out. Sitchin did not wish to endanger the accuracy of his entire body of work based on one exact date that people kept pestering him to reveal. While he was alive in the 1990s Sitchin did reveal, when the question was posed to him, that Nibiru was more than halfway back. With Sitchin no longer with us, we will have to wait for 2078 to see what may appear in our skies....

There are many pictures extant on the Web that purport to show Nibiru almost like a second Sun. NASA is clearly under restriction to deal with even its existence publicly. One of our first projects when we formed our think tank, www.cosmichumanity.org, was to contact academics on the college level, attempting to find those who would be willing to publicly and academically study the alien situation in general and our species' genetic creation specifically, and write critical white papers and articles on those topics to inform the general public. We did not get a single taker. We encountered silence, withdrawal; apologetic retreat. Only one academic, the Dean of a Midwestern College, was honest and brave enough to tell us personally the reason for the silence and refusal. He said that if the funding agencies of the government from which he received financial support came to him tomorrow and asked him to do such studies and papers, he would do so in a "heartbeat" because he already knew it was the most important and essential topic on the planet. But, until the government funding agency actually asked him to do such studies and reports, he would not want to be caught even thinking about it (with another outside organization like ours) because he knew the funding that he already possessed would be cut off within days. I mention these unpleasant items to inform people of what she or he may encounter in studies of what some would call "alternative" or controversial topics.

Although having to admit from the acquired astronomical evidence that there had to be collisional events causing the many anomalous phenomena visible with regard to moons, planets and the asteroid belt of our Solar System, the astronomers who acknowledge these items still are reluctant to acknowledge the cause of them. The Sumerians, 6000 years ago, made clear that collisional events had sculpted the solar system. They were taught and passed on to us that it was Nibiru which was the main cause of the "sculpting." Central to their cosmogony and worldview was a cataclysmic event that they called the Celestial Battle. It was an event to which references were made in miscellaneous Sumerian texts, hymns, and proverbs—just as we find in the Bible's book of Psalms, Proverbs, Job and various others. But the Sumerians also described the event in detail, step by step, in a long text that required seven tablets. Of its Sumerian original, only fragments and quotations have been found; the mostly complete text has reached us in the Akkadian language, the language of the Assyrians and Babylonians who followed the Sumerians in Mesopotamia. The text deals with the formation of the Solar System prior to the Celestial Battle and even more so with the nature, causes, and results of that awesome collision. And, with a single cosmogonic premise, it explains puzzles that still baffle our astronomers and astrophysicists. Even more important, whenever these modern scientists, reluctant as they generally are, have come upon a satisfactory answer—it fits and corroborates the Sumerian one.

The Sumerian word for Earth was KI ("kay" eye). It was applied as a root word or a verb, to Earth for a reason. It conveys the meaning "to cut off, to sever, to hollow." Its derivatives illustrate the concept: KI.LA meant "excavation," KI.MAH "tomb," KI>IN>DAR "crevice, fissure." In Sumerian astronomical texts the term KI was prefixed with the determinative MUL ("celestial body"). And thus when they spoke of mul.KI they conveyed the meaning, "the celestial body that had been cleaved apart." By calling Earth KI, the Sumerians thus invoked their cosmogony—the take of the Celestial Battle and the cleaving of Tiamat.

Unaware of its origin, we continue to apply this descriptive epithet to our planet to this very day. The intriguing fact is that over time (the Sumerian civilization was two thousand years old by the time Babylon arose), the pronunciation of the term ki changed to gi, or sometimes ge. It was so carried into the Akkadian and its linguistic branches (Babylonian, Assyrian, Hebrew), at all times retaining its

Tiamat, after the cleaving. This is how the Pacific Ocean *really* looks, from space—unlike what is depicted on flat maps. North America/Mexico is in upper right. The huge disparity of land to water on one side of the planet makes a cataclysmic impact in the past far more likely to have occurred.

geographic or topographic connotation as a cleavage, a ravine; a deep valley. Thus the biblical term that through Greek translations of the Bible is read Gehenna, stems from the Hebrew Gai-Hinnom, the crevice-like, narrow ravine outside Jerusalem named after Hinnom, where divine retribution shall befall the sinners via an erupting subterranean fire on Judgment Day.

We have been taught in school that the component "geo" in all the scientific terms applied to Earth sciences—geo-graphy, geo-metry, geo-logy, etc.—comes from the Greek Gaia (or Gaea), their name for the goddess of Earth. We were not taught where the Greeks picked up this term or what its real meaning was. The answer is that it came from the Sumerian KI or GI.

Until the Voyager discoveries, the prevailing scientific viewpoint considered the Solar System as we see it today, to be the way it had taken shape soon after its beginning, formed by immutable laws of celestial motion and the force of gravity. There have been oddballs, to be sure—meteorites that come from somewhere and collide with the stable members of the system, pock marking with craters, and comets that zoom about in greatly elongated orbits, appearing from somewhere and disappearing, it seems, to nowhere. But these examples of comic debris, it has been assumed, go back to the very beginning of the Solar System, some 4.5 billion years ago, and are pieces of planetary matter that failed to be incorporated into the planets or their moons and rings. A little more baffling has been the asteroid belt, a band of rocks that form an orbiting chain between Mars and Jupiter. According to Bode's Law (an empirical mathematical "law" that gives the spacing of the planets from the Sun as 0, 3, 6, 12, 24, etc.), there should have been a planet, at least twice the size of Earth, between Mars and Jupiter. Is the orbiting debris of the asteroid belt the remains of such a planet? The affirmative answer is

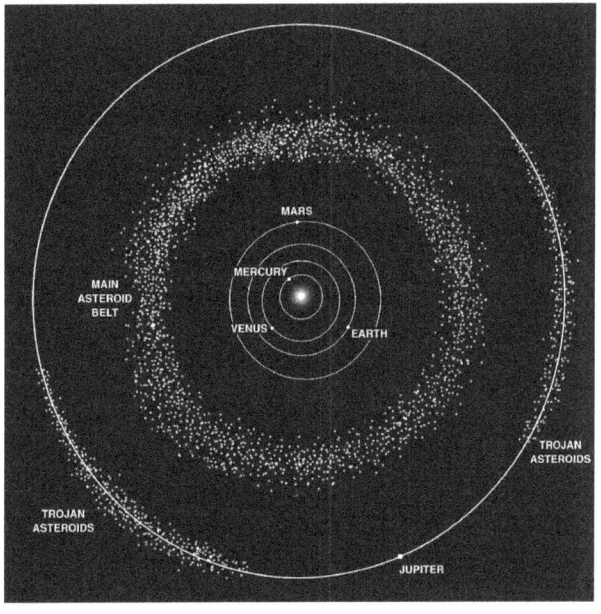

plagued by two problems: the total amount of matter in the asteroid belt does not add up to the mass of such a planet, and there is no plausible explanation for what might have caused the breakup of such a hypothetical planet. If there was a celestial collision, then when? With what? And why? The scientists have no definitive answer.

The realization that there had to be one or more major collisions that changed the Solar System from its initial form became inescapable after the Uranus flyby in 1986. That Uranus was tilted on its side was already known from telescopic and other instrumental observations even before the Voyager encounter. But was it formed that way from the very beginning, or did some external force—a forceful collision or encounter with another major celestial body—bring about the tilting?

The theoretical basis for the answer was enunciated, prior to the encounter with Uranus, by Dr. Christian Veillet (among others). If the moons formed at the same time as Uranus, the celestial "raw material" from which they agglomerated should have condensed the heavier matter nearer the planet; there should be more of heavier, rocky material and thinner ice coats on the inner moons and a lighter combination of materials (more water ice, less rocks) on the other moons. By the same principle of the distribution of material in the Solar System—a larger proportion of heavier matter nearer the Sun, more of the lighter matter (in a "gaseous" state) farther out—the moons of the more distant Uranus should be proportionally lighter than those of the nearer Saturn.

But the findings revealed a situation contrary to these expectations. In the comprehensive summary reports on the Uranus encounter, a team of forty scientists concluded that the densities of the Uranus moons (except for that of the moon Miranda) "are significantly heavier than those of the icy satellites of Saturn." Likewise, the Voyager 2 data showed—again contrary to what "should have been"—that the two larger inner moons of Uranus, Ariel and Umbriel, are lighter in composition (thick, ice layers; small, rock cores) than the outer moons Titania and Oberon, which were discovered to be made mostly of heavy, rocky material and had only thin coats of ice.

These findings by Voyager 2 were not the only clues suggesting that the moons of Uranus were not formed at the same time as the planet itself, but rather some time later in unusual circumstances. Many other anomalies were discovered of which these mentioned were just a few. But the astronomers had to accept the obvious conclusions that, "A likely possibility is that an interloper from outside the Uranus system came in and struck a once larger moon sufficiently hard to have fractured it." Meaning that the debris and effect was the cause of the anomalies. The forty-strong team of investigating scientists had to say that the only plausible answer was that, "We must take into account the strong possibility that satellite formation (moon formation) conditions were affected by the event that created Uranus's large obliquity (tilt). It means that in all probability the moons in question were created as a result of the collision that knocked Uranus on its side. A collision with something the size of Earth traveling at about 40,000 miles per hour could have done it, probably about four billion years ago. But in all the briefings, no attempt was made to suggest what that "something" was, where it had come from and how it happened to collide with, or bang into, Uranus.

With that in mind, there are three important points to remember with regard to the interactions of the planets Nibiru and Tiamat:

1) Tiamat, as part of the original system and located where the asteroid belt is today, orbited counterclockwise. Nibiru, captured into the system, orbited clockwise.

2) During the time of the horrendous disturbance of the Solar System, the most dangerous body to the stability or safety of the other planets was Tiamat's "leader of the host" a large satellite, a moon that was almost planetary size and was about to attain its independent "destiny"—its own orbit around the Sun. Tiamat "cast a spell for him, to sit among the celestials gods she exalted him," meaning that Tiamat's gravitational and magnetic effects controlled this large moon. It was called, in Sumerian, KIN.GU—"Great Emissary." It was the satellite moon, which became our Moon, Kingu, when it was transferred uninjured into our orbit with the remainder of Tiamat that became Earth.

3) There were two collisional events between the Nibiru system and the Tiamat system. In the first event, the moons of Nibiru slammed into Tiamat; Nibiru itself did not hit Tiamat. In the second event, Nibiru did indeed crash into Tiamat.

All this astronomical detail concerning the evidence for some large body, four billion years ago, being captured into the Solar System and slamming into various existing planets and moons, appears in the Sumerian records, according to Sitchin. It shows Nibiru being captured into the solar system from outside and careening through the system, colliding with various bodies until the system settles down. These Sumerian records hold answers to the questions about this evidence of destruction that has baffled astronomers and astrophysicists for decades. It is frustrating that their own evidence clearly points to a massive "body," a planet, as the actual cause, yet they won't acknowledge it and ignore or cover up its existence.

I have written to some astronomers and scientists who have been part of TV documentaries on this kind of topic, always stopping short of admission or even conjecture... one has even admitted privately that he says what the corporate media who put on the documentaries wants him to say because they pay him a lot of money. Notice how the scripts of this type always end with a question rather than a conclusion... so they can do yet another show on the same topic to make some more money. I have been asked to participate in this type of documentary only once—although I have been interviewed or presented on over 300 talk radio and TV talk shows. I turned down the offer on the first one because they refused, as all do, to allow me to review what they had incorporated of my work and what they wanted me to say ahead of time, before it was aired. Word probably gets around quickly if one is not cooperative. But I was not going to allow the editing of my material in such a way that it might have twisted it around to make it say what they wanted it to say. Fine. I don't need that.

Chapter 9 of *The Twelfth Planet* is another example of Sitchin's astute linguistic capabilities. After explaining the astronomical and astronautical capabilities and needs of the Anunnaki for landing and takeoff of their spacecraft, he presents a brilliant analysis and exposition of the planisphere disk, which had puzzled experts for so long. By reading the seemingly meaningless characters not as Assyrian word-signs but as Sumerian word-syllables, the entire piece becomes recognizable as a flight map among the planets. I hold an instrument rated pilot's license and this planisphere flight map reminds me of the route and landing charts familiar to modern pilots. It has only been very recently that the charts and maps have been available through electronic devices and cockpit screens. If indeed the Anunnaki were using clay tablet charts in their cockpits—it seems implausible—they would have been more underdeveloped at that time than we tend to think of them. My personal opinion is that this Akkadian copy is a copy of a Sumerian original, as Sitchin identifies it. It is a copy of a more sophisticated, perhaps paper or even a sort of electronic original, much more fitting for use in a cockpit. Again we see how our reaching an advanced scientific or technological level of development, in this instance our ability to fly in space, enables our understanding of a previously mystifying item—the planisphere in this case.

Another example of the key role our technological advancement plays in our understand of ancient phenomena: Until a few decades ago, the notion that a common mortal can put on some special clothes, strap himself in the front part of a long object, then zoom off the face of Earth, seemed preposterous or worse. A century or so ago, such a notion would not have even come about, for there was nothing in human experience or knowledge to trigger such fantasies.

Yet, the Egyptians—5000 years ago—could readily visualize all this happening to their Pharaoh: he would journey to a launch site east of Egypt; he would enter a subterranean complex of tunnels and chambers; he would safely pass by what may have been the installation's atomic plant and radiation chamber. He would don the suit and gear of an astronaut, enter the cabin of an Ascender, and sit strapped between two gods. And then, as the double doors would open, and the dawn skies would be revealed, the jet engines would ignite and the Ascender would turn into the Celestial Ladder by which the Pharaoh will reach the Abode of the Gods on their "Planet of Millions of Years." On what TV screens had the Egyptians seen such things happen, that they so firmly believed that all this was really possible?

In the absence of television in their homes, the only alternative would have been to either go to the Spaceport and watch the rocket ships come and go, or visit some sort of "Smithsonian" type museum and see the craft on display, accompanied by a knowing guide or by viewing flight simulations. The evidence suggests that the ancient Egyptians had indeed done that: they had seen the launch site, the hardware, and the astronauts with their own eyes. But the astronauts were not Earthlings going elsewhere: they were, rather, astronauts from elsewhere who had come to Planet Earth. So it is easy for us who have indeed watched rockets being launched and witnessed the astronauts flying and operating in the spaceship cockpits or spacewalking outside of the Space Shuttle to accept the reality of rocketships and, for many, the reality of alien "flying saucers" probably operating on antigravity.

The body of evidence is actually quite huge. And still the academics, scientists and astronomers are reluctant to accept the overwhelming evidence of the Anunnaki, our genetic creation, the history of our solar system… and only now are Sitchin Studies reaching the university curriculum.

Chapter 6

SITCHIN'S EXTENSIVE EVIDENCE

It is with *The Twelfth Planet*, Chapters 9, 10 and 11, that we encounter some of the more profound matters of history.

But before we do that I want to take you through the proofs for Sitchin's thesis. Because the thesis is controversial in the minds of some, it would be well for you to have considered the proofs in the event that you become engaged in discussion. There are some scientific objections to the thesis that are serious enough to contemplate. Consider the question, How could the Anunnaki, clearly described as comfortable in Earth gravity and atmosphere, very similar to current humans in all ways—although they did seem to need sunglasses as often depicted—have evolved on a planet within our solar system whose orbital apogee takes it into the deep cold of space, far out from the sun, for much of its orbit? Sitchin has pointed out that the ancient records repeatedly describe Nibiru as a "radiant" planet. This may be understood as having a high core temperature. Although controversial, there is also astrophysical opinion that a large body such as Nibiru in elongated orbit is constantly tending toward a circular orbit. This causes stresses in the planet that could generate a good deal of heat. That their planet is gradually cooling may be indicated by Sitchin's interpretation of their exploiting Earth (which contains most of the gold identifiable in the solar system) for the purpose of obtaining large quantities of gold, needed for molecular seeding of their atmosphere with a reflective gold shielding. Pertinent here is Dr. Robert Harrington's confident statement to Sitchin during their conference at Harrington's office at the Naval Observatory that the tenth planet (X/Nibiru) is "a nice, good planet, could be surrounded by gases, probably has an atmosphere and could support life like ours." The sunlight level there might be quite different than on Earth because of the great distance from the Sun. The Anunnaki were often depicted or sculpted with what seemed to obviously be sunglasses.

If, however, the Anunnaki evolved on a radically different planet from Earth under quite different conditions on which to adapt, why should they have turned out to be so identical to human specie? It's a reasonable question. Sitchin's answer is based on the collisional event between the intruder planet, Nibiru, and the planet Tiamat, the residual part of which recongealed into the Earth after being driven into current Earth orbit. That the two, or at least one, of the colliding planets was sufficiently developed to have evolved basic organic compounds, perhaps even simple life or even more complex life, the cross-seeding of everything from amino acids to more complicated organic compounds or even primitive organisms, could account for the evolutionary similarity. Although I find it a reasonable hypothesis, even trivial, that advanced civilizations would be capable of crossing extremely different genomes, perhaps with even radically different bases, the cross-seeding theory can account for the apparent relative ease with which the Anunnaki impinged their genes on the genes of *Homo erectus*. The Anunnaki genetic skill level, 300,000 years ago, is indicated well by the recorded fact that, in early trials, they succeeded in crossing animal genes with *Homo erectus* genes, obtaining living hybrids but never a satisfactory product—which led them to modify *Homo erectus* genes with their advanced genes.

Professor Paul Davies from the Australian Centre for Astrobiology in Sydney put forth an idea suggesting that there could be, hidden within our DNA, an alien message written in binary code. Which brings up another thoughtful question: If our genome is estimated as 98% to 99% similar to the chimpanzee, how could there be a melding of the *Homo erectus* and Anunnaki genomes, or impingement of the advanced code on the lesser advanced one detectable? This is a major question likely answerable only by the geneticists open-minded enough to attack it. Two of them have—suggesting that there is evidence of alien sequences in our genetic code. Two major scientists who worked on the Human Genome Project for 13 years, Vladimir Shcherbak and Maxim Makukov, have come out publicly and said they believe humans were designed by a higher power, most likely an alien civilization working to plant life on other planets and/or to preserve some kind of message in our DNA. They believe that out of all the

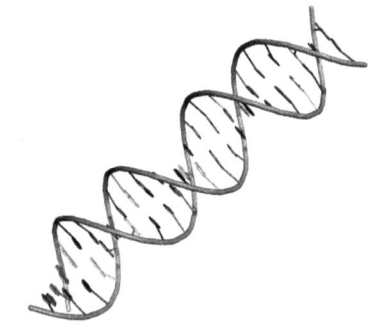

Concealed within our "junk DNA" could be the best evidence for an outside intelligence having been here on Earth in the ancient past.

non-coding sequences in our DNA (otherwise considered "junk DNA"), 97 per cent of it is actual genetic code from alien life, and they claim this to be *verifiable*. Who would know better than these two, who were dissecting and examining our entire genetic code for 13 years? Good for them for speaking up. Said Makukov, "Sooner or later, we have to accept the fact that all life on Earth carries the genetic code of our extraterrestrial cousins and that evolution is not what we think it is."

The Astronomical Evidence

A key underpinning of the Sitchin paradigm is the existence, now and in the past, of the tenth planet in our solar system, the home planet of the Anunnaki, with the size, orbit and characteristics described, as Sitchin has demonstrated, in the *Enuma Elish* and corroborated by Harrington, now deceased, former Chief of the U.S. Naval Observatory.

Tombaugh discovered Pluto in 1930. Christie, of the U.S. Naval Observatory, discovered Charon, Pluto's moon, in 1978. The characteristics of Pluto, derivable from the nature of Charon, demonstrated that there must still be a large planet undiscovered and further out because Pluto could not be the cause of the residuals, the vertical "wobbles," clearly identifiable in the orbital paths of Uranus and Neptune, and signaling the gravitational influence of another large planet in the solar system. Note that was in 1978-9.

The IRAS (Infrared Astronomical Satellite), during 1983-84, produced observations of a tenth planet so robust that one of the astronomers on the project, Ray Reynolds, said in a New York Times interview, that "astronomers are so sure of it that all that remains is to name it"—from which point the information has becomes curiously "guarded." In 1992 Harrington and Van Flandern, both of the Naval Observatory, working with all the information they had at hand and doing parallel computer studies, published their findings and opinion that there is, indeed, a tenth planet, even calling it an "intruder" planet. The search was narrowed to the southern skies, tipped on an angle below the ecliptic—the plane in which the other planets orbit the sun. Harrington, having read *The Twelfth Planet* and translations of the *Enuma Elish*, invited Sitchin to a meeting at his office and they correlated the current findings with the ancient records. As a result, they considered the *Enuma Elish*—a document deemed by "mainstream" scholars as being a mythic tale of a battle between good and evil—to be a real a history of the formation of our solar system, and more.

It is my opinion, after working with Sitchin's material since 1976, that, in light of the evidence already obtained through 1) the use of the Pioneer 10 and 11; 2) two Voyager space craft; 3) the Infrared Imaging Satellite (IRAS, 1983-84) results; 4) the announcements by NASA's John Andersen that there is no twin to our Sun but there is evidence for a large tenth planet; and 5) the clear and unequivocal statements of Harrington when consulting with Sitchin; that the search has already been accomplished and completed. It is also my opinion that the planet has already been found—and is being tracked.

We need to force the issue of the tenth planet being known to exist and part of our solar system, not just to demonstrate the validity of the new paradigm but for a very practical reason. The ancient records are very clear. The passage of the tenth planet, Nibiru, once every 3600 years, through the inner solar system affects the Earth, sometimes in catastrophic ways, as was recorded in the history of cultures worldwide, with the Flood.

The Technological Evidence

Ooparts is the term used to describe Out Of Place Artifacts in time, consisting of tools, technical devices, toys, architecture, artful depictions, and documents which have come to light through archaeological excavation or discovery. Almost everyone is familiar, through published works or documentaries, with the clay pot batteries still containing the electrodes from the Iraqi desert, dated 2500 B.C.; the flyable model airplane from a pyramid tomb; the sophisticated machining of stone requiring the most advanced techniques we know today; the 1200-ton, precision-cut blocks of stone in the Baalbek temple foundation that we could not even handle today; an ancient relief frieze from an Abydos temple depicting rockets, airplanes and even a helicopter, etc.

All of these ooparts, coupled with evidence from many disciplines and the historical records, indicate that an advanced civilization existed in those times that possessed a high degree of technology—and that civilization was indeed that of the Anunnaki.

The Documentary Evidence

The recorded historical documentation (from ancient times) for the existence and deeds of the Anunnaki has become gradually available to us only since the early 1800s. The excavation of the ancient sites of Mesopotamia brought to light the amazingly advanced civilization of Sumer and, with it, thousands of clay tablets containing not only mundane records of commerce, marriages, military actions and advanced astronomical calculation systems, but of the history of the Anunnaki themselves. It is clear from those records that the Sumerians knew these aliens to be real flesh and blood. The library of the ruler Ashurbanipal at Nineveh was discovered to have burnt down and the clay tablets held there were fired, which preserved them for our reading. One of the most impressive finds in recent times has been a sealed, extensive library in Sippar holding, neatly arranged on shelves, a set of some 400-plus elaborate clay tablets containing an unbroken record of the history of those ancient times, a sort of time capsule. The evidence is so overwhelming and robust that, if it weren't for those with power enough to suppress it all (which they did), it would have been accepted and our worldview changed a century ago, or perhaps earlier.

The Genetic Evidence

The recovered records place the location of the Anunnaki laboratory where the first humans were literally produced in east central Africa, just above their gold mines. This falls precisely on the map where the modern mitochondrial DNA "search for Eve" places the first woman *Homo sapiens*, and in the same time period. (The gold mining engineers of Africa have also rediscovered 100,000 year-old gold mines in that area, clearly at a time when man was too primitive to have an interest or use for gold, or possess a knowledge about mining.) The evidence for, and description of, advanced genetic engineering is all there, found in the ancient documents. Our rapid progress from inception to going to Mars so soon, after only 250,000 years, does not correspond to the million-year periodicities of slow evolutionary development of other species, such as *Homo erectus* before us. As so many thinkers have pointed out, we are radically and anomalously different.

My considered opinion is that the evidence is overwhelming. The advances in our scientific discoveries in genetic, mitochondrial DNA research, space and planetary science, archaeology, paleontology, anthropology, and linguistics, as well as even the physics of metallurgy, have enabled Sitchin and Gardner to demystify the advanced technologies of the Anunnaki and identify and explain ooparts and the mind-boggling facts of our creation. We had progressed from being their slave animals to a limited partnership and, since they phased back and off Earth, are now phasing out of a 3000-year traumatic transition to species independence (a rapid metamorphic process), under the imperative of our advanced Anunnaki genetic component.

A primary obstacle to clear meaning is the necessity, on Sitchin's part, to rely sometimes too heavily on the Old Testament versions of historical events rather than original Sumerian and Mesopotamian sources. In fairness, the reason for this is because these particular older original sources were not available at the time he needed them with regard to some topics. *Genesis Revisited*, Chapter 3, is of tremendous service in that Sitchin uses the latest science to sharpen the picture and resolve the questions about our species and its chronology.

Let us return to the central element of our history, our creation in an African Anunnaki laboratory.

The mutiny of the Anunnaki mine workers started the process of our species' initiation when Enki suggested, as an answer, that a slave species be created. Be aware that it may have taken the Anunnaki mining crews up to 100,000 of our years to become rebellious and to mutiny. This is a clue to the time frames within which the Anunnaki operated. But the lengthy creation process, of which Ninlil (Ninhursag) was a key figure, is fascinating not just because it involved complex genetics many thousands of years ago, but that it has only been quite recently that we have understood genetics well enough to follow the processes and their results in our day.

The actual process of genetic science employed by Enki and Ninhursag is so fascinating and engrossing that we sometimes miss the questions generated by it. From the point of view of ethics or with regard to the element of human dignity, were the "birth goddesses" ordered to perform their birthing function or did they all volunteer? It is difficult to determine from the information in the olden texts, but there did seem to be an acceptance of any ethical or moral considerations on the part of the Anunnaki for any and all parts of the procedures—from test tube fertilization to birth goddess function.

With regard to the topic of sexuality: Sitchin points out that "knowing" is the term used throughout the Old Testament for sexual intercourse, usually in the context of a husband and wife doing so to procreate children. After analyzing the Old Testament tale about the Lord forbidding Adam and Eve, Sitchin concludes that the tale is "…the story of a crucial step in Man's development, *the acquisition of the ability to procreate*. The logic here is simple: we were genetically engineered into existence as a slave species. We came into existence as a hybrid and hybrids are sterile. Then the Anunnaki needed and wanted more of us. Our services were increased, so they gave us the ability to procreate so we would do so faster. Once able to procreate and multiply, the source and motivation for migrations were in place.

In light of the tales that detail the creation of us, Sitchin is quite correct in revealing that "knowing" good and evil had to do with the acquisition of the ability to procreate. I personally find it difficult to determine that we can know definitively if there were a Tree of Good, a Tree of Life, a Tree of Evil—if they were literally, biologically real or if they were symbolic.

What about the quest for immortality on the part of humans once we were created? Several questions are prompted by the metaphors used in the Biblical account. Why didn't Enki give the newly created creature immortality? If there was, as stated, a Tree of Life and a Tree of Good and Evil planted and grown in the Garden of Eden by the Lord, were they actual or symbolic trees? If real and not metaphorical what, specifically, were their species and possible fruit? If real, was—or is—the fruit of either of these trees capable of bestowing longevity or immortality on an Anunnaki or human individual?

The short answers are accurate enough: Enki did not include longevity, much less immortality, in the newly created human hybrid genome because we were meant to be slaves to be used by the Anunnaki for their purposes—so our life spans, our shelf life, did not matter if we began to age and wear out.

But the matter did not rest there. In his second book of the Earth Chronicles Series, *The Stairway to Heaven*, Sitchin gives the history of the search for immortality by humans and the actual bestowing of it on special humans. A single example: Enoch was a ruler in the line of Adam. According to the Hebrew tradition he was actually taken up to "Heaven," to planet Nibiru or an Anunnaki space station, and taught various forms of profound knowledge. He was then returned to Earth and, after teaching his brethren for some time, was taken permanently up to "Heaven" (Nibiru), obviously to dwell there. It shows that humans could coexist on an equal basis with the Anunnaki if given the opportunity, and could exist on a foreign planet with suitable conditions.

Some Pharaohs, because of their exalted position, were considered to be almost as "gods," Anunnaki equals, and rewarded with immortality. They were taken up to Nibiru in some type of craft, which has been depicted in ancient writings, as a reward for their service. From the records it seems that a pharaoh's body would be mummified for the purpose of preservation in the "next life," but their soul and personality would be honored instead of the body. Their body would be ceremonially escorted to the spaceport and greeted by Anunnaki in elaborate, ceremonial stages and then transported to Nibiru ("Heaven"), to experience the next life. The preservation of mummies begs the question as to whether or not these pharaohs were brought back to life as a reward for their service and allowed to live among these advanced beings.

It is necessary to clear up what is an apparent error in Sitchin's interpretation: he takes the tale of Cain, son of Adam and Eve, murdering his brother, Abel, at face value, as being accurate and true. His ingrained training in the Hebrew Old Testament took the tale as true and he writes that the line of Cain, who had two sons and four grandsons, was eventually ignored because "...the Old Testament, considering the line of Cain to be accursed, lost all interest in tracking further their genealogies and fate."

Further research by Gardner shows a radically different picture of the "sons of the gods" (the *nene ha-elohim*) in regard to Cain and his line. After the Flood, "when the kingship was lowered from heaven"—when the Anunnaki had reestablished kingship on Earth probably by decree from Nibiru—"the senior royal descent was not the line from Eve's third son Seth, as portrayed in Genesis. It was, in accordance with the earliest matriarchal tradition, the line from her first and senior son, Cain—the character whom the earliest Hebrew Bible texts said was superior to his brother Abel, did not murder him, and who was so maliciously discredited by the Christian Church." This is an important correction, with thanks to Gardner, because it throws light on the nature of the "sacred kingship" of the GR AL, the Grail kingly line, of which Cain was first.

Gardner, in a few paragraphs, clears up another central point: the real nature of Yahweh. "Today's conventional teaching of the Babel incident tells only of the wrath of Jehovah, but the Genesis text does actually cite him along with other gods. Even the King James English-language edition states that when God saw the people building their tower, he said, 'Go to; let us go down...'(Genesis 11:17)" What has occurred over the centuries is that, irrespective of the biblical texts, Jehovah has been sidestepped into a wholly singular identity, the thoroughly non-historical identity of the "One God," which prevails today. In this context (outsides the more traditional esoteric circles), Jehovah has been divested of his wife, his family and his fellow gods, to be left alone in a wilderness of enigma that no one has ever truly understood. There are numerous references in the Old Testament to the "gods" (the *Elohim)* and to the "sons of the gods" (the *bene ha-elohim*) and these seemingly anomalous entries have caused their own confusion through the years because of Jehovah's perceived isolation.

A longstanding puzzle that has loomed in the face of all biblical researchers is God's distinctly split personality. One minute he is the gentle shepherd calling his loyal sheep to his side; in the next minute he is launching fire and brimstone upon his own supporters. In the book of Isaiah (45:7) God is quoted as saying, "I create evil," and in Amos (3:6) it is asked, "Shall there be evil in a city, and the Lord hath not done it?" None of this has ever made any sense—but it makes all the sense in the world if Jehovah (Enlil/El) is removed from the constraints of religious dogma and placed in his proper historical context as one of a pantheon of Anunnaki who had their own ups and downs, their own political disagreements, made their own misjudgments and perpetrated their own wrongdoings. In the original Sumerian tradition, the Anunnaki were just as fallible as ordinary human beings, and in the Canaanite tradition, the Elohim were equally so. One always knew which god to support and which to fault—but Jehovah has been left alone to take all the praise and all the blame, whether deserved or not. It is generally the case that the bad things are simply said to be "His will," and are left unchallenged with wholly inadequate justifications such as, "God moves in mysterious ways."

It is worth covering at length the real nature of the God of the Bible and all the god-fearing religions because it is at the heart of the matter for breaking the godspell. It takes a bit of time for a person who has been brought up thoroughly indoctrinated in one of these religions to assimilate the profound change of thinking required. Perhaps, when the godspell is finally totally dissipated, the generically human focus will be on whether there is a principle or entity beyond the beyond and infinity who/which might be the cause of everything, all universes, etc. But worship—work-ship—will not be involved.

Chapter 13 of *The Twelfth Planet* focuses on another very important matter for each of us individually, and our species collectively—the implications and warning to us from the Flood. It is clear through our studies that, as Sitchin points out, the cause of that planetary catastrophic event was a passing of Nibiru.

The effects on the Earth of a close passing, as with the Flood, when sampled from the ancient records, are horrendous. The Old Testament, relating to the story of Noah, states, "On that day, all the fountains of the great deep burst open… And the waters became exceedingly strong upon the earth and all the high mountains were covered,… fifteen cubits above them did the water prevail,… Both man and cattle and creeping things and the birds of the skies were wiped off from the Earth;… And after 150 days the waters were less;…"

The earlier Sumerian flood story, with Noah previously named Utnapishtim, refers the south-storm, "Gathering speed as it blew, submerging the mountains, overtaking the people like a battle…"

The Mother Goddess, Ninhursag, wept upon seeing the devastation, stating her creatures were swept away like flies and were "taken by the rolling sea." When it was all over, "Stillness had set in. And all of Mankind had returned to clay."

These brief statements from our Bible and the original Flood story sums it up well enough for one to appreciate the horrendous nature of the event, but there are many other details that have been furnished by the legends preserved by peoples all over the planet. Not only humans but the Anunnaki themselves literally had to start over, to rebuild their cities, their flight facilities; just about everything had been wiped out because it was not just a tsunami that had swept up from the South through the Middle East, it was a planetary-wide cataclysm that left only a smattering of humans alive and the Anunnaki survived only because they could get airborne and space-born, to ride it out. It is easy to understand what a turning point in both human and Anunnaki history the Flood was.

A major development following the recovery from the Flood was the opening up of gold producing facilities in South America. In *The Lost Realms*, Sitchin presents the evidence for the Anunnaki presence there, which I will briefly outline here: The huge, intricate stone work in the Peruvian mountains that has mystified so many investigators, along with the impressive ziggurat constructions done by the Anunnaki in the Middle East, are similar in design. The words still in use in the native languages of Peru, even the names of the tribes and groups, are derivatives of Sumerian.

The Anunnaki knew that there were sources of gold there—from almost solid mountains of it to streams full of gold nuggets all along the western coastal mountainous areas, and brought humans there to do the mining. Much later, when the Spaniards came to conquer and pillage, they discovered that the natives had a tradition that mirrored the human/Anunnaki history in the Middle East. Ningishida, son of Enki, was put in charge of the Western hemisphere. He had been known to the Egyptians as Thoth, and to the Mayans and other tribes he was known as Quetzalcoatl. He was the one, they said, who taught them the advanced ziggurat type of construction, the layout of cities, and civilized practices, as well as the astronomy and science they knew.

When the archaeological evidence was beginning to be uncovered in the South American and Mexico regions, the oldest traces of civilization was mystifyingly the Olmec, called the Mother Civilization, copied and adapted by all the others who came afterward. It dawned along the Mexican gulf coast at the beginning of the second millennium B.C. It was in full bloom at some forty sites by 1200 B.C., even possibly by 1500 B.C. Spreading in all directions, but mainly southward, it made its mark across Mesoamerica by 800 B.C. The Olmec, a negroid race, were native to their country on the western coast of Africa. Carvings on stone of various scenes depict the Olmecs as tall, heavily built with muscular bodies—"giants" in stature, no doubt, in the eyes of the indigenous Indian population. All in all, the capabilities, the scenes, the tools, appear to lead to one conclusion: the Olmecs were miners, come to the New World to extract some precious metals—probably gold, perhaps other rare minerals, too. When one compares the faces on the colossal Olmec heads with those of Nigerian West Africans, the gap of thousands of years is bridged by the obvious similarity. It is from that part of Africa that Thoth could have brought over his followers expert in mining, for it is there that gold, tin, and copper (to alloy bronze with), have been abundant. Nigeria has been renowned for its bronze figurines—cast in the telltale Lost Wax process—for millennia; recent research has carbon-dated some of their sites, in which the most ancient ones have been found to date to about 2100 B.C. It is there, in West Africa, that the country now called Ghana bore for centuries the name Gold Coast, for that is what it was—a source of gold known even to the Phoenicians. And then we have the area's Ashanti people, renowned throughout the continent of Africa for their goldsmithing skills.

It was, Sitchin opines, when the Old World order was upheavaled, that Thoth undertook the task of bringing his expert followers over: to start a new life, a new civilization, and new mining operations. In time, these operations and the miners (the Olmecs), moved south, first to Mexico's Pacific shores, then across the isthmus into northern South America. Their ultimate destination was the Chavin area; there they met the gold miners of Adad, the people of the golden wand. This meeting and association brought together the two Anunnaki-directed mining operations.

The Olmec were the source of many firsts in the Mesoamerica area. The first Mesoamerican glyphic writing appears in the Olmec realm; so does the Mesoamerican system of numeration, of dots and bars. The Long Count calendar inscriptions, with the enigmatic stating date of 3113 B.C; the first works of magnificent and monumental sculpted art; the first use of jade; the first depictions of hand-held weapons or tools; the first ceremonial centers; the first celestial orientations—all were achievements of the Olmecs. No wonder that with so many "firsts," some have compared the Olmec civilization of Mesoamerica to that of the Sumerians in Mesopotamia, which accounted for all the "firsts" in the ancient Near East. And like the Sumerian civilization, the Olmecs too, appeared suddenly, without a precedent or a prior period of gradual advancement. In their texts, the Sumerians described their civilization as a gift from the gods, the visitors to Earth who could roam the skies and were therefore often depicted as winged beings. The Olmecs expressed their "myths" in sculptured art. Their tales-in-stone are remarkably similar to the Sumerian.

Who were the people who had achieved these feats? Nicknamed Olmeca ("Rubber People") because their gulf-coast area was known for its rubber trees, they were in reality an enigma—strangers in a strange land, strangers from across the seas, people who belonged not just to another land, but to another continent. In an area of marshy coasts where stone is rare, they created and left behind stone monuments that amaze to this very day; of these, the most baffling are the ones that portray the Olmecs themselves. Unique in all respects are giant stone heads sculpted with incredible skill and unknown tools to portray Olmec leaders. The first investigator to see such a gigantic head called it "a work of art... a magnificent sculpture that most amazingly represents an Ethiopian." It was not until 1925 that the existence of such colossal stone heads was confirmed by Western scholars. One of the first ones discovered measured about eight feet in height, twenty-one feet in circumference and weighed about twenty-four tons. Each head portrays a distinctly different individual.

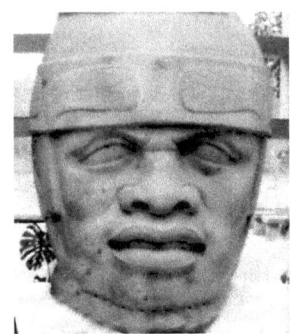

The San Lorenzo Colossal Head #8 stands 7.2 feet high, weighs about 13 tons, and is displayed at the Museum of Anthropology in Xalapa, Mexico. It was found in 1968 buried 16 feet deep, lying on its side next to a large, monumental throne.

The sites at which the colossal heads and other Olmec depictions have been found are no less intriguing; their size, magnitude, and structures reveal the work of organized settlers, not just of a few random shipwrecked visitors. La Venta was actually a small island in the swampy costal area that has been artificially shaped, land-filled and built up according to a preconceived plan. Major edifices, including an unusual conical "pyramid," elongated and circular mounds, structures, paved courts, altars, stelae, and other man-made features have been laid out with great geometric precision along a north-south axis extending for about three miles. In a place devoid of stones, an amazing variety of stones—each chosen for its special quality—was used in the structures, monuments, and stelae, although all of them required hauling over great distances. The conical pyramid alone necessitated the bringing and piling up of a million cubic feet of soil. It all called for tremendous physical effort. It also required a high level of architectural and stone-working expertise for which there had been no precedent in Mesoamerica; the art was obviously acquired elsewhere. The insistence on the employment of great blocks of stone—even if they had to be brought from afar—for monuments, commemorative sculptures, and burials, must serve as a clue to the enigmatic origin of the Olmecs. It is not hard to see the advanced technology of the Anunnaki as the source for the advanced tools and sciences of geometry and mathematics, which the Olmecs exhibited.

But we are still left with uncertainty and many questions with regard to the eventual fate of the Olmecs. The golden age of the New Realms did not last forever. Olmec sites in Mexico underwent destruction; the Olmecs themselves and their bearded companions met a brutal end. Mochica pottery depicts enslaving giants and winged "gods" warring with metal blades. The Ancient Empire witnessed tribal clashes and invasions. In the highlands of Titicaca, Aymara legends recalled invaders who marched up the mountains from the seacoast and slew the white men who were still there.

Were these reflections of the conflicts among the Anunnaki, in which they increasingly involved Mankind? Or did it all begin to happen after the gods had left—sailing off upon the sea, or ascending heavenward? Whichever way it happened, it is certain that in time the links between the Old Realms of the Middle East and the New Realms of the Americas were broken off. In the Old World the Americas became only a dim memory—hints made by this or that classical writer; tales of Atlantis heard from Egyptian priests; even perplexing maps that trace unknown continents. Was it all myth, were there really lands of gold and tin beyond the Pillars of Hercules? In time, the New Realms became the Lost Realms as far as Westerners who lived in other parts of that hemisphere were concerned—with their reality controlled more and more by the Church. In the New Realms themselves, the golden past became only a legendary memory as the centuries rolled on. But the memories would not die and tales persisted of how it all began and where—of Quetzalcoatl and Viracocha, and of how they will one day return.

I submit that Sitchin's analysis and interpretation of the evidence for the presence of the Olmecs and their civilization in Mesoamerica and his correlation of their contact with the bearded ones of Adad's mining group is wholly correct. His work on the "enigmatic" Olmec history has cleared that up and given us a strong picture of the way that the Olmec culture, obviously imported from the western coast of Africa, influenced the entire area, from Mesoamerica down through the northern part of South America. It is amazing that it has been only in the last few decades that serious archaeological work has been done to reveal the Olmec culture and contribution. I've place this consideration of the New Realm or New World here, in this book, because

Sitchin does not give it much direct or detailed mention in *The Twelfth Planet*, and it is well to know that the development of civilization in Mesoamerica and South America runs parallel to that of Sumer and Egypt.

In chapter 10 of *The Lost Realms*, which Sitchin devotes to Mesoamerica, he writes: "Every version of every legend in the Andes points to Lake Titicaca for the Beginning—the place where the great god Viracocha performed his creative feats, where mankind reappeared after the Deluge, where the ancestors of the Incas were granted a golden wand (a gold detector tool?) with which to establish Andean civilization. If this be fiction, then it is supported by fact; for it is on the shores of Lake Titicaca that the first and greatest city in all of the Americas had stood."

It's scope, the size of its monoliths, the intricate carvings upon its monuments and its statues have amazed all who have seen Tiahuanacu (as the place has been called) ever since the first chronicler described it for Europeans. Everyone equally wondered who had built this unique city and how, and puzzled over its untold antiquity. Yet the greatest puzzle of all is the location itself: a barren, almost lifeless place some 13,000 feet—four kilometers!—up among the highest Andean peaks that are permanently snow-covered. Why would anyone expend incredible effort to erect colossal edifices out of stone that had to be quarried and brought from many miles away in this treeless, windswept desolate place?

The waters hide a variety of strange fishes, which contribute to support a population necessarily scanty in a region where barley will not ripen except under very favorable circumstances; and where maize, in it most diminutive size, has its most precarious development; where the potato, shrunk to its smallest proportions is bitter; where the only grain is the quinoa; and where the only indigenous animals fit for food are the biscacha, the llama, and the vicuna. Yet in this treeless world were developed the

The legendary Gate of the Sun in Tiahuanacu, above, considered by some to be the oldest monument on Earth. Carved from a single block of stone, it weighs in at over 100 tons and has what many believe to be the ancient god Viracocha carved above the main doorway (below).

germs of Inca civilization from an earlier, original civilization which carved its memorials in massive stones, and left them on the plain of Tianhuanaco, and of which no tradition remains except that they are attributed to the work of the giants of old, who reared them in a single night.

We know the answer: the advanced Anunnaki were responsible. They were after the gold and, eventually, humans following their technology and architectural examples, settled the place, and it eventually grew. But there are still those who will not accept the clear and detailed history of the Anunnaki and for them, it is puzzling and problematic.

During the mid-1800s local natives, various builders in the capital of La Paz, and even the government itself (for construction of the railroad), had begun to systematically carry off the stone blocks, not for their artistic or archaeological value, but as freely available building materials. In the nearest town, on the peninsula of Copacabana, the church, as well as the villagers' abodes, were built of stones taken from the ancient ruins as if they were quarries. Even the cathedral in La Paz was erected using Tiahuanacu's stones. Yet the little that remained—most because it was too massive to move— impressed all that saw the remains as of a civilization that disappeared before that of the Incas began, a civilization contemporary with that of Egypt and the Near East. The remains indicate that the structures and monuments were the work of a people who were capable of a unique, perfect, and harmonious architecture—yet one that had no infancy and passed through no period of growth. If we see the hands of the Anunnaki in these marvels, the answers are easy... otherwise still a mystery. They opened up the continent for gold and over time, with the multiplying of humans, huge cities evolved.

Skipping far forward in time, by the time the Spaniards arrived—- seeking gold—the Aztec capital, Tenochtitlan, was an impressive metropolis. Their reports describe it as large, if not larger, than most European cities of the time, well laid out and administered. Situated on an island in Lake Texcoco, in the highlands' central valley, it was surrounded by water and intersected by canals—a Venice of the New World. The long and wide causeways that connected the city to the mainland made a great impression upon the Spaniards; so did the numerous canoes sailing the canals, the streets teeming with people, the marketplaces filled with merchants and merchandise from all over the realm. The royal palace was many-roomed, filled with riches and surrounded by gardens that included an aviary and a zoo. A great plaza, humming with activity, was the setting for festivities and military parades.

The records the Spaniards left bespeak their amazement at encountering not merely a cultured people, but also a civilization so similar to their own. Here, across what had been a forbidding ocean, for all intents and purposes isolated from the civilized world, was a state headed by a king—as in Europe. Noblemen, functionaries, and courtesans filled the royal court. Emissaries came and went. Tribute was extracted from vassal tribes, taxes were paid by loyal citizens. Royal archives kept written records of tribal histories, dynasties, and wealth. There was an army with an hierarchical command and perfected weapons. There were arts and crafts, music and dancing. There were festivals connected with the seasons and holy days prescribed by religion—a state religion just as in Europe. And there was the sacred precinct with its temples and chapels and residences, surrounded by a wall—just as at the Vatican in Rome—run by a hierarchy of priests who, just as in Europe of the time, were not only keepers of the faith and interpreters of divine will, but also guardians of the secrets of scientific knowledge. Of that, astrology, astronomy, and the mysteries of the calendar were paramount.

Astounded to discover not just a civilization in the New World, and one so akin to Europe's, and also the great number of people there, the Spaniards were doubly puzzled by the biblical threads in the Aztec legends. The Nahuatl tales of the creation of Man follow a very ancient Mesopotamian version that did not even find its way into the Book of Genesis! There lies a major clue as to the source of such tales extant in Indian cultures of the New World: the Spaniards, being of generally Catholic, Judeo-Christian, background took these legends to be "Biblical," but the simple fact is that the teacher of these cultures was the Anunnaki, Ningishida/Thoth/Quetzalcoatl, who, coming directly from the Anunnaki tradition and history, could have taught them the creation of Man from his own personal, direct experience.

Chapter 7

RETURN OF THE RED SUN

Other cultures worldwide have recorded cataclysms in the ancient past caused by a planetary body appearing in the skies. Some, like the Hopi Indians, have predicted its return. The 1963 book by Frank Waters, *The Book of the Hopi*, tells how a minister named David Young picked up a Hopi elder who needed a ride in 1958 on a deserted stretch of road. After a brief silence he introduced himself as White Feather, a Hopi of the ancient Bear Clan. He said he was old and dying and wanted pass along the nine prophecies of the Hopi elders. Six of them were fulfilled at that time, the seventh and eighth have come true since then, leaving the ninth and final prophecy today. It states, "You will hear of a dwelling-place in the heavens, above the Earth that shall fall with a great crash."

The prophecy continues, saying that a Red Sun will appear in the sky. It continues, saying, "These are the signs that great destruction is coming. The world shall rock to and fro. The white man will battle against other people in other lands—with those who possessed the first light of wisdom. There will be many columns of smoke and fire." It also says that the Red Sun will bring the Day of Purification, and much will need to be rebuilt.

The old man also told Young of the coming of Pahana, "the lost White Brother from the stars." He looks like the white man but is not the same, because he lacks the greed and cruelty. Pahana will come at the end of the Fourth World and at the beginning of the Fifth. "He shall bring with him the dawn of the Fifth World," said White Feather. "He shall plant the seeds of wisdom in their hearts."

What is the "Red Sun" and what are its effects that will "rock the world to and fro," which can cause great destruction and necessitate rebuilding the world, leading to a whole new way of life?

Perhaps without even realizing it, White Feather was speaking consistently with recorded legends of what happens when Nibiru returns, found in religious traditions and histories from over seventy countries on every continent, as well as tribal legends of at least forty tribes from around the world. Fifty names for the Purifier/Planet X/Nibiru are recorded in the research archives of anthropology, geology, and archaeology from all reaches of the Earth. Clearly, the Red Sun of the Hopi is Nibiru/Marduk of the Sumerians, Phaeton of the Greeks, The Lord of Hosts of the Old Testament, Wormwood of the New Testament, the Purifier is the Tenth Planet, X—a member of our solar system.

The return of Nibiru has been reliably recorded throughout history in various cultures worldwide. The growing effects of its return will transform this recurring event from a "fringe" belief into a stark reality.

And what is its "coming," as prophecied by the Hopi? It's on its way back into the inner solar system. It is gravitationally and geomagnetically affecting all the planets and the Sun. Global warming—on all the planets in our solar system—is most probably the early effects of its approach. It's Uranus, perhaps almost Neptune, in size. It was found by the IRAS, the joint Dutch-NASA Infrared Imaging Satellite in 1983 and announced six times in the major media and finally, they said, "...all that remains is to name it." It's the terrible elephant in our solar system living room. It's existence and threat is being covered up because the controllers know they can't do much about it except build underground cities for their own survival (and the rest of us be damned). They are no doubt are tracking it, as is the Vatican. Some of those who know about it at NASA have quietly built domed homes for themselves that can withstand wind speeds of hundreds of miles per hour. The legends and ancient records speak of the Purifier/X/Nibiru/Phaeton/the Destroyer/Frightener/Doomdragon as carrying with it a contingent, a retinue of bodies, moons, and asteroids perhaps, that are dragged behind or pushed in front of it. It's Passing is consistently described as causing a bombardment of the Earth with all sizes of space debris.

Geologist, geophysicist, D. S. Allan and J.B. Delair have given us a profound gift in their book, *Cataclysm!* They have exhaustively catalogued and analyzed both the frighteningly awesome physical evidence of the last time the effects were cataclysmic and they have collected the legends and warnings of the survivors from all over the world.

Two facts are clear from the testimony of the legend keepers combined with the accumulated scientific data: the Red Sun/Purifier/Nibiru comes through the inner solar system regularly, however, although storms and flooding disturbances are apparently always an effect, it does not always cause a cataclysmically severe upheavaling of the Earth. There is also copious balancing testimony in the archives that its coming, apparently at the majority of Passings, can mark the return of the Anunnaki, the transmission of advanced technology by them and a unifying influence on our species.

According to some sources the astrophysical calculations and, of late, computer simulations to determine what the effects on the Earth each time shall be, are extremely difficult to determine. The complexity of the problem is due to so many planets and moons in our system having to be taken into consideration.

The legends and warnings engraved in the memories of the keepers of the legends are traceable to the time the Red Sun came through within relatively recent human memory, causing planetary-wide devastation of the human species almost to the point of extinction through cataclysmic effects on the surface and in the atmosphere. They place the event at circa 9500 B.C. This was the Flood of the Old Testament, found here in an almost children's story form, rewritten from the detailed and precise records of ancient Sumer and Babylon, originally narrated to the scribes by the Anunnaki. These original stories accurately parallel the accounts passed down worldwide, through the centuries, by human survivors. The Sumerian accounts, although more scientifically detailed and socially comprehensive, are only one among the hundreds of narratives of awe, agony, and warning that echo down from the past.

The incontrovertible evidence from geology coupled with the reports of the survivors passed down to us as warnings are the same—whether from the Hopi, Navaho, Choctah, the Cashinaua of Brazil, the Ovaherero, Kanga, Loanga, Wanyoro of Africa, the Maya, Aztecs, the people of Ceylon and India, China or Australia, and more. They all relate that the Purifer/Nibiru/Red Sun brings conflagration, celestial disorder, flood, darkness, hail and fire, hurricanes, bombardment, a collapsed sky, hell on earth. It can also bring pole reversal, crustal slippage, geomagnetic chaos and ice-bound conditions of whole regions, wholesale extinctions, raised mountain ranges, and sunken continents.

The "Red Sun" (an apt title from the Hopis because the ancients described it as dark red) is a planet. Lloyd and Hazelwood and Masters can reduce it all to brown dwarfs, James McCanney can reduce it all to comets, Richard Hoagland can reduce it all to Mars, the neo-Gnostics reduce it all to archetypes, the mythologists to myth. It is not a "sun," not a brown dwarf, it is not a planet or moon of a brown dwarf, it is not a comet, it is not Mars, nor an archetype, nor myth. It is the tenth planet, X, Nibiru (the Planet of Crossing), as Robert Harrington, Chief Astronomer of the Naval Observatory, agreed in his interview with Sitchin when, working from all the accumulated data from the Pioneer and Voyager probes (that have recently exited the solar system), the visual residuals, the computer simulation studies, the IRAS success data, stated confidently that, "it is a nice, good planet, probably having an atmosphere that we could be comfortable in."(!) By then, the early nineties, he knew it was a planet, he knew that it was on the way back in on its huge, elongated, cometary-like 3600-year orbit, coming up from below the ecliptic rotational plane of the other planets at a thirty to forty degree pitch. And he methodically recounted to Sitchin the many effects on the other planets—Uranus tipped over ninety degrees, Pluto, formerly a moon of Saturn, was dislodged to become an independent planet, etc. These anomalies could have been caused when Nibiru was first captured into our system, echoing the details given in the *Enuma Elish*, which was the major document given to us by the Anunnaki, giving a detailed history of the formation of our solar system, their genetic engineering of us as a species, etc. He knew it was a planet and where it was located because he sent a scope and team to the southern hemisphere to get a visual. It should be no surprise to hear that Malachi Martin, as a priest working in the Vatican, reportedly discovered a computer there with a direct link to the Hubble telescope running a program called Wormwood. It should be no surprise that NASA has established an important astronomical observatory at the South Pole.

It is notably ironic that so many will accept the testimony of the tribal legend bearers to the existence and threat of the Red Sun/Purifier/X/Nibiru before they will accept the detailed astronomical and historical data and narratives of the Sumerians and the Old Testament, or even the evidence from contemporary science, because of the cover-up and silence of the astronomers. But, whether from the Hawaiians, the Hopi, or from the Selungs of the Mergui Archipelago or the Mixtecs of Mexico, the legend bearer "prophets" of the Hebrew tribe, or the Sumerians, the legends and warnings form a broad unifying platform for the hard, often grisly evidence from the natural sciences, geology, history, archaeology and astronomy.

How cataclysmic can some Passings be? The Hawaiian narratives say that there was land—a dry land mass of mountains and lowlands, a great continent stretching from Hawaii, including Samoa, Lalaloa (the Hawaiian version of Rarotonga) and reaching as far as New Zealand, also taking in Fiji. All this was called Ka-houpo-o-Kane, the Solar Plexus of Kane, and (afterward) was also called Moana-nui-kai-oo, the Great Engulfing Ocean. (Could this have been the lost Pacific continent of Mu?)

The Mixtecs of Mexico in their legends speak of a now-vanished land to the east of the present American coast: "In a single day all was lost, even the mountains sank into the water, subsequently there came a great deluge in which many of the sons and daughters of the gods perished." (Could this have been Atlantis?) Such a scenario could in fact reflect how cataclysmic these Passings may be. The pushing up of the Andes mountains, with seashells littering their tops, is dated to that horrendous time. The top of Mt. Everest bears astounding evidence: clam shells embedded at the crest. *Closed.* Closed clamshells say they were embedded there alive.

"Bone caves" all over the world bear the grim evidence of those luckless humans—compacted with the remains of plants, trees, animals, insects and birds, often from far away—who took refuge in cave shelters but perished in devastating floods and upheavaling. The stories of the lucky who took refuge in caves are informative. The Navajo legends that speak of their ancestors "coming out of the earth" used to seem like quaint little "genesis" myths. But one can understand them in more detail and context. "...at one time all the nations—Navajos, Pueblos, Coyoteros and white people—lived together underground, in the heart of a mountain, near the San Juan. Their food was meat, which they had in abundance, for all kinds of game were closed up with them in their cave; but their light was dim, and only endured for a few hours each day." When they emerged from the cave, digging their way out, they found themselves on the outside of a mountain surrounded by water which shortly afterwards ebbed away leaving a sea of mud. This is no naive, quaint, primitive tribal myth: it is hard-survival history. Allan and Delair cautiously estimate from the planetary evidence that we, the species *Sapiens*, survived that last cataclysmic Passing only in a handful of hundreds, maybe a thousand or so, in small pockets worldwide.

I have only touched on examples and histories here for the sake of bringing a single, crucial, unifying point, critical to our future survival and prosperity as a species, to our collective attention: we have all the evidence (and more than we need) to grasp the nature, scope and profundity of the potential threat of species extinction we face every 3600 years from the incoming Purifier/Planet X, Nibiru. It is inbound now: the IRAS findings show it.

White Feather's message mentions that there will be messengers that will precede this coming of the Purifier. We can be victims of the cover-up and the imposed silence of the astronomers, waiting for confirmation—as with alien disclosure, from some "official" "authority" or government that is doing the cover-up in the first place—of the knowledge and the danger, or we can be messengers to stir up the people to be aware and take thought about where the safe places will be, how to provide for the safety of the maximum number of the populations worldwide on a unified, coordinated basis, and come together as a species for survival. Denial is not an acceptable option.

The astronomers and those surely doing computer simulations, working from the IRAS data in 1983-84 to the present, must be freed, allowed and encouraged, indeed compelled to contribute. We can spin in analysis paralysis or we can prepare ourselves to contribute intelligently and maximally, whether this next Passing is of the cataclysmic kind or of the, apparently more common, milder kind that can certainly bring flooding (melting of the ice caps) and turbulent storm systems. Either kind will be White Feather's "alarm clock" kind of wakeup call to peaceful planetary unity and a new way of life. That is only fundamental terran, human to human, common sense politics and compassionate concern.

But what of the exo-politics of the matter?

The warning, worry and concern of aliens of various types who have communicated with remote viewers is that the computations involved in solving the multi-body problem as to where all the planets will be at each stage of Nibiru's inward passage, through the inner solar system to perigee, is so complex that it taxes even their advanced "computers"—so they may not be able to predict anything valuable until the "last minute." The position of the Earth, whether it is on the same side or somewhat protected on the opposite side of the Sun, when X the Purifier comes to perigee between Mars and Jupiter, is most likely the critical variable that determines the severity of the effects of any given 3600-year Passing. It is claimed that some advanced aliens are trying to "adjust" the orbits of some of our planets to minimize the horrendous effects of its Passing this next time around despite, as they have stated, that it "takes an awful lot of energy." Jim Marrs in *Alien Agenda* has done us a favor by cataloging the skilled remote viewer reports from various alien groups on this topic. Is this awesome fact, or fiction? I believe it's important enough to work hard together for a determination.

The records and legends of the Sumerians, passed down through the various Semitic tribes and still available on entire libraries of clay tablet records, knew Nibiru/X as the home planet of the Anunnaki. There is little record of it or them being effected by its Passing in the way the Earth can be or the way Mars, even closer to it when it passes through the adjacent Asteroid Belt, has been devastated. Possibly because it is much larger than Mars and the Earth, because it travels so rapidly, slingshotting through the Hammered Bracelet (the ancient's name for the asteroid belt, as taught to them by the Anunnaki... rediscovered in 1801). But the Anunnaki knew how to predict what degree of devastation was about to occur here on Earth 11,500 years ago from their observations and, no doubt at all, they could today afford us valuable information and perhaps even help towards our survival and rebuilding. The exopolitical choice between potential species extinction and asking for help (from an alien species of the demonstrated benevolent kind, the Anunnaki) seems quite clear and simple. This choice may avail itself should Nibiru appear in our skies, with the "Day of Purification" coming fast upon us.

We clearly need to exert as much pressure for clean, full disclosure of the facts about the Red Sun/Nibiru/Phaeton/Purifier as we work toward full disclosure of the real alien situation and the release of advanced technology, free energy, antigravity—all of which would be of high benefit for emergency survival and rebuilding. We need especially to free the scientists and geologists and astronomers from their prison of silence so they can eagerly inform us of the real nature of the situation. We need to know the position of the Red Sun/X/Nibiru on its incoming orbit, when it will cross the ecliptic, when it will come to perigee, what is the best estimate of potential effects of this Passing—the aliens supposedly talking to remote viewers say this will be a rather bad one— where the safest locations are, if indeed it's going to be a bad one. We need the intelligent, scientific, evaluation of the data to be shared with us if it is indeed being gathered. We need to know the year it will return to perigee. Sitchin stated publicly that he calculates, working from all the detailed ancient data, that it could be around the year 2078. Allan and Delair say the geophysical evidence for the Flood gives a period between 11,500 to 13,000 years ago. If we take the 2078 date and subtract 3600-year single orbit periods, we get a potential date for 8722 B.C., when compared to Allan and Delair's 9500 B.C. projection (less than an 800 year difference). The point is, there were major Earth changes that happened around this time. Today, we need to know what the best computer simulations indicate, taking into their scope all the potential variations of orbital shape and speed due to complex interactions with the other planets, actual data from the IRAS, (probably) withheld visual observations, and the judgments of experts who are not afraid to speak.

We can be passive, uncertain victims or we can be proactive messengers and teachers and promoters of unity for survival and rebuilding—whether this is a cataclysmic or milder Passing. We are all painfully aware of the problem that peaceful unity of all of us on this planet (critical to matriculation into stellar society) is difficult to achieve. But unity of intelligent understanding and action is even more pressing because of the proximity of the Purifier's potential threat. Acknowledging the perennial problem is insufficient. We can be exopolitically passive or exopolitically active in seeking intelligent contact with those species that can "help us to help ourselves." (What did Carl Sagan know and when did he know it?)

There is an upside. Whether we accept the existence of the Red Sun/Nibiru/the Purifier from the testimony of the elder legend keepers of the world or from the testimony of the NASA affiliated, head astronomer of the Naval Observatory, that very recognition of the Red Sun as what it really is, a planet in our system that constitutes a dire threat to our existence, affords us a context that contributes to the resolution of a major problem in anthropology and archaeology. The crux of the matter is focused on the actual age of the human species. Cremo and Thompson in *Forbidden Archaeology* state it thus: "We identify two main bodies of evidence. The first is a body of controversial evidence (A), which shows the existence of anatomically modern humans in the uncomfortably distant past. The second is a body of evidence (B), which can be interpreted as supporting the currently dominant views that anatomically modern humans evolved fairly recently, about 100,000 years ago in Africa, and perhaps elsewhere." Taken in the context of the repeated effects of the Passings of the Red Sun/Purifier, there is no inherent contradiction between these two bodies of evidence. Neither is there any intrinsic conflict between possible intervention by alien species in the genetics of humanoid species over the vast past, and the specific genetic creation of our species by genetic engineering some 200,000 years ago.

Consider that, when the geological evidence is examined and studied from over the entire planet in the context of repeated disturbances and upheavalings that have rocked the Earth "to and fro," tilted the entire globe into precession of its axes, instantly made species extinct or froze them in their tracks, literally raised mountains, emptied seas, raised and sunk continents, we can finally understand the profound anomalies and seeming contradictions.

The upheavaling of this cataclysmic type, literally churning, exposing, reversing, burying of whole segments of continental surfaces, tsunami waves of unbelievable height, burying entire living continental forests under fifty feet of earth, gives an invaluable key to one of the most confusing factors in archaeology and anthropology: the puzzling, often suppressed evidence in the fossil records for the existence of anatomically "modern" types of humanoids in the extremely distant past. It is trivial that a more recent "modern" human skull or skeleton could be unearthed from a strata of earth far below the surface because of the churning. This realization leads to an even more fundamental point: humanoid species, from perhaps millions if not a billion years ago on this planet could have evolved anatomically and culturally, repeatedly, to a point close if not equal to our species today, then been rendered extinct by a Passing of the Purifier/Nibiru of the cataclysmically upheavaling kind, perhaps leaving recognizable traces of a higher cultural level and an evolved anatomy. The process could have begun again, repeatedly, from a very primitive base of cellular organisms or, in some cases of near (rather than total) extinction, perhaps bootstrapped by a few survivors. The single cardinal fact of the potential for repeated extinctions by cataclysmic Passings could be responsible for the puzzling trace evidence of seemingly anatomically "modern" humans in the far distance past.

Further general obfuscation around the topic of anatomically "modern" types of humans existing in the very remote past is unnecessarily generated by the use of the term "human" in too general a way, allowing it to be applied to a variety of species indiscriminately. If a fossil footprint next to a dinosaur print says the maker's foot indicates a being with anatomical characteristics similar to ours, then that is reasonably all that should be inferred. In light of what we know of our anomalous genetics and the clear history of our synthetic inception, we should properly discriminate by concluding that there may well have been a humanoid species that evolved in the very distant past to a point where their anatomical characteristics were very close, perhaps even almost identical, to ours—although we, as a specific species, *Homo Sapiens sapiens*, did not come about by an evolutionary process.

White Feather's narrative raises another question: Who is Pahana?

More than one reference to the coming of a teacher who will help in the reconstruction after the devastation is found in the worldwide legends. White Feather speaks of one Pahana, who will return, "...and bring with him the dawn of the Fifth World." Other legends in Central America speak of a teacher who wore a long white robe, showing up soon after the devastation and traveling about, teaching the rudiments of organized civilization and technologies. These individuals could easily be identified as Anunnaki teachers assigned to do just that. The Anunnaki had originally decided to let the human species go extinct when they realized that the Passing would be of the cataclysmic kind, referring to the Flood found in the Old Testament story of Noah. The Sumerian histories tell in detail how Enlil, upon landing after the devastation, was furious that his brother Enki had warned and saved a handful of humans. He relented, however, under Enki's insistence that we were needed in the rebuilding. It would have been at that point that emissary teachers were dispatched over the world to seek out surviving humans and help in their recovery and rebuilding.

White Feather's reference to the "white people" taking refuge with the tribes in caves are spoken of by Allan and Delair as being described in "... numerous traditions distributed globally" as "culture heroes," consistently said to be "white, tall, bearded, and invariably superior to the aboriginal people among whom they appeared—often suddenly—to impart laws, crafts and useful information." Pahana could easily have been an Anunnaki "culture hero" assigned to the North American West.

Chapter 8

HUMAN EVOLUTION ON STEROIDS:
THE DNA OF THE GODS

Over the last one hundred and fifty years, the sciences of Anthropology, Archaeology, Paleontology, and Genetics, as well as the disciplines of History and Linguistics, have developed an explanation of our origins and evolution as the species, *Homo Sapiens sapiens*. More data is accumulated faster and faster and new techniques of discovery, interpretation and refinement become available frequently. Yet, after a century and a half, there are still serious disagreements among peers concerning even basic principles and criteria.

Between 1976 and 2008 the Sumerian scholar, Zecharia Sitchin, published, in his seven-volume Earth Chronicles series, a detailed account of the origins of our species derived from the same archaeological, historical and linguistic material. This scenario says that we were genetically engineered as a cross between the genes of an indigenous species, *Homo erectus*, and an alien species, the Anunnaki (Sumerian: those who came down from the heavens), who came from the tenth planet in our solar system. Sitchin was one of about two hundred scholars in the world who could read the Sumerian language. He was also well versed in all of the Semitic languages and has demonstrated consistent, excellent scholarship. Although his thesis has been summarily and preclusively rejected by those in the anthropological and archaeological arenas, it has gained the attention and interest of a few astronomers of note. This is because Sitchin's translations and interpretations of the major recovered document, the *Enuma Elish*, show a detailed account of the formation of our solar system, and have already provided detailed information about what the newest astronomical discoveries concerning our tenth planet are beginning to reveal.

This chapter presents the reasons why the sciences of Anthropology, Archaeology and Genetics should re-examine Sitchin's material concerning our origins on its own merit, as Robert Harrington of the U.S. Naval Observatory did in 1992, concerning the astronomy of our solar system and its direct connection to Sitchin's research. A scientific protocol for verifying or disproving Sitchin's material is suggested and the ramifications, if true, are examined.

A fundamental question, seldom considered due to our conditioning to look to the three classic criteria bases, theology, philosophy and science which are themselves brought into question by it: Is it possible to arrive at a new world view which corrects, completes and subsumes all our previous worldviews? Explains all our previous explanations? The answer is, unequivocally, Yes. But Kuhn, who examined the nature of scientific revolutions is painfully correct. We almost have to wait for the older generation to die off rather than see an orderly and rational transition to a new paradigm. Those with vested, academic teaching or scientific reputations or religious, political or economic interests are not going to acquiesce easily or at all. We operate far behind the evolutionary leading edge in this regard because of this inertia.

The Status Quo of the Sitchin Paradigm of Our Own Half-Alien Species' Origin and History

The Sumerian scholar, Zecharia Sitchin, published his first book, *The Twelfth Planet,* in 1976, the product of some thirty-five years of investigation. From his knowledge of Sumerian, the Semitic and other ancient languages and his research and study of the archaeological and Biblical data acquired over the last one hundred and fifty years he put forth his thesis that the transcultural gods known to all the ancient cultures were not mythological but real flesh and blood humanoid aliens, very much like humans, who had come here from the tenth planet in our solar system, Planet X in the popular press, called Nibiru by the Sumerians. They subsequently genetically engineered our species, originally as slave animals to work in their gold mines, by crossing their genes with those of *Homo erectus*.

The objections to Sitchin's thesis come from Mythology, which traditionally holds the gods to be mythic beings; from Archaeology, which has accepted the traditional Mythological interpretation; from Anthropology which would hold strictly to a natural evolutionary model; from Genetics which doubts it *apriori* on the basis of our limited current analysis and understanding of our genetic code:

Historical Background for the Sitchin Paradigm

There was literally no such thing as the discipline known as Archaeology in Western culture until the 1800s. The Roman Church controlled and determined the view of the past. Bishop Ussher's view, that the entire planet and life on it as described in Genesis came into existence through the auspices of a cosmic creator in 4004 B.C., was doctrine and one could be branded a heretic for disavowing it. Not until paleontological findings forced that view to be reevaluated and Schliemann, a wealthy German merchant, refusing to admit that the ancient cities and peoples were legend, found the actual city of Troy, was a window into the past opened and the mythic view questioned. Scientific Archaeology as we know it came into existence only when academics reluctantly had to acknowledge the past being dug up and collected by amateurs in the Middle East. Archaeology was born... and archaeologists rapidly came to be mistrusted and hated by the religious institutions that feared solid, physical revelations that could contradict their teachings and the accuracy of the "history" of the Old Testament.

Zecharia Sitchin at Troy, late 1990s, on top of a huge megalithic stone that was yet to be excavated. According to legend, the gods were instrumental in the building of Troy.

Now that we've walked on the moon, are exploring the solar system, and have probes going starward, the possibility of an alien civilization coming here is taken for granted and one coming here from inside our solar system seems trivial, rather than an impossible myth. "Mythinformation," accepts what could well be history as being nothing but stories and fantasies—but its practice has gradually eroded over time. After two hundred years of increasing failure, although still hiding behind tenure in the university, it has become a relatively dead issue. It's often been said that there's a core of truth in every myth, and we've been finding that core to be bigger than we thought in a large number of cases.

Consider what a typical reaction to this analysis would be from a religionist. What is said here by this author has been presented as carefully and reasonably as possible. However, *by the very fact of it being an analysis of our history and, almost incidentally, religion*, it will often first be perceived as the breaking of a taboo, perhaps a suspect attack, perhaps atheistic, or somehow less than "American" in its spirit, perhaps even "against God"—even though the evidence brought is no different in kind than that brought in any other archaeological area and, perhaps, is even more robust. This kind of objection is set aside here by religionists/fundamentalists in the same way in which religious objections to the general notion of evolution are dealt.

The Demise of the Mythological Explanation of the Gods

It is trivial that quaint local myths concerning many subjects exist all over the world among both more and less primitive peoples. We consider here only the latter day *interpretation* of the transcultural "gods" involved in human history as mythic, or unreal. We note also that the ancient civilizations did not call the Anunnaki "god" or "gods." They referred to them as masters, lords, in the sense of rulers.

Those still holding to the mythological interpretation are in an unenviable position. They find themselves having to hold that the same citizens of the first civilizations who, they claim, invented—or hallucinated—the gods through their primitive imaginings and naive proto-scientific projections of personality on the great forces of nature, were the same so-called primitives who somehow could build the stupendous Giza pyramid; also to somehow quarry, cut and move into place the one-thousand ton stones of the Baalbek "temple" (rocket platform), which even our modern technology cannot begin to lift; or to somehow know the great precessional cycle of the heavens, the existence of all ten of the planets of our solar system, and how our solar system was formed. (*Enuma Elish*) "Tenure tetanus" is always a serious block to accepting this—for what does a Mythologist do whose Ph.D. was written under these basic assumptions, and who is not about to burn rubber through the halls of academia while making a complete 180 degree u-turn with their beliefs....

To escape this awkward dilemma, some fall back on the explanation that there "must" have been an even earlier civilization, lost now in the mists of time, the identity of which we cannot know, but "must" have been destroyed or declined—yet still somehow left enough technology and knowledge lying around to jump-start the early civilizations we know. They must also hold this interpretation against the clear declaration of the Sumerians and all other ancient peoples that the gods were real flesh and blood beings, present to them, with whom they could communicate and who gave them civilization. This is the last ditch holdout point of the mythological camp: they will not concede that the Sumerians knew, and said clearly, that the Anunnaki were real. The point, as far as they are concerned, is not even up for discussion.

The supposed mythic nature of the physical locations spoken of in the ancient legends has been gradually disproven, beginning with the work of Schliemann and others, and completed with the re-discovery of nearly all the ancient cities and centers on all continents.

The supposed mythic nature of the events involving the "gods" of ancient times and the technology attributed to them has been gradually disproven, beginning with the discovery of documents from the most ancient cities and reinforced with the discovery of the great library of Ashurbanipal at Nineveh. In addition to this we have with the gradual accumulation of some two million artifacts and documents confirming many of the same events in great detail. The discovery of ooparts (high tech tools, toys, artifacts, and technology seemingly out of place in time), along with documentation of advanced scientific knowledge ostensibly out of place in time, along with astronomical knowledge of the entire solar system beyond our current level, has reinforced the negation of the mythic interpretation.

The supposed mythic nature of the "gods," the Anunnaki themselves, as unreal beings (according to academic mythologists) or Jungian archetypes (per Joseph Campbell), or the relegation of them to schizophrenic hallucination (Julian Jaynes), has been gradually disproven, beginning with the acknowledgment of the reality of the events attributed to them *and* the discounting of arguments for their unreality due to the seeming fantastic deeds, technology and weapons attributed to them. Our development of the technologies of rockets, lasers, radio communication, genetic engineering, and atomic and particle beam weapons, allow us to duplicate many of those feats.

Some Contexts Advanced

ancient astronauts	vs.	precocious predecessors
ancient astronauts	vs.	mythic beings, archetypes
Egyptologists	vs.	New Age investigators

The mythologists believe that our same ancestors who were so naive that their groping, proto-scientific attempts at explaining the basic forces of nature led them to project anthropomorphic mythic persona and deeds on the sun and moon, the wind, the thunder, the lightning, the forest and the ocean were, at the same time, so knowledgeable about the physical laws of that same nature that they could easily cut, move and place the 1200-ton stones at Baalbek, build the pyramid of Giza, know the 21,600 year precessional cycle of the Earth, and knew how to process gold that we know came out of extremely ancient mines.

Or they must claim, as mentioned above, that those human ancestors were indeed naive, had no technology for creating those monumental constructions and advanced artifacts, so there must have been an advanced civilization back in history somewhere which was capable of doing so. This advanced civilization apparently left just enough strategic technology and knowledge laying around to jump-start the earliest "sudden" civilizations—but somehow, in the intense investigation of the last 150 years, we still haven't got a clue as to who they were.

Having made that firm assumption then some practical proofs of the possible historical nature of it are usually precluded. Why bother to verify the existence or non-existence of a tenth planet as a preliminary verification of whether the purported physical home planet of the Annunaki is really there? Why do a detailed scientific genetic investigation to see if, indeed, there might be a genetic link between us and what "must be" mythological beings that don't exist? Are these just made up stories that talk about these genetic connections? Mythologists say yes, but science will eventually prove otherwise.

The mythological position cannot address the existence of ooparts, except indirectly. The existence of monumental constructions of astounding precision and advanced techniques and the data and artifacts from highly advanced sciences must be separated off from the mythological explanation and attributed to some highly advanced human civilization, which left the stuff laying around but about the identity of which we have no clue.

We could not have understood the recently uncovered and discovered depictions—call them hieroglyphs or pictures if you will—to possibly be of rockets, helicopters, and airplanes, or the gold objects with wings and tail and cockpit as found in South America, or the unearthed ancient Turkish "object" to clearly be a manned flying craft, except for our own advances in those areas. One hundred fifty years ago there wasn't any such thing as Archeology in Western culture, so only now are we finding these things and disproving the Mythologists.

The entire scope of history as taught in the schools was the version dictated by the Roman Church, which said, following Bishop Ussher's opinion, that the world and everything on it had come into existence in 4004 B.C. on October 29th somewhere around 9:30 in the morning. And you could get into deep trouble if you argued with it. There was no use doing archeology if everything was already known and you could find it all in the Bible. But in the late 1800s, as previously mentioned, Heinrich Schliemann, a German merchant, went down to the Middle East armed with ancient maps and dug up the so-called mythological city of Troy. The point is that no one could any longer say these cities were fantasies of the mind of some ancient writer of heroic fiction. Quite rapidly then, European tourists began to collect artifacts and clay tablets found in the sands in the Middle East. More cities were discovered and the academics were forced to recognize the evidence—and suddenly, there was Archaeology.

The religious authorities, and the academic community which they controlled, hated and feared archaeologists because they might discover something that contradicted their doctrines. Other sciences like astronomy, geology, paleontology, and anthropology have contradicted the doctrines of the Church over time. Geology has shown that the earth is billions of years old—not just six thousand. Anthropology has focused on ancient primitive humanoid species millions of years old. Yet, I just recently watched a "Doctor Somebody" on a Christian channel explaining how the dinosaurs were around within the last six thousand years and the Christian view was still right. Not long ago the Church apologized to Galileo, whom they put under house arrest for saying that he could see other planets out there and that Copernicus was right in saying that the Earth revolved around the Sun. They still haven't apologized to Giordano Bruno, the monk who said he thought there had to be other planets around other suns and probably other civilizations out there among the stars. They burnt him at the stake for that just sixteen years before the founding of Harvard University. No apologies for that.

This interpretation of other life in the universe has been implemented further by the pioneering exploration and questions posed by von Daniken and then completed by the comprehensive and brilliant demonstrations of Sitchin and Sir Laurence Gardner, the English historian and genealogist. The opposing mythic interpretation has been supported by religions because to recognize the Anunnaki as real would open the door to a radical reinterpretation of the entire phenomenon of religion and put into question the real identity of the very deity at the center of their belief system. Gardner has brought to light, however, the fact that there exists a robust, highly documented history carrying all the way back to the Anunnaki, possessed by the heterodox tradition of Christianity. This tradition is the one branded as heretical and was murderously persecuted by the Roman Church before and during the Inquisition. There was no Dark Ages for those who kept to this tradition and were able to survive the persecutions. The Dark Ages existed for the vast majority of those whom the Church was able to keep in the dark about the real nature of human history.

Just as the Archaeological data from the past 150 years in the form of site identification, documents, artifacts and ooparts, reinforced by the developments in our own science, has gradually demolished the mythological interpretation, so have those very developments given basis and reinforcement to the Sitchin paradigm.

Archaeology, Biogenetics, Anthropology and Astronomy

The archaeological synthesis of the Sumerian scholar, Zecharia Sitchin, proves that the gods (Sumerian: Annunaki; Egyptian: Neter; Hebrew: Anakim, Nefilim, Elohim) from the ancient civilizations came here from space, created humans and gave us civilization, were flesh and blood humanoids from the last planet in our solar system (Nibiru, Planet X) who genetically engineered us as slave animals by splicing their genes with *Homo erectus* genes and, eventually, accepted us as limited partners. A half-million pieces of archaeological proof corroborates the evidence for Planet X/Nibiru, which has been independently developed by NASA, JPL, and the Naval Observatory. Each organization is now searching the southern skies, where the gravitational pull of Planet X on Uranus and Neptune flags it as being part of our solar system. Interesting evidence has also surfaced from the mitochondrial DNA "search for Eve" and anthropology's "out of Africa" data, placing our genesis in Central Africa some 250,000 years ago, which matches other ancient records.

The gradual accumulation of astronomical data concerning the existence, physical characteristics, orbit and orbital periodicity, points of perigee and apogee of the tenth planet in our solar system, gradually reinforces the plausibility and attractiveness of Sitchin's paradigm. At least a few astronomers are open minded enough to consider it, and this number cannot help but grow over time.

The situation is different with anthropologists and archaeologists, at least to date, because there does not seem to be any evidence, regardless how patent and robust, that would cause those in these disciplines to allow themselves to consider the Sitchin paradigm. The major obstacle is the traditional mindset that it preclusively couldn't be so, *a priori*. Peer pressure is the second major obstacle. No one wants to go first, to be the first who says that this could be possible, that the evidence could be clearly construed this way, and it should be objectively examined.

But there may be a breakpoint even for Anthropology and Archaeology. In claims that are due to the establishment's attitude rather than the material, we may one day see these fields come to the same or similar conclusions as Sitchin, based on the further study of mounting evidence. It is also a matter of interpreting ancient texts as accurately as possible, rather than depending on dogmatic religious versions that offer little explanation beyond the fact that it must be accepted at face value, without question.

For example, because of the somewhat cryptic nature of the text in Genesis concerning the creation of the human female, let us sort out the details. This tale of the creation of Man's female counterpart relates how the Adam, having already been placed in the E.DIN to till it and tend its orchards, was all alone.

"And Yahweh Elohim said, it is not good that the Adam is by himself; let me make him a mate."

This obviously is a continuation of the version whereby The Adam alone was created, and not part of the version whereby Mankind was created male and female right away. (It seems there were several writers giving somewhat different versions of the tale.) In order to resolve this seeming confusion, the sequence of creating the Earthlings must be borne in mind. First, according to the Sumerian version, the male *lulu*, the "mixed one," was perfected; then the fertilized eggs of ape woman, bathed and mixed with the blood serum and sperm of a young Anunnaki, were divided into batches and placed in a "mold," where they acquired either male or female characteristics. Re-

Cylinder seal shows mother goddess, Ninti, presenting the newly created Adapa (Adam) to Enki. Note the laboratory-type flasks and Tree of Life.

implanted in the wombs of Birth Goddesses, the embryos produced seven males and seven females each time. But these "mixed ones" were hybrids, which could not procreate (as mules cannot).

To get more of them, the process had to be repeated over and over again. At some point it became apparent that this way of obtaining the serfs was not good enough; a different way had to be found to get more of these humans without imposing the pregnancies and deliveries on female Anunnaki. That way was a second genetic manipulation by Enki and Niniti, giving The Adam the ability to procreate on his own. To be able to have offspring, Adam had to mate with a fully compatible female. How and why she was brought into being is the story of the Rib and the Garden of Eden.

The tale of the rib reads almost like a two-sentence summary of a report in a medical journal. In no uncertain terms it describes a major operation of the kind that makes headlines nowadays, when a close relative (for example, a father or a sister) donates an organ for transplant. Increasingly, modern medicine resorts to the transplantation of bone marrow when the malady is a cancer or affects the immune system. The donor in the Biblical case is Adam. He is given general anesthesia and is put to sleep. An incision is made and a rib is removed. The flesh is then pulled together to close up the wound, and Adam is allowed to rest and recover.

The story continues elsewhere. The Elohim now use the piece of bone to construct a woman—not to create a woman, but "construct" one. The difference in terminology is significant; it indicates that the female in question already existed, but required some constructive manipulation to become a mate for Adam. Whatever was needed was obtained from the rib, and the clue to what the rib supplied lies in the other meanings of IM and TI—life, belly, clay. Was an extract of Adam's bone marrow implanted in that of a female Primitive Worker's "clay," through her belly? Regrettably, the Bible does not describe what was done to the female (named Eve by Adam), and the Sumerian texts that have dealt with this point in a legible way have not yet been found. But the purpose for Adam's rib seems clear and something happening with Eve regarding this rib seems likely in the Sumerian texts. The best available translation of the *Atra Hasis* text into Early Assyrian contains other lines that parallel some the Biblical verses. The tablet that carries this text is too damaged, however, to reveal all that the Sumerian original text had to say.

Chapters 12, 13, and 14 of *The Twelfth Planet* gives an interesting picture of not just newly created human psychology, but also of Anunnaki psychology.

From the beginning of the possession of humans as a slave race, we witness the difference—often outright conflict—of agenda and attitude toward the new humans between Enlil and Enki. In its most basic form the conflict was, as we have seen, that Enki was benevolent towards humans and their interests because he had created them in the first place (in one text, the Most High God, Anu, states that Adapa, the model man, or Adam, was "the human offspring of Enki"); whereas Enlil insisted that humans keep to their lowly position and he had no interest or intention to further the human condition. He considered and treated humans as domestic animals. It was Enlil/Yahweh who laid down the rules when humans were brought from Africa to Mesopotamia to work as slaves for the Anunnaki there. It was Enlil who commanded the humans working in his orchards to eat any fruit they wished except from the Tree of Good and Evil.

My personal understanding concerning the nature of the Tree of Good and Evil is that, although possibly only symbolic, it might have been some real plant or tree of which the fruit was possibly psychedelic or mind-opening in some way. In the Mesopotamian story of the fall of man called The Myth of Adapa, Enki sent Adapa (Adam), to Anu (the "Most High" god, so that Anu could see and appreciate Adapa. Before leaving on this journey, Enki instructed Adapa to refuse the Bread of Life and the Water of Life if he was offered them, because Enki thought they might try to get rid of Adapa by poisoning him, if he were not satisfactory to them. These food and water items certainly appear to be real because of the nature of the situation. Perhaps that is indication that the Tree of Good and Evil was also a real plant. I emphasize that this is pure personal conjecture and opinion. The other main point is that Enlil had no interest at all in mankind becoming smarter or wiser; he prevented that whenever he could.

So with the prompting by Enki (the Serpent) to "eat" of the forbidden fruit of knowledge and sexuality, we can readily see that humans were in a hapless position from the beginning—not because of anything

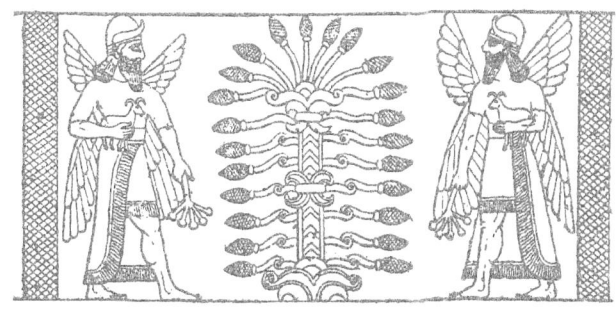

Copy of a Sumerian relief, the Tree of Life image flanked by two opposing gods (Enlil and Enki?)

they had done, but because of the conflict between Enlil and Enki. What Enlil may have considered the Fall of Man, Enki may have considered the upgrading of Man. Those who have emulated Enlil's restrictive attitude and actions, I have called Enlilites. They have been the power players down through the ages, male chauvinistic elements such as the orthodox Rabbis and the Bishops and Popes of the Catholic Church. The notion of sin, from the Enlilite perspective, dictates that sin must be forgiven through the confessional and that humans are essentially flawed by Original Sin and must be saved through their Jesus. Their entire doctrines, beyond this one example, are typically dictatorial and controlling, mirroring Enlil's attitude.

A question, not too often asked is as follows. If Adam and Eve were the two first individuals created, if we take the Old Testament story as literal, and Eve bore two sons and then the sons took wives, *where did the wives come from*? This kind of question brings into focus the modern science that Sitchin and Sir Laurence Gardner have brought to bear on the ancient history. The important, indeed inescapably surprising fact is that, when modern methods of genetic analysis, anthropological dating, and stratigraphy, are combined with the data given in the ancient records, the puzzling gap stands out between the far older time of the advent of the human line and the sudden advent of modern man, *Sapiens sapiens*—us. This is another indicator of the arbitrary decisions the Anunnaki made as to when and how they determined to make changes or upgrades to the human situation. They also assumed that they had the prerogative to wipe us out as a species. Since they regretted having altered/invented us because we were becoming too numerous and annoying at one point, the decision was made to let us be obliterated as a species when they knew a planet-wide catastrophic Flood was immanent—caused by Nibiru, their home planet, coming in through the inner solar system.

For clarity of the evolutionary sequences leading up to us, we should mentally separate ourselves from the progression of hominid species up to and including *Homo erectus*. The divorce, paradoxically, may not be easy—but that simple change of perspective will immediately show us that the normal process of evolution, subject to the usual pressures and influences on the organism, may be learned from the fossil records and actual observation of existing species undergoing change, just as we are doing now. But the patterns are indeed very gradual. They take a very long time, and the changes in any individual species even over millions of years are mild, to say the least, being a little more noticeable, perhaps, as with *Homo erectus*. The term "paleocultural" has been coined to differentiate the prolonged stability in morphology and behavior manifest in all species preceding us, from our own rapid cultural progression.

A secondary but important part of the differentiation between us and our predecessors on the evolutionary tree are some noteworthy physical characteristics. A relatively naked skin rich in sweat glands, a turned-down nose, an unusual head and large brain, a cleft-shaped depression in our upper lip, a system of laryngeal muscles that allow us to use a very complex communication system of sounds, are all unique. A beginning in this kind of research would undoubtedly lead to another level of work with subtler features, eventually producing a detailed genetic analysis of our makeup.

We now know that the first of our kind were produced by biological engineering, not mating, and the gestation was provided by officially appointed "birth-goddesses," Anunnaki females, assigned to the task. The records also say explicitly that, once we were given the ability to procreate, eventually there was ordinary sexual activity between humans and humans, and humans and Anunnaki—indeed the dilution of their racial purity was a result. This became the primary reason for their decision to destroy us. It seems reasonable to assume, therefore, that, there was procreation between individuals of all degrees of human and Anunnaki lineage. There conceivably could have been procreation between humans and *Homo erectus*. Reflection on these combinations shows the variety of genetic proportions and features that would carry down to our time, the knowledge of which would provide potential maps for genetic researchers concerned with differentiating them. Against that background occurred the expulsion of unwanted humans into the "outback" (grown too numerous for the work requirements through the acquired ability to procreate). What have been called "regressive" types of humans may be seen in this context, as the possible result of having been expelled into more primitive conditions where they had to fend for themselves with little, even rudimentary, technological knowledge or experience. The ancient records clearly state that, when first created, we drank from the ditch and ate the grasses with our mouths. That suited the purposes of the Anunnaki well enough, since apparently they only desired a slave-animal. A human of that level of development and self-awareness most probably would not develop a high culture. The details we have about Enkidu, the "Wildman of the steppes" who became a friend of Gilgamesh, are valuable clues, found in the Sumerian *Epic of Gilgamesh*. Primitive (before being literally civilized in a short period of time), he seems to epitomize the "regressive," outcast human type. He was not simply *Homo erectus*.

124   Ancient Gods and Human Origins

Enkidu, right, as shown on ancient Akkadian cylinder seal.

But the best specimens (by Anunnaki design or by genetic probability) were, or rapidly became, far more developed than that and already showed a dominance of Anunnaki hereditary traits. It appears clear from the records that the Anunnaki tended to keep the better specimens. Obviously there would be a greater chance that those who were kept would mate with other humans or even Anunnaki—more so than the outcasts who may even have mated with the more primitive *Homo erectus*.

Since the potential existed for the superior specimens to appear, however, some of those that were pushed into the outback, who eventually migrated or were distributed to all the continents, would have been capable of forging and sustaining a higher culture. This is the key to the understanding of the puzzles presented by advanced art and traces of sophisticated astronomical knowledge and technology that we have discovered at very ancient sites. It is the key to why rudimentary to high culture is always found where humans are found—no matter how far back we trace ourselves. The puzzle of ooparts, advanced items "out of place in time," may be examined in this context of human cultural development. The artifacts were not actually out of place; our understanding was simply inaccurate. The information gathered by von Daniken and Maurice Chatelain finally takes on clear and logical meaning and is set in proper context. Both have acknowledged the conclusiveness of Sitchin's synthesis. The other part of the puzzle of ooparts, beyond our cultural development, is explained by the fact that actual traces of Anunnaki technology have survived in the items themselves. The entire area of archaeology and historical re-search and analysis becomes one of the most significant human endeavors, and should be given the highest priorities. Archaeology becomes the textbook of human Sociobiology 1A.

Only part of our genetic background was geared originally and directly to the environment, time, circadian rhythms, and biorhythms of this planet—that of *Homo erectus*. This of course matched the original genetic imperative of the planet. The other half of our genetic background is the product of a planet on which a "year" is 3600 times as long as Earth's, and which has passed far beyond Pluto in its outer orbiting. It is driven in all likelihood by a different set of genetic imperatives. It is no wonder we exhibit the often-conflicting characteristics of a genetically tampered-with race—characteristics that are perhaps unavoidable in such conditions at this level of complexity.

It seems reasonable to assume that if there were the possibility of partial incompatibility or incompleteness, then genetic defects could result. At any rate, we only need to look in the mirror to find someone who can tell us exactly what it is like to be the product of genetic engineering. Science has not officially accepted the proof, or is hiding it, so we must explore this fact for ourselves. Genetic science currently lists identified human genetic defects and diseases well into the thousands... *the thousands!* So the level of complexity is high.

I propose a systematic sorting of the known genetic defects and diseases and any further discovered to determine which are caused by obvious identifiable external agents, such as exposure to radiation for example, and those which might have their origin in the bicameral programming which, under certain circumstances, might issue contradictory or conflicting instructions in the code. The most valuable clue might come from evidence garnered in the course of paleo-archaeological evaluations of signs of pathological conditions in recovered ancient skeletons. If a genetic defect can be traced back as far as the very beginning of our unique species, it would be quite significant.

The percentage of the race, at any given time, that is afflicted with incapacitating insanity, serious or fatal diseases such as heart failure, cancer, deadly epidemics, and handicapping neurosis, is far too high compared to a species that evolved "naturally." It is difficult although not impossible to make at least approximate comparisons in this case. To approach the investigation of the genetic causes of these serious afflictions with our bicameral uniqueness in mind is not without merit, and systematic scientific investigation of the topic is certainly worthy.

It is reasonable to speculate that before a final satisfactory model of us was produced, subtler intellectual faults, conflicting psychic characteristics or genetically tolerable defects (any of which did not affect basic performance or "product" life to an unacceptable degree), may well have been passed over.

In view of the level of technological skill possessed by the Anunnaki and the details of the information about our creation described in the ancient texts, the following scenarios may be projected as to their intentions and actual success in the project:

1. They intended and accomplished a straightforward, genetic cross using the highest level of technology they were capable of at the time, and produced a product that satisfied their expectations and needs. The result was as genetically perfect as a merging of these two codes, *Homo erectus* and Anunnaki, could be for their intended purposes.

2. They deliberately manipulated the structure of the coding of the two strains, producing a stable product that was also modified further for traits such as docility and subservience, resistant to disease and physical endurance. Gold and diamond mining are very stressful occupations and, even today, miner-candidates are screened for endurance under high temperatures in the South African mines.

3. They possessed enough advanced genetic knowledge to even modify the coding to program us to respond to external command cues of some sort. These could be visual, verbal, electromagnetic, etc. Although it may seem an extremely far-fetched possibility to some of us now, all indications are that our capability to do precisely that level of genetic engineering is already, or soon will be, available to us.

The bottom line here is that it is not inconceivable that there might be an element of inherent incompatibility between the *Homo erectus* and Anunnaki gene codes. The basic general postulate is that cross-seeding between the two planets due to the recorded collisional events in the early solar system was the cause of the compatibility of the codings, but the separation over a lengthy period of time under different conditions may have allowed some differentiation leading to partial incompatibility.

It is important to understand the peculiarity of the genetic rules that the Anunnaki followed, and which were also followed by imitation by the people of the Old Testament. Much of what has happened on Earth, and especially with its earliest wars, stemmed from the Succession Code of the Anunnaki that deprived the firstborn son of the succession if another son was born to the ruler by a half-sister. The same succession rules, adopted by the Sumerians, are reflected in the tales of the Hebrew Patriarchs! This practice is so unique that it becomes unlikely for it to have had a different source. The Bible related that Abraham (who came from the Sumerian capital city of Ur) asked his wife Sarah (a name that meant "Princess") to identify herself when meeting foreign kings, as his sister rather than as his wife. Though not the whole truth, it was also not a lie, as explained in Genesis 20:12: "Indeed she is my sister, the daughter of my father but not the daughter of my mother, and she became my wife."

Abraham's successor was not the firstborn Ishmael, whose mother was the handmaiden Hagar, but Isaac, the son of the half-sister Sarah, though he was born much later.

The strict adherence to these succession rules in antiquity in all royal courts, whether in Egypt or the Old World or in the Inca empire in the New World, suggest some "bloodline," or genetic assumption that appears odd and contrary to the belief that mating with close relatives is undesirable. But did the Anunnaki know something that modern science has yet to discover? Or was this close mating more of an effort to maintain their status more easily?

In 1980, a group led by Hannah Wu at Washington University found that, given a choice, female monkeys preferred to mate with half brothers. "The exciting thing about this experiment," the report states, "is that although the preferred half brothers shared the same father, they had different mothers." *Discover* magazine (December 1988) reported studies showing that "male wasps ordinarily mate with their sisters." Since one male wasp fertilizes many females, the preferential mating was found to be with half sisters: same father but different mother. It appears thus that there was more than whim to the succession code of the Anunnaki.

What do we have, at the grosser socio-biological level from the relatively advanced Anunnaki? It is an important question. To begin with, we seem, obviously, to have inherited the traditions of war, violence, slavery, caste, and territorial dominance. They were relatively advanced in their science, but were, it seems, in continual violent conflict among themselves in some way.

Slavery was what we were created for as a species, apparently agreeable to them. Their social structure marked out a sort of worker caste in the mining community and we humans were certainly a separate caste. The human workers were assigned territories and jealously guarded them. It may be argued that *Homo erectus* was violent and perhaps warlike and was the genetic source for these traits. But we directly witnessed the Anunnaki doing horrendous, documented things, even as advanced as they were. It is true that the Anunnaki could also manifest love, affection, kindness. So we can carefully choose, individually, what positive or negative things we wish to allow in our nature by looking to their example.

Chapter 14 of *The Twelfth Planet* gives the grim details of our species' near demise. Allan and Delair's book, *Cataclysm!*, is also a remarkable account of that ancient event. The authors went around the world discovering and documenting numerous locations, caves, crevasses and fissures where the worldwide flooding pressure and tremendous earth upheaveling had jammed the remains of plants, trees, animals, debris and humans, often from other parts of the world, into these places, compacted into a grisly record. They estimated that we survived as a species perhaps only as a thousand plus over the entire planet.

The effects on the Earth of a close passing, as with the Flood, when collected from the ancient records, are horrendous: "Both man and cattle and creeping things and the birds of the skies were wiped off from the Earth;… And after 150 days the waters were less;… (OT)

The earlier Sumerian flood story refers to the south-storm, "Gathering speed as it blew, submerging the mountains, overtaking the people like a battle...," with the Mother Goddess, Ninhursag, weeping from the devastation.

As recounted in the ancient records, when Enlil (who, unlike Enki, never sided with humans) became aware there were a few humans still alive, he became very angry. But even he could be turned around by common sense when Enki pointed out to him that it would require many humans to help the Anunnaki recover from the devastation.

At this current time we have become convinced that Nibiru is on the incoming leg of its orbit and already we are seeing earth and climate changes becoming stronger all the time, due to early effects of Nibiru's gravitational and electromagnetic influence. Nibiru's incoming orbital position is being ignored or suppressed by the powers-that-be because there is nothing much they can do about it. But why are the powers-that-be building underground, secure and reinforced cities for themselves in the countries where they can locate and afford them? It may occur to you that this topic seems to be more tangential to the basic topic of the Sitchin paradigm. I mention it here because of the nature of the potential threat of species extinction, and I do not use that word casually. It would be well if those who know will take precautions against the danger and warn others who have an open mind.

And how can we take precautions against such extreme conditions as tidal waves flooding above mountain tops, violent storms tearing up whole forests of large trees, etc.? I call it the Ark Project, fittingly. Hopefully some will have better solutions, but my thinking is that floating on the waters, no matter how high they rise, is the better solution for survival. Vessels that are strong, secure, capable of being made tight and navigable, steerable with sufficient capacity for a large compliment of adults and children, seem the most feasible and safe. If it took 150 days before the waters began to recede during the Flood—taken as worst case—we would need probably 10 months of stable food supply and a plentiful supply of drinking water for each vessel, as well as basic medical and first aid supplies, navigation charts, signaling and communication equipment, and agreed upon destination points. Although this may be the best solution, it is obviously a very limited solution because it cannot handle an entire population. Major innovation is desperately needed in time. Governments should be involved and cooperate.

The chronological chart as the last page of *The Twelfth Planet*, Chapter 14, is very helpful and I recommend that one become familiar with it. The hundreds of thousands of years of time frames were more familiar to the Anunnaki than they are to us. The periodic ice ages and alternating warming periods seem due to the periodic passings of Nibiru. There are many of us who think that the nearing of Nibiru is the current cause of earth changes and climate change. The ice sheets over the world are melting rapidly and the seas are rising. Will we subsequently enter a new Ice Age? Be aware.

We apparently have been fortunate during the three subsequent passings since the disastrous one called the Flood in the Bible around 9500 B.C., according to Sitchin's calculations. If the Earth is on the opposite side of the Sun from Nibiru when Nibiru slingshots around at perigee in the Asteroid Belt area between Mars and Jupiter, we may be protected enough to make it a relatively mild passing.

It is on this general topic of the discovery, existence, orbit and threat of Nibiru that the extraordinary 13th chapter of *Genesis Revisited* is based, and which I summarize here. Moving into the present, beyond the ancient records, Sitchin does an exhaustive analysis of the rapid changes that the United States and Russia have gone through politically, showing a plethora of information that would indicate that the two countries were moving into a time of accelerated cooperation, especially in space and space exploration. Sitchin is convinced, as he states emphatically at the beginning of the chapter, that, although not informing the public, the governments of the world are aware of the existence of the Tenth Planet, Nibiru, and are searching for it—or already monitoring it. They are well aware of the significance of that information, know of the possibility of the existence and probable return to Earth of the Anunnaki, and are aware of the threat to our planet by a passing of Nibiru. I have to agree with him on that point: all evidence and signs indicate that is the case. It is not difficult to sense the acute problem that a government, which is committed to tolerating various religions, faces if it attempts to inform the public that the incoming Nibiru is home planet of the Anunnaki. It immediately brings up the facts about the Old Testament being a rewrite of a three thousand year *older* Sumerian historical writing, and that the God of the god-fearing religions is an Anunnaki, alien individual.

With regard to governmental involvement: As Sitchin points out in the last chapter of *Genesis Revisited,* in 1985 the "working committee," formed of representatives of several nations in coordination with the U.S. State department's Office of Advanced Technology, hammered out a set of guidelines, a Declaration of Principles Concerning Activities Following the Detection of Extraterrestrial Intelligence. Interestingly enough, this whole thing was put together shortly after the incident at Mars where the Phobos probe was interfered with… and probably shot down. As he points out, the intention of establishing the guidelines was to maintain control by certain authorities in the face of potential panic on the part of the public, upon revelation of the existence of alien intelligence. It restricts any individual or group from disclosing publicly any detection of, or contact with, alien intelligence and requires said person or group to inform the working committee, which in turn would inform the proper authorities and the Secretary General of the U.N., among others. It is difficult to determine if these rules are a matter of law or not. But this is, nevertheless, a very heavy restriction. There is no indication that it has subsequently been lifted. But I suggest that it has some inherent problems of implementation. If a person who has been in contact with an alien intelligence—for example, an astronaut—makes it known to the committee in keeping with the restrictions, then the committee must determine what to do about it and if it should indeed notify everyone within its circle.

As Sitchin discusses, it's one thing if a signal or a message has been detected from another star system, no big rush really. But if an astronaut reports that she or he has encountered and met with an alien inside the space shuttle— which has been rumored to have happened—it's an entirely different matter. It would seem that the committee has decided to remain silent regardless of what reports they receive, just to keep the information from the public. On reflection one may ask, Does not Sitchin's exposition of the Anunnaki reality fit the category of knowledge of alien contact, which is spelled out in this restriction? It is easily seen that Sitchin's paradigm and information must create a major problem for the Committee. If they were to come down on Sitchin for not reporting to them first, would they be admitting that the alien Anunnaki are real? Of course Sitchin published before the Committee was even formed, so these examples show what ambiguities face the Committee.

Sitchin's presentation of the scientific, NASA and JPL reports and statements about Nibiru's discovery is very impressive. When the materials are put together it is difficult to accept the cover-up statements of the government. My personal take on that mass of evidence is that it clearly points to the conclusion that Nibiru was found by the IRAS (Infrared Imaging Satellite) telescope in 1983 and has been tracked ever since. *Genesis Revisited* was published in 1990. The IRAS team had 600,000 images to "blink" then, but it should have been done by now and only a few images seem to be available to the public (blinking is when two images are made in the same area of night sky, and alternating between them will cause any differences or moving objects to "blink"). Yet we have no definitive, official statement about the existence of Nibiru except for a totally spurious, canned statement from the White House, which is the only "official" word so far. And it seems disconcertingly clear that Harrington lost his life over his planned disclosure.

Clearly, we should not wait for official disclosure. The potential for positive change, indeed revolutionary change, to our species, is so great and important that it should be pursued vigorously. When one looks at the evidence we can, in effect, safely say that disclosure has already become a fact. We should not wait for "official" disclosure.

All signs point to another return passing in the near future. According to some, Sitchin calculated an approximate return of 2078 A.D., others claim is was 2058, while others who knew him claim he would not give an exact date. It is helpful to be aware of the chronology of the passings and the potential variance of such an elongated orbit—which has, on occasion, shifted the time of previous passings to within 50 to 200-year windows in either direction. All told, 2078 could easily be within this window.

The early effects of Nibiru's return are already being felt as climate and earth changes. Sitchin indicates that there have been several passings previous to the Flood passing that were relatively mild enough so that the Earth was not significantly affected. The logic of the situation points to a catastrophic passing happening to Earth if Nibiru passes close enough for the gravitational and electromagnetic forces to cause that kind of effect. It seems obvious that Earth would have to be on the same side of the Sun as Nibiru when it comes closest, therefore we'd be unprotected from the catastrophic effects it would bring.

In the words of the Sumerian King Lists, "the Deluge has swept over" 120 shars (orbits of 3600 of our Earth years each) after the first Anunnaki landing on Earth, 450,000 years ago. This places the Deluge at about 13,000 years ago, around 9,985—10,000 B.C. in Sitchin's calculation. It is exactly the time when the last Ice Age ended abruptly, and when agriculture began. It was followed 3600 years later by the New Stone Age (as scholars call it), the age of pottery. Then, 3600 years later, civilization all at once blossomed out—in the "plain between the rivers," in Sumer. No mention is apparently made of any of those passings, those 120, 3600-year orbits before the Flood, as being catastrophic for the Earth. If some of them were indeed cataclysmic we may have found the cause for many of the climate and earth changes that can be read embedded in the geological records.

We do have the evidence that the three passings since the Flood, around 6800 B.C, 2800 B.C., and 800 A.D., were innocuous. If that is indeed true, then we can perhaps take a bit of comfort in knowing that every 3600-year passing is not going to be that dangerous. But where are the astrophysicists and the astronomers when we need them… to warn us ahead of time if this next passing will bring a threat of species extinction? Ultimately, we have (or soon should have) sufficient computer power to model the entire solar system and be able to determine precisely when Nibiru will come within catastrophic proximity to the Earth, or the other planetary bodies, once again.

The Flood was of such a cataclysmic nature, requiring even the Anunnaki to start over in all ways from a new beginning, that Sitchin's use of the terms "pre-Deluge" and "post-Deluge" is both practical and logical. Post–Deluge, the Anunnaki attitude toward humans changed to a significant degree. Food sources such as new grains and domesticated animals that had developed on Nibiru were literally sent down to Earth. The planet was divided into four areas, each under an Anunnaki ruler. Human kings, like chief foremen for the Anunnaki, were put into place, answering to their Anunnaki overlords but exercising authority of their own. It is easier to understand the full spectrum of the history of the Anunnaki and the human species if one keeps in mind the radical break that took place because of the Flood/Deluge.

If today there are controllers or censors who are suppressing the information about Nibiru and it's nature, its orbit, and potential threat of annihilation to our species, it is the most serious of crimes. I recommend to those suppressing this information that they cooperate with those all over the planet who are working to disclose the reality of Nibiru and the threat it presents, and to help protect the population from annihilation. There may well come a day when they wish they had done it sooner.

Summary

By this point in the book, you may have developed a sense of the profundity of the reality of the Anunnaki and their genetic creation of us. I will summarize the essential thesis here, with the intent that it will crystallize your conceptions and enable you to formulate the questions that will expedite your confident mastery of the subject.

We know now that before the Hittite and Egyptian civilizations, before Assyria and Babylon, even before Akkad, there arose in southern Mesopotamia the high civilization of Sumer. All the others were offshoots of that first-known civilization.

It is by now established beyond doubt that it was in Sumer that the tales of gods and men were first recorded. It was there that numerous texts—more numerous than can be imagined, more detailed than could be expected—were first inscribed. It was there that written records of the history and prehistory of our planet Earth had originated.

The discovery and understanding of the ancient civilizations has been a process of continuous astonishment, of incredible realizations. The monuments of antiquity—pyramids, ziggurats, vast platforms, columned ruins, carved stones—would have remained enigmas, mute evidence to bygone events, were it not for the written word. Were it not for that, the ancient monuments would have remained puzzles: their age uncertain; their creators obscure; their purpose unclear. We know that the Anunnaki put this "sudden" civilization in place, taught humans the many advancements of sophisticated civilization. Writing was essential for documentation, for record keeping, for information exchange, as it is in any complex society. The Anunnaki were always in control and could have obliterated the records—and even the evidence and traces of the entire civilization if they so wished. But it is clear: they allowed Sumer to flourish, deteriorate, and fall into ruin on its own course, with the records, libraries and archives all there. If we were able to ask the Anunnaki if they believed that the documentation, records, and personal archives would be of high value to future generations (as they have become to us), I am certain that their answer would be Yes.

We owe what we know to the ancient scribes—a prolific and meticulous lot, who used monuments, artifacts, foundation stones, bricks, utensils, weapons of any conceivable material, as inviting slates on which to write down names and record events. Above all there were the clay tablets: flattened pieces of wet clay, some small enough to be held in the palm of the hand, on which the scribe deftly embossed with a stylus the symbols that formed syllables, words, and sentences. Then the tablet would be left to dry (or be kiln-dried), and a permanent record had been created—a record that has survived millennia of natural erosion and human destructiveness.

In place after place—in centers of commerce or of administration, in temples and palaces, in all part of the ancient Near East—there were both state and private archives full of such tablets; and there were also actual libraries where the tablets, tens of thousands of them, were neatly arranged by subject, their contents entitled, their scribe named, their sequel numbered. Invariably, whenever they dealt with history or science or the gods, they were identified as copies of earlier tablets, tablets in the "olden language."

Astounded as the archaeologists were to uncover the grandeur of Assyria and Babylonia, they were even more puzzled to read in their inscriptions of "olden cities." And what was the meaning of the title "King of Sumer and Akkad" that the kings of these empires coveted so much? It was only with the discovery of the records concerning Sargon of Agade that modern scholars were able to convince themselves that a great kingdom, the Kingdom of Akkad, had indeed arisen in Mesopotamia half a millennium before Assyria and Babylonia were to flourish. It was with the greatest amazement that scholars read in these records that Sargon "defeated Uruk and tore down its wall.... Sargon, King of Agade, was victorious over the inhabitants of Ur.... He defeated E-Nimmar and tore down its wall and defeated its territory from Lagash as far as the sea. His weapons he washed in the sea. In the battle with the inhabitants of Umma he was victorious...." The scholars were incredulous: Could there have been urban centers, walled cities, even before Sargon of Agade, even before 2500 B.C.?

As is now known, indeed there were. These were the cities and urban centers of Sumer, the "Sumer" in the title, "King of Sumer and Akkad." It was, as a century of archaeological discoveries and scholarly research has established, the land where civilization began nearly six-thousand years ago; where suddenly and inexplicably, as though out of nowhere, there appeared a written language and literature; kings and priests; schools and temples; doctors and astronomers; high-rise buildings, canals, docks, and ships; an intensive agriculture; an advanced metallurgy; a textile industry; trade and commerce; laws and concepts of justice and morality; cosmological theories, and tales and records of history and prehistory.

Because we tend to have a Western focus and the discoveries of ancient Sumer are so astonishing, learning about them is engrossing and preoccupying.

We don't pay sufficient attention to the other centers of civilization brought about by the Anunnaki. The Indus valley civilization, rediscovered only in the latter half of the 20th Century, was extensive, developed, and contained large cities. Sitchin's linguistic expertise helped him make the cross correlations of words, symbols and names between the traditions and tales of the three main cultures and centers of civilization. His scholarship enabled him to determine that Sumerian was the "olden language" and the source of all the subsequent languages, and of the Indus region as well as Chinese. It is interesting that he speculates that the variety of languages were the direct effect of the Anunnaki confusing human languages for crowd control, found in the Tower of Babel tale in the Bible. Based on Sitchin's analysis, I've become convinced that the emulation of Enlil's tyrannical behavior gave rise to the god-fearing "religions" of dictatorial suppression. The lesser influence of Enlil experienced in the Far East and Indus civilizations allowed the development of the more philosophical and consciousness-oriented disciplines.

There is a theme running through human culture, the source of which is not so evident as that of the hero: the cult of the sex goddess. The tradition from which it has sprung is Tantric in its roots, has always been suppressed in the West and clearly has its beginnings with Inanna, who was given domain in the Indian subcontinent. Merlin Stone's work in *When God Was A Woman* is a brilliant presentation of the feminine culture, which Inanna engendered. That cultural orientation traveled the trade routs from India through the Middle East, found its way into Europe through the Moslem influence in Spain and the traveling Troubadours with their cult of "love," influenced the French women who had freedom, responsibility and leisure when their men went off to the Crusades, and eventually became woven into the patterns of culture that we have assimilated through our European heritage. It has finally manifested in our male-dominated and inhibited society in the decadent and distorted Hollywood sex symbol, embodied in such figures as Marilyn Monroe. If the roots of the Tantric tradition began with Inanna/Ishtar, as seems clear, then we are looking at yet another well-defined Anunnaki element in our culture.

We were the "black-headed ones" from the beginning. The fact that the Anunnaki were tall with light complexion, and light-colored or blond-haired, is in accord with the features so prominent in the latest cinematic models. The focus on the "blond goddess"—or the blond Adonis—perhaps is even partially genetic… simply another manifestation of the prepotency of the Anunnaki gene component of our human nature. The general male-dominant character of our society, the roots of which we can easily see, is responsible for the distortion and cheapening of its opposite image. The ancient source of the sociological phenomenon of women's liberation is clear.

Another cultural icon that is embedded in our social structure is that of the hero. The concept of hero originally was of a god or demi-god who could command mysterious technology, do great deeds, and was often recognized as the furnisher of new inventions of great value. In the new historical perspective, these elements take on a new meaning. Certainly the Anunnaki possessed advanced technology that was awesome and totally mysterious to humans and they used it for peaceful as well as destructive purposes. The Anunnaki certainly did teach us civilization and technology. It was not until they began to withdraw that the human king/hero began to come into prominence—sometimes very benevolent, other times despotic and cruel.

But the concept of royalty and that of hero has become confused through the gradual association of wealth as the common denominator of status. Western culture tends to elevate the entrepreneurial achiever, the risk-taking capitalist hero who's of the jet-setting, privileged class—"royalty" in the minds of the media and the masses, without any relationship to personal qualities, which is a confusion indeed. So the role models are distorted and tend to perpetuate subservience and class divisions—subjugation rather than independence.

But because of our genetic heritage we are all royalty; we have "instinctively" (genetically) sought that dignity and status for millennia; we have known it as ours all along. Breaking the slave godspell and realizing that dignity and independence will take some time, but it is the inevitable step to the integrated status of new human.

Chapter 9

BEYOND THE ILLUSION

It is important to emphasize that the two main components of the alien phenomenon, when understood as "problems," are really artificial problems, not valid ones. The two components are:

1) The presence and interaction with the greys, and probably other species, from other star systems.

2) Our own species' history as a genetically engineered, bicameral race (having two full species of gene codes—alien Annunaki and indigenous *Homo erectus*).

The reason I have categorized these two "problems" as being artificial is because they should not be covered up or hidden from the public. The "problems" they create by being hidden have put our thinking and progress on a frustrating "hold." The real problems we face are dealing with these issues, but they can't be dealt with effectively until the artificial problems are removed. The artificial problems stem from the cover-up and the damaging effects it brings. Vested interests exist that do not want the reality contained in each of these truths to be acknowledged.

The "vested interest" group or groups involved with the extra-solar system alien phenomenon, the greys and probably others, are difficult to identify because they have determinedly and purposefully kept hidden. It seems clear, however, that they were and are the successors to the original group of military and scientific personnel of the MJ-12 (or similar groups) as identified, in a single example, by Col. Philip Corso in his book, *The Day After Roswell*. It is generally held that they do not want the presence and contact with the greys acknowledged because they judged initially, and probably rightly, that such news would cause the "invasion from Mars" panic effect that they anticipated. As a result, they seem to be trying to break it to us gently—not only for this reason, but also because, sooner or later, they will have to admit that they were lying to the public all this time. As astronaut Edgar Mitchell has said publically, "it isn't that they have been keeping it a secret for fifty years, they haven't, they have just been letting it out a little bit at a time." Only those who've been paying attention have noticed.

But the bottom line is that the evidence for the grey's presence and interaction with us is overwhelming—from the documents pried out under the Freedom of Information Act, to the videotaped evidence from Mexico and elsewhere and, if it was a murder trial, the defendant would have been found guilty on the basis of circumstantial evidence in half an hour. But the "problem" of proof is sustained as such, artificially, by the deliberate manipulation of the vested interests that continue to patronize the population. The supreme irony is that the deep programming for us to be docile and submissive to authority that we have inherited from our aboriginal relationship to the Annunaki, makes us look to the authorities of today for final validation and vindication—but they have been manipulating us in this matter all this time.

The "vested interest" groups involved with suppressing our true history as a genetically engineered species are a bit easier to identify than those hiding the truth of the greys. They are the power elite of the religions, from the conservative Jewish factions of Levite priests who promoted the monotheistic, one-god supremacy of Jehovah, to the politically savvy Christian groups who melded with and subverted the Roman Empire to become the Roman Church. They clearly did not and do not want the knowledge of our "invention" by the Annunaki/Nefilim allowed to be disseminated because it would show religion, as we generally know it, to be a sublimated continuation of our subservient slave relationship to the alien masters, who had phased off the planet.

But, again, the evidence is overwhelming. The work of Zecharia Sitchin, who should have been awarded a Nobel Prize for his core research and thesis, has restored our true history to us from as far back as our genetic creation in the Annunaki laboratory in central east Africa. This is exactly where the mitochondrial DNA search for Eve was pinpointed, as being the first home of our species. I may disagree with Sitchin on a detail or two—concerning the precise identity of Yahweh, and what attitude we should have toward the Annunaki—but that does not affect the immense importance of the full body of his work and its main thesis. Sir Laurence Gardner has recently begun to fill in the edges of Sitchin's fundamental paradigm, correct a few details, and map out the Annunaki agenda to create a purpose-bred line of human leaders and kings—a bloodline which was enhanced by further enrichment with Annunaki genes.

Is there overlap or relationship between these two vested interest groups? I don't see overlap between the individual persons involved in either group, although some investigators would have it that it's just one big alien-directed conspiracy.

I believe these groups, primarily militarily and nationally oriented, are controlling the "grey" phenomenon, and are not primarily motivated by religious power concerns. The religious power players, from Popes to Cardinals to Queens and Kings, are the ones who have suppressed the outspoken dissidents throughout history who knew of our true genesis—along with the development of the bloodline of David, through Jesus, leading to the royal houses of Europe. These dissidents were dealt with by inquisition and the slaughter of thousands who were conveniently branded as heretics, apostates, witches, and were generally accused to be instruments of the devil.

The MJ-12 type of group(s) surely take careful note of the power and status of the main orthodox religious groups like the Vatican because they recognize them as very powerful political groups. So the two tend to reinforce each other for mutual interests. But I must disagree with those who would have it that the Annunaki were and are seven-foot tall, shape-shifting reptilians who eat raw flesh and babies for breakfast and control the world from the so-called "lower fourth dimension." I mean, what is the "lower" fourth dimension? It's now been sub-divisioned? It seems possible that some alien species of the extra-solar system kind are probably of reptilian extraction. But it seems even clearer that the Annunaki are true humanoid, like us—and we are half them—just as depicted on thousands of cyliinder seals, clay tablets, carvings, reliefs, statues and wall paintings. I think Gardner has the most accurate and complete explanation of the terms "dragon," "draco," and "serpent," regarding their true meaning and symbolism.

The main point is that we see ourselves in a philosophical quandary when it comes to so many of the "big" questions of life—in this case, the determination of the nature of our true history and whether the UFO/alien phenomenon are real or not and, if real, what is the nature of it? But, from the perspective I am suggesting, this is also an artificial quandary because the entire thrust of the agenda of both power groups we have been talking about here is to keep the ordinary person from making up his or her own mind, and to instead accept their absolutistic authority—preferably as the unquestioned word of God or, at least, as an unquestioned political authority with privileged information. The entire philosophical quandary we think we are in can be reduced to a simple question of criteria. Criteria may be defined clearly as the unquestioned assumptions we make to start our logical processing from. Our logic can be impeccably correct, but, if we begin from false premises or assumptions, we will not come to correct conclusions. A man assumes unquestionably that he is a chicken and, therefore, acts as a chicken: pecks at the ground for food, flaps his arms, crows like a chicken, does everything just as if he *were* a chicken. Aside from the fact that he might be a certifiable looney, we cannot fault his logic, which is correct when based on his assumption, but we can see that his beginning assumption is incorrect. *The beginning assumptions we have been taught by the vested interest groups are where the problems lie.*

The theologian and religious authority would have you assume without question that there is a proprietary authority to represent the intentions and wishes of a cosmic God, whom you had better respect under pain of something really bad. The notion of a cosmic God turns out to be a sublimation of the old Annunaki masters, further enhanced by the scholastic philosophers like Thomas Aquinas, through the addition of fancy abstractions like infinite wisdom, omniscience, etc. If you buy into the false starting point, you lose—even if the ensuing logic is correct. The godspell we have been under for these thousands of years is the deepest dye in the fabric of our cultures.

The scientist must assume that there is an objective universe that is lawful for the scientific search to even begin. If it is not a lawful, objective, orderly universe, then there are no scientific laws for her or him to discover in the first place. That whole question is up for grabs in that the situation is far more complex than that. Leon Lederman, a well-known physicist, asks the question, "If the universe is the answer, what is the question?"

The philosopher works from the assumption that reason is the supreme tool to discover everything about the universe, and puts all of philosophy into a division between the objective view of reality and the subjective view. My personal opinion about this is that this approach is a traditional attitude that has been the result of the manipulation of the religious vested interests. They need to promulgate an objective reality, held in existence in the mind of their God, and in which the subjective view must always be subordinate and is correct only in so far as it corresponds with their official teaching on the objective order.

This is not atheism as such: it is only the straightening out of some significant intra-solar system politics, the true relationship between us and our former creators, the Annunaki. It doesn't address the question as to whether there is some unthinkable principle that is "responsible" for the universe or universes, and can create an infinite number of them and play games with them on Wednesday afternoon. Atheism, as we traditionally know it, is precocious adolescent rebellion against the false notions of an anthropomorphic, peevish male chauvinist sublimation of the Annunaki master, Yahweh.

As a cumulative result, the ordinary person, who is kept in a position where he or she has little time to devote to thinking about these things in order to make up his or her own mind and who has been conditioned to suspect any subjective opinion in the first place, thinks there is no way to come to a conclusion about the big ticket items like religion, UFOs and aliens.

Individually and collectively, we need to break the hold of this "godspell," the ancient subservient attitude we have retained since we were subject to the Annunaki masters, and to break the hold of the dominating authority controlling the alien phenomenon. Until we restore our true history and attain a generic definition of what a human being is, we will not be allowed into stellar society because we are not mature enough. More and more each day we are finding in deep space that life is teeming throughout the universe. We are clearly not alone and many advanced races undoubtedly know of us (and have visited). But as long as we remain ignorant, immature, and hostile among ourselves, we will be relegated to being shunned as primitives and outsiders. It is time we grew up.

All the signs are there: they indicate that disclosure of the general alien presence by our government may be close at hand. England has just released thousands of pages of classified material to that purpose and Denmark even more recently—both following Spain, Belgium, France, Brazil, India, which have already acknowledged the presence and contact of alien species in our neighborhood. Even the Vatican, as a state, will be pressured to disclose… as unaccustomed as it is to transparency.

Chapter 10

THE VATICAN CONNECTION

In early April of 2000, Zecharia Sitchin attended the International Convention on the Mystery of Human Existence in Bellaria, Italy, as a guest speaker. A friend of mine who is an engineer and technical writer was invited by Sitchin to be part of a small group to accompany him.

Local, national, and international news media covered the event, and Sitchin was interviewed by Italian national radio and television. Sitchin had arranged to meet with Monsignor Corrado Balducci, who worked in the Papal offices of the Vatican and would also be a speaker, but the night Sitchin arrived he said that Balducci was nowhere to be seen. Sitchin spoke the following morning to an audience of about 1000 people and afterward was approached by Balducci, who said, "I drove the whole night from Rome to hear you." He also told Sitchin, "We have much to talk about. I have great esteem for your scholarship."

Monsignor Balducci met twice with Sitchin and his group for lunch and discussions during the course of the convention, answering a number of questions on the

Vatican's views on extraterrestrials. Balducci's impressive presentation was also on this same subject, giving hope that the Vatican has become more open to the alien question.

After 2000 years of suppression and denial, it seems the Church is no longer so eager to cover up the fact that intelligent life may well exist elsewhere, considering that after 350 years, in 1992, they admitted that Galileo was right.

The Monsignor, in his talk, stated the Vatican's *official* position on extraterrestrials.

First, extraterrestrials have been taken off the Vatican's list of demons.

Second, he acknowledged Sitchin's research and called him his friend.

During discussions, he implicitly admitted (according to my friend who was there) that *the Vatican is in agreement with Sitchin's findings*. Of course this wasn't announced on the news or anything like that, it was confided in their private discussions.

And last, but certainly not least, the Monsignor stated that these beings, who look like us, have not only been on this planet since historical times, but have been here in recent times—that is, in our lifetime. According to the Monsignor, the Niburians will be returning here *soon*, and thus, the Vatican needs to find a way to prepare the Christian community around the world if the Catholic Church wants to preserve its role in the lives of their people.

It seems to me that this preparation has less to do with preserving the church's role and more to do with how the Vatican can undo years of lies, as well as lessen the shock that will accompany a world-wide announcement. Interestingly, Monsignor Balducci had expressed these same ideas on Italian national TV in 1998, but then retracted his statements—only to renew them at this convention in Bellaria in 2000.

The problem we have here in the USA seems to be that, as we are supposedly the "most advanced" country in the world, and we have the most to lose in terms of our economy, religious beliefs, and scientific beliefs, these disclosures will raise *Cain* within our communities. Obviously the creationists and Darwinists will have a hell-of-a-time dealing with this when they realize we were genetically cloned, which actually combines both creationism and evolution! Maybe that's why ETs were on the Vatican's demonology list to begin with (*they* were our "creators" within the context of this genetic upgrade, instead of our singular version of God). They have been controlling us and we can't control them! While this has been theory all along, an eventual disclosure by the Vatican makes it far more interesting!

Those who remain skeptical of Sitchin or are open to the debunkers should pay close attention to those who have had access to sensitive supporting material and/or expertise in specialized fields that have come out in support of Sitchin's work like Monsignor Balducci from the Vatican, Dr. Robert Harrington, former Chief of the Naval Observatory, two respected Ph.D. professors who wrote advanced research papers in the book *Of Heaven and Earth*, among others who have risked, in many cases, their esteemed reputations. This only scratches the surface. We are starting to move away from primitive ways that correspond to the more primitive parts of our genetic make-up.

We are still so Babel-factored under the godspell that otherwise normal looking gentlemen in tweed jackets and ties can be seen on TV propounding that the world was popped into existence by a cosmified Jehovah/Yahweh in 4004 B.C. and the dinosaurs somehow appeared and died out since then.

The *New York Times* still finds it fit to print that the Roman Church has just reiterated officially that the Pope is still the only one with a direct red phone line to Yahweh's kabod while, at the same time, the Pope's friend, Msgr. Corrado Balducci, unofficially, but neither unfrocked nor poisoned, goes about publicly acknowledging that Sitchin is right and the Anunnaki are coming back soon and Catholics are to be gotten ready for that event. And, oh yes, the Pope wants to make a pilgrimage to Ur.

First Sitchin Studies Day text includes advanced technical papers from two Ph.D. scholars in support of his work; other noted contributors include Sitchin himself.

Thinking about the rapidity of the changes we have seen in the last quarter century, I clearly remember standing in our living room in Woodstock, NY, in 1976 and reading in the Kingston Freeman—a most improbable newspaper for this sort of thing—a pre-publication article about a book called *The Twelfth Planet*, by someone named Sitchin who could read Sumerian, demonstrating that the ancient "gods" were not mythic, but flesh and blood humanoid aliens who had come to earth and genetically altered our species.

I knew right there, on the spot, that this man had put the last pieces of the human puzzle in place. How did I know? I had been a Catholic, studied for the priesthood, and was a Trappist monk. I had fortunately gotten free of all that, done graduate work in philosophy, taught history of religion and philosophy on the college level, and read widely in all the pertinent subjects. But I realized that there was a serious flaw in the entire fabric of western academics and religions and in the New Age culture, which I had embraced.

So it wasn't by intuition or dry logic that I knew that Sitchin had achieved the seemingly impossible, but by the coherence of his thesis. It was immediately apparent that this was the only explanation that made all the pieces of the puzzle dance together in harmonious consort. I was deeply grateful for that then, and appreciate the continued opportunity to reacknowledge that debt of gratitude for the breakthrough he has made.

My focus has always been more on the present and the future, so I became preoccupied with the ramifications of this new worldview. I was privileged that Sitchin wrote the introduction to my first book in 1987, *Breaking the Godspell*, and again, in 1996 when he asked me to participate in the International Association for New Science symposium in Denver, which resulted in the book *Of Heaven and Earth* at the First Sitchin Studies Day. In a clear demonstration of his open-mindedness, he wrote the introduction for my second book in 1998, *God Games*. One thing I have contributed to him in this friendship was suggesting *Genesis Revisited* for the title of that excellent book.

Sitchin has always had my admiration for his dedication and clarity of focus. For decades, the more ruthless and couthless of both the establishment and the New Age have attempted to get him, quick and nasty, just outside the fact forum because they recognize that they could not refute his work and his thesis subsumed theirs. He has my deep respect for never descending to that level of un-scholarly, primitive personal attack.

In a revolution as profound and relatively far more accurate than that of Darwin's, Sitchin has singlehandedly given us a data "launch platform" from which to re-evaluate mythology as myth-information, to unmask the gods, to repossess our true history, to take archaeology off hold, and to see that the creationists were only half wrong and the evolutionists only half right. He has facilitated the pressurized launch that is pushing us back into our seats as we take off out of our primitive position on Earth and feel our three thousand year traumatic transition out of racial adolescence take us beyond the Babel factor, beyond religion, beyond the old New Age. The high view that we approach is of ourselves, planetarily unified as generic humans, species-independent, and impatient to step into stellar society.

The coherent comprehensiveness of his work provides keys to developing topics as diverse (and yet related) as Gardner's recent dusting off of Petrie's monumental 1904 discovery of the Anunnaki gold processing plant on Mt. Horeb (dedicated to Hathor), the acute anomalies of anthropology, and the genome project. And he certainly gets a ten for his revelation of the planetary history of our solar system. Indeed he has given us a new stylus for a rewriting of the entire history of the planet.

Of course I would be less than accurate to characterize my friend as a saint... unless, perhaps, his friend Msgr. Balducci can convince the Pope, in a dizzying pryotechnic of ecumenicism, to canonize one who characterizes himself as a practicing Jew who says that God is an alien humanoid who gets around in a flying saucer.

It is inevitable that the Sitchin paradigm will totally replace the current academic context. It may even be possible that Tom Kuhn's thesis will be contradicted this time—that scientific revolutions are not smooth, pretty transitions, but see the old guard giving it up only by fighting and convulsing in spasms of tenure tetanus. It is my sincere conviction that Sitchin be awarded a Nobel Prize, and I believe this will become evident to many more of us once the Sitchin paradigm takes hold.

Sitchin has said that we are just scratching the surface. Hopefully, his work will mark the beginning of a new phase of intensive study, offering discussion, refinement of detail, and expansion that will last for many years as we continue to discover who we are and how we got here.

Chapter 11

THE OOPART DILEMMA

Michael Cremo and Richard Thompson, gathering 900 pages of evidence for their masterful book *Forbidden Archaeology*, have given us a huge volume of evidence from various sources of erroneous or suppressed interpretation of geological and archaeological evidence, based on presuppositions and/or professional protectionism. For example, far too often, to the point of common practice, an artifact or skeleton will be dated according to the stratigraphic evidence if it matches the presupposed template of the investigative scientist, or the stratigraphic evidence will be interpreted according to the presupposed template of the investigator about the age and nature of the artifactual or skeletal remains therein. Carbon dating and more advanced methods of chronological determination notwithstanding, far too often the dating processes are manhandled.

Cremo and Thompson are formidable researchers when pointing out the widespread and often blatantly manipulative, suppressive acting from evolutionarily prejudiced "knowledge filters" by scientists in their handling of data and evidence. It is difficult, however, to refrain from pointing out the rather obvious "information filter" operant in *their* thinking. This would be simply amusing if it were not for the fact that the promulgation of their understanding of the "template Vedic spiritual cosmology" concerning the origins of undifferentiated "humans" as non-physical consciousness principles who have generally devolved down into the material world, has prompted some to accept their rejection of the historical interpretation of the genetic creation of the human species by the Anunnaki. There is an awkward and unfortunate confusion of dimensionality in this, and the use of the words "spirit" and "soul" contributes to the sublimation of the flesh and blood gods of the original Vedas who, the Hindu tradition says, composed the original 100,000 verse Vedas themselves in the age preceding the present one.

"When, in the nineteenth century, scholars began to decipher and understand forgotten languages and trace the connection between them, they realized that the Vedas were written in a very ancient Indo-European language, the predecessor of the Indian root-tongue, Sanskrit, of Greek, Latin, and other European languages. When they were finally able to read and analyze the Vedas, they were surprised to see the uncanny similarity between the Vedic tales of the gods and the Greek." (Sitchin, *Twelfth Planet*, p.63) The Greek traditions and "religion" arrived on the Greek mainland from the near East and the Greek pantheon of gods is derived from the earlier pantheon of the Sumerian tradition. Neither Cremo nor Thompson give consideration to the demonstrated thesis of Joseph Campbell's master work, *The Masks of God*, that the genealogies of the "gods" the world over, from the Vedic to the Norse traditions, are the same. The names may be different due to the usages of various languages—but who married whom, who were cousins, who were the sons and daughters of whom, all are the same in all the major "mythologies" worldwide. In the first volume, *Primitive Mythology*, of his exhaustive study, Campbell points out that these parallel genealogies negate the traditional doctrine of the mythologists that the various myths were engendered simply by naive human minds attributing supernatural or divine characteristics and identities to the awesome forces of nature—the lightning, thunder, wind, etc., and claims that "something happened in that little Sumerian mud garden and spread all over the world."

Although Sitchin and other scholars present evidence of clear cross referencing of the "gods" of the middle eastern histories with those of the Vedic histories, neither Cremo nor Thompson make any such acknowledgement. Across all three books by them (*Forbidden Archaeology*; *Devolution*; *Alien Identities*) the words Sumerian and Sitchin each appear only once in an index (*Alien Identities*) and together, on pages 186-7. Even though Thompson, in his *Alien Identities*, draws extensive parallels, comparisons and identifications between the Vedic classes of deities and alien descriptions and actions in more modern times, he dismisses the entire Sumerian history and Sitchin's identification of the "gods" of the ancient Sumerian records as aliens in less than three short, rather vague paragraphs, lumped together with channelers dealing with "the genetic intervention theory."

The author of the Foreword for *Forbidden Archaeology* states, "*Forbidden Archaeology* does not conceal its own positioning on a relativist spectrum of knowledge production. The authors admit to their own sense of place in a knowledge universe with contours derived from personal experience with

Vedic philosophy, religious perception, and Indian cosmology." All their books are dedicated to "His Divine Grace" A .C. Bhaktivedanta Swami Prabhupada, their guru who encouraged their research and possibly directed them to write *Forbidden Archaeology*, according to some references. Their direction of research tends to take them toward a rejection of Darwinian-type evolution and, indeed, Cremo wrote a book of his own, *Human Devolution: A Vedic Alternative to Darwin's Evolution*, which, in less theological tone, uses their understanding of the "template Vedic spiritual cosmology" in effect, as a superior standard for comparative analysis, analogous to the use of the Bible as a "template of Judeo-Christian spiritual cosmology" for comparative analysis by various sectarian theologians.

Cremo and/or Thompson in *Forbidden Archaeology* and their individual subsequent books, not surprisingly, do not mention the Flood event. "Baalbek," the pre-flood monumental Anunnaki landing platform containing 1200-ton finely cut stones in its foundation, does not appear in their indexes, among a myriad of other facts and ooparts of our history. They do not integrate the archaeology of the early Middle Eastern civilizations. Their indoctrination in this latter day sublimated Vedanta template is little different than the indoctrination of Christians in the sublimated Biblical template. Both their Vedanta version and the Christian version are simply just two of the major godspell babel-factors that keep us radically divided and crippled. Vedic, Christian, and other similar templates, pre-cancel being able to explain and synthesize the total planetary picture.

In the sixties, with so many people waking up, coming out of spiritual comas through activism, meditation, LSD, or anti-war pacifism, we opened up, broadened and "rediscovered" three great books from the East: *The I Ching*, a set of 64 gestalts modeling the parameters of human psychology, based on chaos theory and a dynamic with the assumption that the only permanent thing is change. Each of the 64 gestalts or hexagrams can and do turn into any of the others. Then there is *The Tibetan Book of the Dead*, a psychic version of the Baedeker tourist guide, read to the dying or the tripping, which taught one how to make the transition from the level of opposites, the level of the I Ching, to the level of death or to the state of being described in the third book, *The Book of the Tao*. This book lays out a map to the "Buddha" level of consciousness beyond opposites, by keeping focused and conscious, by not getting caught in anyone else's trip. For example, remember the rooms down the hallway in the Yellow Submarine, where one could open a door and step into the middle of a big argument or a train wreck or some seductive situation—but one must keep flowing like the river, for which there are no rocks. And then, after "coming down" from that vision and the experience of beyond opposites, we are gently cautioned to stay "high," open, and metaconscious—knowing that, as we chose something good we created something else as bad; seeing something as true, something else is differentiated as false.

The balance of enlightenment affords harmony at all levels. A young teacher of meditation and two of his kind go over to visit the Dalai Lama. At the end of the congenial visit, the young teacher, expecting some word of approval, is taught a lesson when the Dalai Lama says to him considerately, "Perhaps you should eat more." What do you do after enlightenment? Chop wood, carry water, is the classic Zen saying. The point, or non-point, being simply that each level of consciousness has it's own inherent epistemology, logic, and rules of appropriate action. One may certainly learn to attain and remain in that level of consciousness, beyond opposites, but that enlightenment had better subsume enlightenment on the level of opposites because ignoring a red light will getcha really hurt (or you'll hurt somebody else). Yes, certainly, unequivocally, expanded loving consciousness is the way to get to the Fifth World where fourth, maybe some fifth-dimensional perception and communication will be ordinary, and the educational process of children will include training towards it. But the level of expanded cosmic consciousness must balance itself in an enlightened harmony with the level of consciousness on this level of opposites. If one is riding the cosmic wave in the middle of the night and your child suddenly vomits in his sleep—sick, opposite of well—you (appropriately) do not just focus Buddha consciousness on him from the other room, you get up and gently, reassuringly, consciously care for, clean up, change, treat, comfort, and perhaps even learn from the heightened, intense, sensory and conscious experience.

On the three-dimensional level of opposites involving Cartesian-Newtonian physics, the concept of equal and opposite reactions applied to rocketry, and the general concept of gravity applied respectfully at that same level, will get your rocket launched, threaded through the Van Allen Belt, through the asteroid belt, slingshot around Jupiter, and safely out of the solar system. If you wish to go much faster than the clunky primitive anti-gravity rockets, one better pay attention to *The Book of the Dead* kind of advice, using relativity equations that allow one to deal with and take advantage of the changes in time and space, and the governing principles of light speed. Relativity does not contradict Cartesian-Newtonian level physics; it subsumes it as a special case. If you want to explain the formation of the stars and galaxies, then listen to the plasma explanation. It does not contradict the level of relativity physics, it simply subsumes it as a special case. If you want to explain how and where the ubiquitous plasma "comes from," then the quantum level of virtual particle theory can contribute. If we want to know the source of the virtual particle level then, so far, it looks like the zero point energy level is it. So far. We are just beginning to learn.

The point is, we need to be aware of all facets and components of the historical origins of both ourselves and the planet. We must remain open to any and all possibilities in regard to these matters that may make sense outside of our "reality tunnels." I've used higher consciousness as an analogy, since it's required baggage for entry into stellar society. If there is an enlightening precursor toward higher consciousness, then that enlightenment had better include the appropriate understanding of the lower level opposites involved in the ramifications of the potential purification of the red sun (Nibiru). If we maintain only the level of high conscious focus, as essential as that is, and disdain the astronomical traffic signals, the possible red light of species extinction, and deal with it for ourselves and the species appropriately at that level; if we don't get up off our transcendental pillow and deal with the vomit and comfort the kid, the Fifth World may indeed come and the 7-billion, cell-slime human "mold," clinging tenuously to her surface, too often insulting mother Earth, may not be part of it.

If we do not transcend and integrate the opposite absolute templates of the Vedantic and Biblical, or Biblical and Darwinian, or Vedantic and Darwinian, or Christian and Muslim, etc., at the appropriate level of historical, physical, three-dimensional reality, we could well destroy ourselves as a species. At this point, it's pretty obvious that we may never be allowed into stellar society. The turning point into the Fifth World must include not only the required consciousness upgrade, but also a resolution of the opposites that cripple us. Consciousness as we conceive it, not to make a pun, is quite obviously a facet of the universe which, at the appropriate level, spontaneously manifests, like electrons and planets manifest, at certain stages of the evolution of the universe. We might say that individual personalities have existed from the very beginning of the universe, from the Big Bang (or whatever concept they come up with next), but to maintain that template level of concept without respecting the evolving level of more and more opposites—which dictate that on the level of three-four dimensions we get conceived, gestated and born—would be imposing the epistemology, logic, rules, and science of one level inappropriately on another.

One does not negate or contradict the other. If in fact we do exist from the beginning of time, or even before "time," as unique consciousness principles, that level of reality does not contradict the level of three-dimensional genetic engineering that can produce a synthesized species—as the history and genetics quite clearly show us to be. It simply subsumes it as a special case, just as relativity subsumes Cartesian-Newtonian physics as a special case. The reverse imposition of a three-dimensional sublimation template (such as Roman Christian theology, or Vedantic "spiritual" cosmology) on higher-dimensional consciousness is just as inappropriate.

We can well go on slamming our antique templates together like they were shields while we jihad each other with righteous dogmatic swords—but only for so long, before we perish by them. I'm not much for that. As you likely are, I am for constantly transcending consciousness, the maturation of the species, and for the matriculation into stellar society. I am for transmuting from competition to cooperation, from babel-factored to species unity, in this century of potential transcendental transmutation. We have the consciousness of the higher-dimensional kind to do it. But we have to have the lesser level appropriate consciousness to deal with the nuisance and inconvenience of a very real and possible cataclysmic, physical threat of survival and therefore, to be aware enough to implement nanotechnology and free energy to achieve the fastest transition at the survival levels, when it arrives, so that everybody, planet-wide, gets taken care of and makes it into the Fifth World.

Chapter 12

PREPARING FOR NIBIRU

I knew Zecharia Sitchin well. I talked often with him by phone, have spoken at his conferences, he wrote the introductions for my first two books, and we discussed at length the matter of Planet X/Nibiru. I highly recommend that one watch the video of his meeting with Robert Harrington at Harrington's office at http://www.xfacts.com/x1.htm (an excellent site full of great, supporting info and research), or Google it to find other options. This meeting is also found on Sitchin's excellent video entitled Are We Alone? The quality of the on-line segments may not be good as the videotape, but either way, one can see that the maps of the solar system that each drew independently from each other during their own separate research are very similar. Harrington states that when he read Sitchin's *The Twelfth Planet*, he realized that he had to talk to him because his research, just like Sitchin's, was all there in the Sumerian records. He and Sitchin are therefore discussing the same body, same orbit, and same pitch of 35-40 degrees to the ecliptic plane of the other planets. Harrington says that the Sumerians knew more than even he and "they" (the modern astronomers) did about the details, giving, as an example, the fact that the ancient records give precise sight lines off of planets for a visual when Nibiru comes into the inner solar system in a rotation opposite the other planets (perhaps one of the astrophysical reasons, besides its size and relative velocity, for it causing so much geomagnetic and geophysical disruption; whereas, from the relatively small time frame in which they had been observing it, he could not be sure of that counter rotation). It is clear from the video and all of Sitchin's writings and communications that he and Harrington were always talking about the same X/Nibiru/Tenth Planet body.

I submit that we have to differentiate between the existence/nature/orbital characteristics and the separate matter of when it will actually come to perigee between Mars and Jupiter on the next passing. Sitchin has said some time ago publicly, at a conference I believe, that it would be, by his calculations from the details of the Sumerian information, around 2078. He waffles around in *The End of Days*, however, comparing three different chronological systems... and I think I don't blame him. Obviously, the world controllers are not going to communicate with him to confirm or deny anything about the anticipated year of the next passing. In the video, he and Harrington pretty much agree on approximate position in orbit, although Harrington did not have sufficient information in the early nineties to know the precise orbital periodicity, saying only that if, indeed, it is as long as Sitchin says, 3600 years, it would allow their final determination of the size of it—up to the size of Neptune, in that case.

Sitchin's *Genesis Revisited* gives images of the actual maps that Harrington sent to him, marking the areas of the sky they were looking in, because they had maintained additional communications beyond the above-named videotaped conference. *Genesis Revisted* also includes references and quotes from all the other announcements made by the IRAS team and other astronomers, the newspaper articles, etc., all very good sources.

A Catholic "archaeologist" lady at Notre Dame University says publicly that Sitchin's work is "total rubbish," while experts in the field have told him privately that he is right. But they won't go public due to "tenure tetanus," peer pressure, and all else that goes with it. Harrington was the only government official who would go public that I know of and, although I know of no connection between this and his death at a rather young age, he did say he knew that he might "get into trouble" over it. We could also talk about Malachi Martin as a possible casualty, or the twenty observatory people from the southern France observatory site where they were claiming to have pictures—who died in an inexplicable cable car accident going to or coming from the observatory. I think Bob Dean also had a picture from this same French observatory.

The IRAS (a NASA-Dutch joint project) was sent up to look for Planet X in the infrared, found it, six announcements to this effect were made by the team, then silence. But Tom Van Flandern, who worked closely with Harrington at the U.S. Naval Observatory, told me himself that some 50-60,000 images that were taken by the IRAS are still uninspected, a pretty clear indication that they found what they were looking for, including sufficient details to give them a complete picture (which they shelved and refused to look at?). Again, it's clear: it's not a matter of whether Planet X/Nibiru exists or has the characteristics, size, or orbit, as given in detail and as taught to us by the Anunnaki. There are only two remaining questions—at least for us out here, who are left hanging in the breeze. 1) When will it come to perigee? And 2) When it does come through, will this next passing be a milder one (with some flooding and earthquakes) or a major cataclysmic one?

Although it cannot be verified, it's been rumored that one researcher from the 1970's claimed there exists a one-in-seven possibility of major cataclysmic effects from each passing of Nibiru. This is interesting for two reasons: it would indicate that before Sitchin published, or almost as he did, in 1976 (when *The Twelfth Planet* appeared), there was interest and some knowledge on an international scale of this planet and its potential threat. It may have been prompted by the already-noticed up and down (relative to the flat plane of the ecliptic), wave-like motions in the orbits of Uranus and Neptune, indicating the presence of another very large body out there, which gives some indication of location. Secondly, it points out the variations of effects. Allan and Delair give exhaustive worldwide evidence and description of the truly cataclysmic passing somewhere between 13,000 and 9500 B.C.—called the Flood in the Old Testament, and described in greater detail in the Sumerian records. It included the descriptions of the Anunnaki women weeping as they watched from hovering craft, or in orbit, as humans were washed away or killed "like flies," etc.

Simple arithmetic shows that there must have been three more passings since then, 3600 years apart, and all apparently of the milder type. Where are the astronomers when we need them? A further consideration is the possibility that, depending on the intricacies of the 12-body problem presented by the solving of the positions of all the planets at the time of any given passing, the precise duration of Nibiru's huge elliptical orbital periodicity might vary each time by a greater or lesser amount. Further, there might be a variation of it's actual passing at perigee through the Asteroid Belt region between Mars and Jupiter, perhaps closer to Mars or Jupiter, or even the occurrence of collisional events with asteroids. An even worse case might be some weird configuration of the planets that one might speculate would bring Nibiru in at a passing between Mars and Earth (but that is pure speculation on my part).

State of the art computer simulations using the high-powered computers of today should be able to model all variations of passings from "mild" (relative to Earth, since Mars' devastated surface shows a good deal more effects) to cataclysmic, and that certainly is a task that should be of utmost priority. I cannot help but think that those simulations have been done for some time and are being continually improved due to the complexity of the situation.

Whether true or not, it is interesting to note that technically advanced aliens have supposedly told remote viewers that the computations and modeling involved with this challenges even their computational power, due to so many planets being involved.

It is critical that we know the two simple facts: 1) We need to know when Nibiru/Phaeton/the Destroyer/Frightener/Doomdragon/Purifier/"Red Sun"/Planet X will come to perigee as precisely as possible for our species' safety and survival. 2) It is also critical that we know as precisely as possible whether this next passing will be of the "milder" kind or the cataclysmic kind, for the sake of our species' survival. It is critically important enough to get our ducks in a row as accurately and quickly as possible, and rule out inaccurate theories through earnest discussion and solid scholarship. If we subscribe to the idea that it's a brown dwarf in an orbit perpendicular to the ecliptic plane as a twin failed star of our Sun, or some variation of that, we will be looking in the wrong places for it. We will make the wrong predictions about where, how and when it will come through, and unnecessarily handicap our computer simulations and calculations as to whether it will be a mild or cataclysmic passing.

If we ignore or deny the most precise and detailed information taught us directly by the Anunnaki—that Nibiru is their home, a habitable planet—we play directly into the agenda meant to keep us Babel-factored, isolated, at odds, ignorant, separated and disposable. Religions as we know them can be still played (like Karl Rove does so masterfully) like a violin, kept in conflict and controlled, with the entire religo-cultural context of the world kept in a perpetual state of war, because it's all too easy for the powers that be to ask, "Your alien gods live on the 1000-degree surface of a brown dwarf?" If we accept their lies, we'll be still trying to unite the species as generic humans to survive when Nibiru/Phaeton/the Destroyer/Frightener/Doomdragon/Purifier/"Red Sun" comes through. It's our survival that we're likely talking about, and the time gets shorter and shorter. Sitchin, referring to President Reagan's interactions with Russia, stated, "If Planet X exists, we are not alone in this Solar System. And the implications for Mankind, its societies, its national divisions, and its arms races are indeed so profound that the American president was right to apply the consequences to the superpowers' confrontation on Earth and cooperation in space." (p. 322, *Genesis Revisited*)

Let's talk about the facts we know that can unite us. We have gone from Tombaugh rediscovering Pluto in 1930 to the modern-day installation of the observatory at the South Pole and whistleblowers talking about the elite building of underground survival shelters. We've gone from Tombaugh freezing his butt off, squinting through an eyepiece and laboriously blinking photo plates, finding no Planet X in the regions of the sky he investigated, leading him to conclude that X has a "highly elliptical and highly inclined orbit and is now far from the Sun," to John Anderson of NASA reporting at a news conference, June 25th, 1987, that the Pioneer space craft, cruising outward in opposite directions through our system's planets looking for Planet X, "found nothing." That, he explained, was good news, for it ruled out once and for all the possibility that the perturbations of the outer planets were caused by a "dark star" or "brown dwarf." *But the perturbations were there...* the data had been checked and rechecked and there was no doubt about it; indeed, the perturbations were more pronounced by the records of a century ago, when Uranus and Neptune were on the other side of the Sun. This led Dr. Anderson to conclude that Planet X does exist; it's orbit is much more inclined that that of Pluto—Pluto is inclined by about 15 degrees to the flat plane of the ecliptic of all the other planets [inclined means swinging in a plane below the ecliptic—in the case of Planet X, about 40 degrees, not perpendicular to the ecliptic], and it has about five times the mass of Earth. (from Sitchin, *Genesis Revisited*, p. 323) I submit that the public announcements and technical papers coming from authorities both in and out of NASA, the Naval Observatory, JPL, and Ames, being of the caliber of Anderson, Reynolds, and Harrington, as examples, are as "official" as we are going get, and holding our breath for some "statement" from the powers that be to make it "official," might well lead to suffocation.

Let's examine the sources of information from the point of view of chronology and terran politics. Sumer was peaking at around 4000 B.C., a high civilization, with all the institutions in science, medicine, astronomy, writing, learning, that we consider "modern," with a knowledge of the full solar system, including Planet X, a knowledge of the history of the formation of our solar system and of our beginnings as an invented slave species. They attributed it all to the Anunnaki who they knew as alien, humanoid, superior in evolution and technological advancement. That was 6000 years ago. The Exodus was 1433 B.C., which was 2500 years later. The Old Testament books, accounts written by Jewish "prophets," scribes and Levite priests, were later yet. I think it is clear that this chronological perspective affords us a way to differentiate some critical information concerning our general topic of X/Nibiru's passings. The Old Testament, appearing 2500-plus years later, would obviously be a poor place to start learning the accurate details about the physics of Planet X. We already know it to be a rewrite of the original

Sumerian that warps and skews the original facts. *The Kolbrin Bible*, 2500 years after the Sumerian, does not purport to be a version of our traditional bible, but a collection of completely different books. If authentic, it may give us a "purer" history of the Exodus and other events and a description of what can happen in a "mild" passing, and even compare a mild one to a cataclysmic one, but it is also a poor place to start learning about the astrophysics of Planet X, due to its shortage of information along these lines and its questionable origins. To say that, "Were it not for *The Kolbrin Bible*, much of this ancient knowledge would be lost to us." is simply inaccurate. The Greek accounts of the same type of events, even later in time, calling the passing body Phaeton, is an even poorer place to start. The Sumerian is the most detailed, concise, and voluminous source. It includes the testimony and teachings of the Anunnaki themselves, and serves as a totally adequate, superior source, even if we were without the Old Testament, Kolbrin Bible, Greek accounts, New Testament, Allan and Delair's extensive work, whistleblower bits and pieces of testimony, or any of the other worldwide, cultural and tribal accounts.

Putting things together in chronological sequence, we have the Sumerian accounts, the Mayan advanced astronomy taught to them by Quezecoatl (aka Thoth the Anunnaki), with discriminating use of the Old Testament, *Kolbrin Bible*, the Greek testimony about Phaeton, the New Testament, added to the hundreds of accounts from worldwide, "mythological" survivor tales and warnings from peoples, nations, and tribes, we reach the present-day research of Allan and Delair in *Cataclysm!*, putting much of it together, along with the data accumulated from archaeology, anthropology, paleontology, genetics, and astronomy, giving us a robust, historical and scientific detailed accounting, stretching over more than 6000 years. If we add to that the bits and pieces of whistleblower testimony, contactee reports, and the indirect evidence from those who have been ridiculed, silenced, and eliminated because they dared to explore it or speak up, then we do not have to stretch any farther to consider the doomsday-type predictions of Nostradamus, Mother Shipton, and Cayce. Their rather cryptic prophecies become bolstered when put into a detailed context.

We should be trying to get answers to the two essential questions, noted above, as if our lives depended on it (bad pun not intended). We need to exert terran political pressures to get access to the undoctored information from the south polar observatory, the computer modeling and the astronomical findings to know when Nibiru will come to perigee and to know the best estimates and predictions as to whether it will be a "mild" or cataclysmic passing. Marshall

Master has put together a practical survival guide. The Internet is one of our most powerful survival tools.

We can contribute, expolitically, by thoroughly investigating the modalities by which we can open direct contact with our parent species. They may have already started the process, from their end, in 1991, with the eclipse of the Sun over central Mexico. On that day, wonders in the sky appeared all over Mexico, where hundreds of unidentified sightings of craft were videotaped all on the same day and collected together on one amazing video called The Masters of the Stars (now almost impossible to find), produced by the Elders in conjunction with Haime Mausson. Some of the craft led investigators to the crater of Popocatepetl, a huge volcano dormant since the time of Cortez, which was undergoing a major earth change, coming awake. This seismic awakening has caused Popocatepetl to completely lose its glaciers by 2001 and it has continued to warm and rumble ever since the time these craft led investigators there in 1991. It seems whatever intelligence was behind these craft wanted, at least in part, to warn us and make us aware of an eventual eruption that could devastate Mexico City.

Whether the actual coming to perigee, the nest passing of Nibiru, is in 2040, 2058, 2078, 3157, whenever the complex astrophysics resolves to hard data, let us unite to work for the survival of the species, ourselves, and our children (whether we have help from elsewhere or not). Let us treat with compassion—but begin to isolate—the 20% anti-species of us who would choose the downward path of devolution and desperately and myopically try to save themselves at the expense of the rest. In the meantime, let us expand and upgrade our collective and individual consciousness. Let us use all means and power and information at that higher conscious level to influence and create the new post-passing human society—one befitting of our part-alien genome as new humans, already eager and ready for stellar society.

Chapter 13

APPROACHING GODHOOD: WHAT HAPPENS NEXT

The ramifications of the fact that the alien humanoid, Enlil, an Anunnaki, is the cosmified monotheistic "God" of the Bible and of the god-fearing religions are so profound that many have difficulty assimilating them. Does that mean that the Vatican and the Catholic Church must be not just rethought, but disbanded? Theology as taught must be discarded? That all the offshoot sects and religions are outmoded? What about the Hebrew and Muslim religions based on faith in the God of Abraham? The answer to all those questions can only be Yes. But, hopefully, graceful rather than disruptive transitions can be made. The changes, whenever they finally come or begin to come, will be difficult because they will deeply affect each individual life as well as institutions worldwide.

Nevertheless, the rewards will overshadow the difficulties. Relieved of the conflicts between the absolutes of the erroneous religions, we will gradually realize that we are the same; that no one was "better" than anyone else simply because of their belief system, and we will reach a state of generic humanity. This, in turn, will lead to the discarding of primitive competition among faiths and races, and to the establishing of planetary peace—the essential condition for us as a species to be accepted for entrance into stellar society.

It is worth reiterating here: this is not atheism. Nor does it question whether or not there is some cosmic Entity that can create universes by thinking of them. It simply sets the record straight about the Anunnaki and our creation. Scott Jones and I, as a think tank team, are working diligently to motivate the academic and scientific communities to inform the public of the mind-boggling facts that relate to this, but have met with general resistance.

In 300,000 years we have come up from our earliest form, the "black-headed ones," eating the grasses with our mouths, drinking from the ditch, going about unclothed—to flying the space shuttle, exploring the planets, deciphering the mysteries of quantum mechanics and analyzing the first split second of the expansion of the universe. The expanded context in which we can now envisage that progress requires certain critical adjustments of our understanding of it.

We will realize the sources of the abhorrent, inhuman practices we are outgrowing. We were created as a slave race: we still practice forms of slavery to this day. We are involved in continual internecine wars, as the Anunnaki were among themselves. They involved humans as their soldiers, just as our governments, rulers or officials use our young as cannon fodder. It is not difficult to see what models we have been following. The shifting worldwide phenomenon of the often-oppressed ruled, rising up against the tyrant, the ruler, can be viewed as a beginning stage of an evolving politic for the better. It is no accident that it is the younger, upcoming generations that are revolting. The ancient and more brutal model, in this case, is being cast aside for a more civil and democratic paradigm.

In *Breaking the Godspell, God Games* and *Sapiens Rising,* the three books that I have written, I've presented the vision of the next stage in our species' evolution, which we are already entering. Indefinite and immortal life spans will be ours to accept; we will, as generic humans, develop a world society—not the primitive world order desired by the powers-that-be—that will see substantial subsistence wages and means for every individual, whether working or not, from birth; we will, are already, moving beyond money, credit, economic, political and social competition; we will be in peaceful contact and interaction with alien species; we'll learn paranormal techniques for flexible communication; develop highly advanced modes of information-handling and direct-brain educational transfer; artificial intelligence will be used extensively to afford us a leisure society—to mention a few items only. The old primitive modalities are disintegrating and becoming obsolete and the process is difficult, even sometimes violent, but free, conscious evolution will prevail. Perhaps our Anunnaki parent species will soon see fit to contact us and perhaps donate some advanced technology, as they have in the past, during some passings.

Of all the mind-boggling ramifications of the reality of the Anunnaki and our genetic relationship to them as our parent species, is the possibility of direct contact with them again. They can easily travel here and have been capable of doing so for thousands of years. I think it is significant that they have not made overt contact yet. It can be assumed that they have made careful decisions as to why and when they should make overt contact again. I say "overt" contact deliberately because there is constant rumor that they—and perhaps other advanced species—have made contact with governments, select individuals in places of influence, the Vatican, etc. It is said that advanced aliens which we could not distinguish from humans may be walking the corridors of the Pentagon. It is even suggested by some that certain Anunnaki individuals or group are controlling the political or social powers-that-be and are directing human affairs. Richard Dolan covers this topic well in his books on modern UFOs and it integrates to a certain extent with Sitchin's information found in *The Twelfth Planet* and *Genesis Revisited*.

As one assimilates Sitchin's history-restoring thesis and its revolutionary ramifications, one can be appalled by the realization that so much of what has been taught in so many areas is simply wrong, erroneous—or sometimes deliberately false. This is the case from an evolutionary perspective. If one can understand the situation as our species gradually evolving past our subservient, indeed slave status, and stepping now out of species adolescence, then the facts may one day be corrected. With this in mind, one can actually contribute to the process of conscious evolution as we individually and collectively step into species independent maturity.

It is an important and open question as to whether the Anunnaki have themselves evolved in conscious evolution, and how they perceive "evolution."

Another immediate question is whether they have maintained the same level of violent conflict as they manifested when here overtly, 2000 years ago, as part of their lifestyle. The question, in a cosmic form, asks if it is part of the evolutionary process in this universe that species of whatever form, regardless of how savage and primitive initially, inevitably evolve to a more peaceful, benevolent and non-violent status, perhaps to a highly transcendent socialistic status, perhaps even more transcendent than we can conceive of in our current mentality.

Contemplating the history of the Anunnaki themselves as portrayed in the ancient records is a very productive exercise. We, ourselves, are in the early stages of developing artificial intelligence robots and androids more and more like ourselves. There quite probably are at least a few thinkers, innovators, inventors who already have conceived of genetically creating an intelligent, biological android as a slave creature. Which would put us almost precisely in the same position as the Anunnaki were 200,000 years ago, when they "invented" us genetically as a slave race. Would they now consider creating a slave race again, as they did with us? Is that really an ethical or moral thing to do? Before we allow ourselves to invent such things, we should—or must—study and discuss any undertaking of this nature because we have the historical precedent of our relationship with the Anunnaki, with all its complexity and serious side effects to contemplate.

It is fascinating that the very last sentence in *The Twelfth Planet* is the question, "…if the Nefilim (Anunnaki) were the "gods" who "created" Man on Earth, did evolution alone, on the Twelfth Planet, create the Nefilim?" Is the creation of a species by an advanced species, for whatever purpose, a general phenomenon in this universe? Sitchin has done us, as a species, a great service in definitively restoring our true history because it allows us to freely and intelligently formulate and deal with these novel questions.

The perspective afforded us by the overview of our beginnings, giving our history a coherent and elevated meaning, should be welcomed with relief by intelligent persons. It frees us to take our place in an ongoing process of an aware and conscious mode, rather than a blind, groping, and often conflicted one. It integrates our past with our present and our future; inevitably we "shall be as gods" and attain to relative immortality as they did, and humbly—but in a mode which will be mostly of our own intelligent doing unless, perhaps, we receive some assistance directly from our parent species. The possibility of future contact with our "makers" seems quite probable but, due to the independence we have achieved, our relationship with them will be a major determinant in the future politics of our development.

The readjustment of our perspective is mirrored in a natural adjustment of jurisdiction among the academic disciplines. Because we have been civilized from the literal beginning of our existence, our "evolution," now still seen against its roots in natural evolution but understood as a unique rapid metamorphosis, becomes our known history. That history (now a context rather than a puzzle, and integrated into our present), together with archaeology, becomes a sociology. That extended sociology becomes an expanded context for our psychology. The liberated character of that psychology allows it to become again the integrated context of the entire spectrum of all phases of our minds' activities, including transcendent experience, philosophy, and science—now understood as generic functions of our inherent philotropism. Philotropism is a word I invented: it means "wisdom-seeking," or "wisdom "tracking," much like the word phototropism means light tracking (as plants do). The sciences expand so that re-search acquires a new dimension, as often found in history, but in this case it is due to the evidence of technology and information in the ancient records, which may be worth much to us in the present.

Previously, we may have been able to remain somewhat blasé to the fact that pioneering archaeologists have repeatedly uncovered the physical reality of cities and civilizations that formerly were considered to be only the content of legend or myth. Previously, we may have been able to hold in skeptical suspension our judgments concerning the reality of gods, demigods, kings, dynasties and high cultures of great sophistication and splendor, of whose material remains and records now lie in our museums for all to witness. We may have been able to previously marvel, without drawing conclusions, at the stupendous feats of monumental engineering and organization, written large across now remote or barren landscapes. We may have been awed, but in unresolved puzzlement, over the contradiction of mature law, trade, education, travel, economics, and advanced medicine, science and technology clearly evident in remote times, of which the scholars have insisted were primitive. We may have been able to labor as students and scholars, docilely submissive to the righteousness of "authorities," naively viewing the bulk of the history of the world previous to the Greeks as somehow being the irresponsible and unreliable figments of innocent, ignorant, even primitive peoples, probably somehow less human than ourselves. We may have previously been able to sidestep the multitude of discovered out-of-place artifacts, ooparts, whose tangible logic speaks eloquently of our predecessors as being technologically and socially like ourselves, rather than the grunting savages that the cloistered savants would have us believe. We may have formerly taken refuge from the responsibility and risks of personal education and evaluation behind the robes of ecclesiastical or institutional dogmas, acknowledging their "facts" as unquestioned inspired authority, and continued to be educated with their approved tests and quizzes that are designed to shape our beliefs, yet were produced by less developed minds centuries ago. Formerly, we may have been able to leave to the "expert" the explanation of the gross inconsistencies of our species' developmental patterns when viewed against the known sequences of previous species. Previously, we may have capitulated to the hive pressure not to judge for ourselves what we could glimpse over the academic and religious barriers. *But all of this should be over.*

Our racial, species childhood must come to an end. It is now over for the more intelligent and aware of us and, as a whole, we are coming, typically reluctant and turbulently, out of our racial adolescence, faced with the responsibility of self-determination and mature action. The point of critical mass of information about our unique genetic creation and who we really are *is inescapably upon us*. The last pieces of the puzzle have fallen into place. Poets and scientists, visionaries and philosophers, explorers and scholars have sensed it, glimpsed it, suggested it—but we, thanks to Sitchin's definitive synthesis, can say it simply and without equivocation: we are a unique product of genetic engineering, a mutant species which has reached a relative state of development, both psychologically and technologically, where we can reflexively appreciate that concept of ourselves and act on it. The mutant slave-animal awakens from an ancient sleep, from an amnesia caused by taboo; sapiens unbound and rising. All of our science fiction projections are fulfilled, yet cannot match the amazing fact that we are *Homo-Erectus-Nefilimus* (Nefilim is used in place of Anunnaki). We become truly sapient on recognition of the full import of that simple genetic fact.

A bit of reflection about what you and I are accomplishing as a major facet of this book is actually implementing disclosure. We know that there are other species on other planets, that they do come to Earth, and that they do interact with us. The Anunnaki fulfill those conditions: we are part of them. There is no need for the pretense of SETI telescopic or electronic searches, no need for speculation by scientists or cover-ups by the powers-that-be: it's done. Disclosure is accomplished when ample evidence is there. We should not wait for "official" admission or "disclosure." The most important element in the disclosure process is the revelation of our true history—that being the alien nature of the Anunnaki and us as part alien, through genetic incorporation with them. We should be moving forward as generic humans, thinking about how we can contribute to breaking the godspell, to bringing about a peaceful species unity on Earth, and work towards being accepted into stellar society. We should be confident enough to request contact with the Anunnaki, resolving any issues we have with them, and develop a habitual cosmic perspective.

Because of the revolutionary nature of this subject, the undisputed factual material was balanced with considered interpretation of the ramifications. I have previously indicated what Sitchin's position was in any given matter and where my subjective understanding was in agreement with his or differed. The only major difference I had with Sitchin's position was his acceptance of the Old Testament's recounting of the history of Adam and Eve's son, Cain.

Gardner's recounting of the tale of Cain, as we have seen, presents him as the founding member of the Grail Bloodline of Kings, initiated by Enki, promoted and supported by the Enki faction and opposed by the Enlilite faction. From your own perspective, I recommend that you exercise your best discrimination and critical judgment about both the factual material and the interpretations of others, myself included, as a matter of course, and when studying any subject for that matter.

The purpose of this book has been to introduce you to the essential thesis of Sitchin's masterwork and help integrate the key aspects into your life. There is a broad spectrum of topics covered in his Earth Chronicles series because the historical revolution he is promulgating involves so many facets of human nature. I have added commentary in this book on some of the more important factors presented by Sitchin. This was meant to clarify the incredible importance of his work and to add knowledge that Sitchin did not necessarily cover. Having assimilated an introduction to Sitchin's masterwork, I hope that you will continue to explore this subject on your own.

Humanity is slowly learning of its true origins but for now, as a whole, remains lost and ignorant. It knows not who it really is. We have at hand the common understanding of our racial beginnings, of our bicameral nature, of our common history and expansion over the face of the planet, of our relationship to the Nefilim and to each other. The awareness and comprehension of this fundamental, generic, racial self-knowledge I have called genetic enlightenment. It is the basis for a profound unification of all humanity. Not some superficial social homogenization of peoples and cultures and philosophies, but a unification that frees us to be one race and explains and enhances our diversity of adaptations and cultures and contributions.

When society and we, as a species, comes to accept the truth of who we are, the godspell will be broken, the Babel factor canceled, and we can finally enter stellar society as a mature race which knows who and what it is, what is good for it and what is not; with whom or what it could interact; with whom and what it would be dangerous to make contact; with the minimum of preconceptions as to how things should be. I invite you to participate in an exploration and mapping out of the post genetic enlightenment context of collective and individual existence in terms of the unique genius, the sometimes disconcerting accelerations, and precocious proclivities of our bicameral genetic heritage.

INTRODUCTION TO APPENDIXES

The White Papers found in the Appendixes contain some sections of information already found earlier in the book. These papers appear here, in their entirety, so one may see these ideas in their full, original context almost exactly as presented to the various organizations and/or people, worldwide, who received them. They have been edited in minor ways for the sake of clarity, only when needed, and to correct minor grammar or spelling. Otherwise, they appear exactly as submitted.

APPENDIX I

The Alien Question: An Expanded Perspective

A White Paper

Addressed to

The Arlington Institute
The British UFO Research Association
The Brookings Institution
The Center For The Study Of Extraterrestrial Intelligence
Extraterrestrial Phenomena Political Action Committee
The Fund For UFO Research
J. Allen Hynek Center For UFO Studies
The Human Potential Foundation
Institut des Hautes Etudes de Defense Nationale
The International Association For New Science
The McClendon Study Group
The Mutual UFO Network
The National Institute For Discovery Science
The National UFO Reporting Center
Operation Right To Know
Paradigm Research
Program for Extraordinary Experience Research
Stargate International
Skywatch International

By

Neil Freer

Author of *Breaking the Godspell*
God Games: What Do You Do Forever?
Sapiens Rising: The View from 2100

For the most part, UFO researchers try to deal with the micro, they are event oriented. That is important, but someone also needs to be looking broadly, excluding nothing. —C.B. Scott Jones, Ph.D.
Human Potential Foundation

The most successful tyranny is not the one that uses force to assure uniformity but the one that removes the awareness of other possibilities, that makes it seem inconceivable that other ways are viable, that removes the sense that there is an outside. —Allan Bloom
The Closing of the American Mind

Synopsis: The current context within which The Alien Presence Paradigm is viewed and dealt with is too narrow and limited. The Alien Presence Paradigm should be seen as having two parts, separate but related:

1> the recognition of the presence of an alien culture or cultures from outside our solar system, and the ramifications of that presence and contact. In this paper this part of the paradigm will be called the UFO/Alien phase.

2> the recognition and restoration of our true history as a genetically engineered species, half alien Annunaki, half indigenous *Homo erectus*, according to the thesis paradigm of the Sumerian scholar, Zecharia Sitchin, and its ramifications for our future. In this paper this part of the paradigm is called the Human History phase.

These are two artificial problems because the overwhelming evidence for both is patent but the obstruction of both by vested interests prevents closure. The same type, sometimes identical, patronizing vested interests and authorities obstruct the processes of revelation of the alien presence as obstruct the restoration or our half-alien history for similar and identical reasons. The resolution of the latter "problem" will relieve the political pressures on the obstructing authorities and facilitate the revelation of the former "problem."

Only by regaining our true species identity and a generic definition of human nature will we attain the global unity and unassailable integrity that will allow us to interact with an alien culture no matter how strange. Without prejudicial religious or cultural filters, we will be able to know what is good or bad for us and able to understand what is good or bad for the alien species. We may not be accepted into stellar society until we reach that level of species maturity.

The two parts of the paradigm are defined, developed, their ramifications examined, and their interrelationships explicated. Practical measures for expediting and accelerating both processes are outlined and suggested, and species beneficial goals, in keeping with the fullness of human dignity and freedom, are defined in an evolutionary progressive context.

The intention of the author in this paper is not to instruct but to suggest. The following is based on fifty years of interest, research, intense study, involvement, and reflection on the human condition as a generic human and professional philosopher. It is respectfully submitted for consideration as a means of facilitating a breakthrough to resolution of these matters which are now effectively and detrimentally at a standstill.

The Status Quo of the UFO/Alien Phenomenon

A preliminary caveat: it is fully recognized that some of the sighted UFOs, reported abductions, encountered "aliens" may be not alien but human action, technology and human events. This paper focuses only on the actual alien presence, technology and interactions.

The position of the author regarding the UFOA presence paradigm agrees with that held by the majority of the organizations addressed herein: alien civilization(s) from outside of our solar system have been visiting the Earth for an indeterminate time, the current one in focus being the grey type(s). The author has been intensely interested in the phenomenon since 1947 when, at the age of 17, he read the first report issued from Roswell, AZ of a saucer being captured after crashing. Some 50 years of research and study of the subject leaves no doubt in the mind of this author that contact by probably multiple alien races with humans has been made (the military first because of the danger of aggressive response). Information and technology has been exchanged, the population of the world gradually acclimated to the alien presence by both the aliens and the human command structure given charge of the matter.

The entire UFOA subject has been covered up and disavowed, at first because of fear of the unknown and possible anarchy and chaos on the part of the population, subsequently because of the difficulty of revelation and taking of blame for cover-up. The alien bodies that have been examined, autopsied and the live aliens interacted with have demonstrated that some are humanoid at least in appearance if not in physiology and some are actually androids. The "problem" is artificial in that it is only a problem because of the obstructive denial by the government. The evidence for the alien presence has developed to such a robust degree and the data is so vast that the government's final acknowledgement is hardly needed.

Even though we have the testimony of Maj. Donald E. Keyhoe, Capt. Jesse Marcel, Maurice Chatelain, Command Sgt. Major Robert Dean, Col. Phillip J. Corso, Admiral James Woolsey, Astronaut Gordon Cooper, to name only a tiny government, military and NASA handful, the supreme irony of this situation is that we continue to look to the very government which has been covering up the phenomenon for validation, verification and authentication. The reason why we have done so is due, to a great degree, to the conditioning, over thousands of years, to submit to authority stemming from the peculiar nature of our origins in subservience as brilliantly elucidated by the thesis of the Sumerian scholar, Zecharia Sitchin. The perpetuation of this subservience in the form of a sublimated "fear of God" through the religious institutions founded on it has shaped our world so profoundly that we fear to even reconsider it. We therefore rely on authority when we should not and we tend to look to anyone showing up here from off planet as masters or saviors.

A fundamental question, seldom considered due to our conditioning to look to the three classic criteria bases, theology, philosophy and science which are themselves brought into question by it: Is it possible to arrive at a new world view which corrects, completes and subsumes all our previous worldviews? Explains all our previous explanations? The answer is, unequivocally, Yes. But Kuhn, who examined the nature of scientific revolutions, is painfully correct. We almost have to wait for the older generation to die off rather than see an orderly and rational translation to a new paradigm. Those with vested, academic teaching or scientific reputations or religious, political or economic interests are not going to acquiesce easily or at all. We operate far behind the evolutionary leading edge in this regard because of this inertia.

The Status Quo of the HH (Human History) Sitchin Paradigm of Our Own Half-Alien Species History

The Sumerian scholar, Zecharia Sitchin, published his first work in 1976. From his knowledge of Sumerian, the Semitic and other ancient languages and his research and study of the archaeological and Biblical data acquired over the last one hundred and fifty years he put forth his thesis that the transcultural gods known to all the ancient cultures were not mythological but real flesh and blood humanoid aliens, very much like humans, who had come here from the tenth planet in our solar system, Planet X in the popular press, called Nibiru by the Sumerians. They subsequently genetically engineered our species, originally as slave animals to work in their gold mines, by crossing their genes with those of *Homo erectus*.

The Historical Background Necessary for an Understanding of Sitchin's Thesis

Consider a typical reaction to this analysis: what is said here, by this author, has been presented as carefully and reasonably as possible. However, *by the very fact of it being an analysis of our history and, almost incidentally, religion*, it will often first be perceived as the breaking of a taboo, perhaps a suspect attack, perhaps atheistic, or somehow less than "American" in its spirit, perhaps even "against God"—even though the evidence brought is no different in kind than that brought against the UFOA conspiracy and, perhaps, is even more robust. The godspell is the deepest dye in the fabric of our culture.

As mentioned earlier, there was literally no such thing as the discipline known as Archaeology in Western culture until the 1800s. The Roman Church controlled and determined the view of the past. Bishop Ussher's view, that the entire planet and life on it as described in Genesis came into existence through the auspices of a cosmic creator in 4004 B.C., was doctrine and one could be branded a heretic for disavowing it. Not until paleontological findings forced that view to be reevaluated (as with Schliemann, who dug up Troy), was a window into the past opened and the mythic view questioned. Scientific Archaeology as we know it came into existence only when academics reluctantly had to acknowledge the past being dug up and collected by amateurs in the Middle East. Archaeologists came to be mistrusted and hated by the religious institutions that feared revelations that would contradict their teachings and the history of the Old Testament.

The Demise of the Mythological Explanation of the Gods

Note: It is trivial that quaint local myths concerning many subjects exist all over the world among both more and less primitive peoples. We consider here only the latter day *interpretation* of the transcultural "gods" involved in human history as mythic, or unreal. We note also that the ancient civilizations did not call the Anunnaki "god." They referred to them as masters, lords, in the sense of rulers.

Those still holding the mythological interpretation are in an unenviable position. They find themselves having to hold that the same citizens of the first civilizations who, they claim, invented—or hallucinated—the gods through their primitive imaginings and naive proto-scientific projections of personality on the great forces of nature were the same primitives who somehow could build the stupendous Giza pyramid; somehow quarry, cut and move into place the one thousand ton stones of the Baalbek "temple" (rocket platform) which even our modern technology cannot begin to lift; somehow know the great precessional cycle of the heavens, the existence of all ten of the planets of our solar system and how our solar system was formed (*Enuma Elish* document).

To escape this awkward dilemma, some fall back on the explanation that there "must" have been an even earlier civilization, lost now in the mists of time, the identity of which we cannot know, which "must" have been destroyed or declined—but which somehow left just enough technology and knowledge laying around to jump start the early civilizations we know. But they must hold this interpretation against the clear declaration of the Sumerian and all other ancient peoples that the gods were real flesh and blood, present to them, who gave them civilization.

Sitchin at a wall in Hattusas, capital of the Hittite Empire in central Turkey, established about 2000 B.C., showing how the huge megalithic stones closely resemble the advanced building style of the Incas.

The physical locations of the ancient legends as mythic has been gradually disproven, beginning with Schliemann, who literally broke open the seal of myth, and completed with the re-discovery of all the ancient and often "mythic" cities and centers on all continents.

The events involving the "gods" of ancient times and the technology attributed to them, considered as myth and naive legend, has been gradually disproven, beginning with the discovery of documents from the most ancient cities and reinforced with the discovery of the great library of Ashurbanipal at Nineveh and the gradual accumulation of some two million pieces of artifact and document confirming those events in great detail. The discovery of ooparts, high tech tools, toys, artifacts, and technology along with documentation of advanced scientific knowledge ostensibly out of place in time along with astronomical knowledge of the entire solar system beyond our current level has reinforced the negation of the mythic interpretation.

The interpretation of the "gods," the Anunnaki themselves, as mythic, unreal beings (academic mythologists) and Jungian archetypes (Joseph Campbell) and the relegation of them to schizophrenic hallucination (Julian Jaynes) has been gradually disproven beginning with the acknowledgment of the reality of the events attributed to them; the discounting of the arguments for their unreality due to the seeming fantastic deeds attributed to them by the development of our technology (rockets, lasers, radio communication, genetic engineering, atomic and particle beam weapons) that duplicate those feats. This interpretation has been implemented further by the pioneering exploration and questions posed by von Daniken and then completed by the comprehensive and brilliant demonstrations of Sitchin and Sir Laurence Gardner, the English historian and genealogist. The mythic interpretation has been supported by religions because to recognize the Anunnaki as real would be to open the door to a radical reinterpretation of the entire phenomenon of religion and put into question the real identity of the very deity at center of their belief system. Gardner has brought to light, however, the fact that there exists a robust, highly documented history carrying all the way back to the Anunnaki, possessed by the heterodox tradition of Christianity. This tradition is the one branded heretical and murderously persecuted by the Roman Church before and during the Inquisition. There was no Dark Ages for this tradition, only for those whom the Church wanted to keep in the dark about the real nature of human history.

Now that we have begun by walking on the moon and exploring the solar system and have probes going starward, the possibility of an alien civilization coming here is taken for granted and one coming here from inside our solar system trivial, rather than unreal myth. "Mythinformation," after two hundred years of failure, although still hiding behind tenure in the university, is a dead issue.

The Essence of the Sitchin Paradigm

Working from the same archaeological discoveries, artifacts, and recovered records as archaeologists and linguists have for two hundred years, Sitchin propounds—proves, in the opinion of this author—that the Anunnaki (Sumerian: "those who came down from the heavens"), an advanced civilization from the tenth planet in our solar system, splashed down in the Persian gulf area around 432,000 years ago, colonized the planet, with the purpose of obtaining large quantities of gold. Some 250,000 years ago the recovered documents tell us their lower echelon miners rebelled against the conditions in the mines and the Annunaki directorate decided to create a creature to take their place. Enki, their chief scientist and Ninhursag their chief medical officer, after getting no satisfactory results splicing animal and *Homo erectus* genes, merged their Anunnaki genes with that of *Homo erectus* and produced us, *Homo sapiens*, a genetically bicameral species, for their purposes as slaves. Because we were a hybrid we could not procreate. The demand for us as workers became greater and we were genetically manipulated to reproduce.

Eventually, we became so numerous that some of us were expelled from the Anunnaki city centers, gradually spreading over the planet. Having become a stable genetic stock and developing more precociously than, perhaps, the Anunnaki had anticipated, the Anunnaki began to be attracted to humans as sexual partners and children were born of these unions. This was unacceptable to the majority of the Anunnaki high council and it was decided to wipe out the human population through a flood that was predictable when Nibiru, the tenth in our solar system and the Anunnaki home planet, came through the inner solar system again (around 12,500 years ago) on one of its periodic 3600-year returns. Some humans were saved by the action of the Anunnaki, Enki, who was sympathetic to the humans he had originally genetically created. For thousands of years we were their slaves, their workers, their servants, their soldiers in their political battles among themselves. The Anunnaki used us in the construction of their palaces (we retroproject the religious notion of temple on these now), their cities, their mining and refining complexes and their astronomical installations on all the continents. They expanded from Mesopotamia to Egypt to India to South and Central America and the stamp of their presence can be found in the farthest reaches of the planet.

Around 6000 years ago they, probably realizing that they were going to phase off the planet, began to gradually bring humans to independence. Sumer, a human civilization, amazing in its "sudden" and mature and highly advanced character was set up under their tutelage in Mesopotamia, human kings were inaugurated as go-betweens, foremen of the human populations answering to the Annunaki. Some humans were taught technology, mathematics, astronomy, advanced crafts and the ways of civilized society. The high civilizations of Egypt and Central America arose.

The Anunnaki became somewhat more remote from humans. By around 1250 B.C. they had gone into their final phase-out mode. The human population and the foremen kings, now left on their own, began to fend for themselves. For some three thousand years, subsequently, we humans have been going through a traumatic transition to independence. Proprietary claims made by various groups of humans as to who knew what we should be doing to get the Anunnaki to return or when they returned, perpetuated the palace and social rituals learned under the Anunnaki and sometimes disagreement and strife broke out between them. Religion, as we know it, took form, focused on the "god" or "gods," clearly and unambiguously known to the humans who were in contact with them as imperfect, flesh and blood humanoids, now absent. It was only much later that the Anunnaki were eventually sublimated into cosmic character and status and, later on, mythologized due to remoteness in time.

What Evidence Supports the Sitchin Thesis?

The Astronomical Evidence

A key underpinning of the Sitchin paradigm is the existence, now or in the past, of the tenth planet in our solar system, the home planet of the Anunnaki with the size, orbit, and characteristics described, as Sitchin has demonstrated, in the *Enuma Elish* and corroborated by Harrington.

Tombaugh discovered Pluto in 1930. Christie, of the U.S. Naval Observatory, discovered Charon, Pluto's moon, in 1978. The characteristics of Pluto derivable from the nature of Charon demonstrated that there must still be a large planet undiscovered because Pluto could not be the cause of the residuals, the "wobbles" in the orbital paths of Uranus and Neptune clearly identifiable. The IRAS (Infrared Astronomical Satellite), during 1983-84, produced observations of a tenth planet so robust that one of the astronomers on the project said that "all that remains is to name it"—from which point the information has become curiously guarded. In 1992 Harrington and Van Flandern of the Naval Observatory, working with all the information they had at hand, published their findings and opinion that there is, indeed, a tenth planet, even calling it an "intruder" planet. Andersen of JPL later publicly expressed his belief that it could possibly be verified any time. The search was narrowed to the southern skies, below the ecliptic. Harrington invited Sitchin, having read his book and translations of the *Enuma Elish*, to a meeting at his office and they correlated the current findings with the ancient records and Harrington acknowledged the detail of the ancient records while indicating where the tenth planet may now be in the solar system.

The Technological Evidence

Ooparts is the term used to describe the purportedly out of place in time artifacts, toys, tools, technical devices, depictions and documents which have come to light through archaeological excavation or discovery. Almost everyone is familiar, through published works or documentaries, with the clay pot batteries still containing the electrodes from the Iraqi desert dated at 2500 B.C., the flyable model airplane from a pyramid tomb, the sophisticated machining of stone requiring the most advanced techniques we know today, the

1000 ton precision cut blocks of stone in a temple foundation that we could not even handle, an ancient relief frieze from an Abydos temple depicting rockets, airplanes and even a helicopter, etc. The most recent and quite amazing oopart is the rediscovery of monoatomic gold by David Hudson (monoatomics are superconductors at room temperature, have anti-gravitic properties and are only now being investigated by the advanced physics community). Hudson's discovery, correlated with the bringing to light, by Gardner, of the suppressed discovery of the Anunnaki gold processing plant on Mt. Horeb by Sir Flinders Petrie in 1889, demonstrates that the monoatomics were already known at least 3000 years ago.

There are also ooparts that date, apparently, to millions of years ago that require serious evaluation and interpretation. Relative to the purpose of this paper, however, consideration is focused on that constellation of ooparts dating from no more than 450,000 years ago, the approximate time of the first Anunnaki arrival on Earth, and primarily on those from the time of the first "sudden" civilizations, 6000 years ago. We have accumulated almost an encyclopedia of such ooparts.

These ooparts, coupled with evidence from many disciplines and the historical records indicate that an advanced civilization existed in those times possessing a high technology and that that civilization was indeed the Anunnaki. Sitchin has no doubt that, all the evidence and the testimony of the early humans themselves, indicate that that civilization was, indeed, the Anunnaki.

The Documentary Evidence

The documentary evidence, i.e. the historical documentation for the existence and deeds of the Anunnaki, has been available to us since the early 1800s. The excavation of the ancients sites of Mesopotamia brought to light the amazingly advanced civilization of Sumer and, with it, thousands of clay tablets containing not only mundane records of commerce, marriages, military actions and astronomical calculation systems but of the history of the Anunnaki themselves. It is clear from these records that the Sumerians knew these aliens to be real flesh and blood. The library of the ruler, Ashurbanipal, at Nineveh was discovered to have burnt down and the clay tablets held there were fired, preserving them for our reading. Even to this day, more and more records are discovered. One of the most impressive finds, in very recent time, has been a sealed, nine foot by 6 foot room in Sippar holding, neatly arranged on shelves, a set of some 400 elaborate clay tablets containing an unbroken

Appendix One: The Alien Question 181

In addition to written cuneiform text, clay tablets were created pictorially through the ancient form of a "rubber stamp" (left), that could be rolled onto wet clay. This image, known as the Adda Seal, shows four gods in their typical roles, including Enki, with water streaming from his shoulders, giving life to the Earth.

record of the history of those ancient times, a sort of time capsule. Again, the evidence is so overwhelming and robust that, if it weren't for those with power enough to suppress, it would have been accepted and our world view changed a century ago or perhaps sooner.

The Genetic Evidence

The recovered records place the location of the Anunnaki laboratory (where the first humans were literally produced) in east central Africa, just above their gold mines. This falls precisely on the map where the mitochondrial DNA "search for Eve" places the first woman *Homo Sapiens sapiens*, and in the same time frame. The evidence of advanced genetic engineering is all there in the ancient documents. Our rapid progress from inception to sending craft to Mars, after only 250,000 years, does not correspond to the million-year periodicities of slow evolutionary development of other species, such as *Homo erectus* before us. The HH paradigm shows that the Creationists were only half wrong and the Evolutionists only half right: there was a creation event but it was a genetic engineering process; there is an evolutionary process but it was interrupted in our regard by the Anunnaki for their own practical purposes. We shall be forced to introduce an additional category: a synthesized species.

Two Definitive Protocols for Proving or Disproving the Sitchin Paradigm

A straightforward approach to prove or disprove the Sitchin paradigm is available from astronomy. A thorough, professional search of our solar system should be able with current technology to determine the existence or non-existence of a tenth planet with the characteristics of size, orbit, orbital periodicity, declination from the ecliptic, as Sitchin has determined from the translations of the ancient records and particularly the *Enuma Elish* document. If that planet is not in our solar system or no evidence can be found for an ejection or cataclysmic destructive event then the Sitchin paradigm falls. This search should be undertaken with highest priority. The matter is sufficiently important to clearing up our historical situation that the academic world should be involved as well as the scientific community. It is the opinion of this author that, in light of the evidence already obtained through the use of the Pioneer 10 and 11 and two Voyager space craft, the Infrared Imaging Satellite (IRAS, 1983-84) and the data available to Harrington when consulting with Sitchin that the search has already been accomplished, in fact that the planet has already been found. It is interesting that Harrington dispatched an appropriate telescope to Black Birch, New Zealand to get a visual confirmation, based on the data leading to the expectation that it would be below the ecliptic in the southern skies at this point in its orbit. On Harrington's early death the scope was immediately called back—as one observer noted, "almost before he was cold." To acknowledge a tenth planet is to open up the possibility of the Anunnaki's existence. The reason for the downplaying of the data, the difficulty of obtaining it, the performance of the scientists publicly speaking about it, all have the same flavor as the Air Force's handling of the Roswell matter.

Obviously, even before any official confirmation of the existence of Nibiru/Planet X in our system and certainly afterward, a focused scan in its direction by a modified SETI type search that used all appropriate parts of the energy spectrum including our own radio and TV common frequencies would be productive in determining the existence of intelligent life continuing to exist thereon. To anticipate a possible mystery: even if the planet it confirmed, it is possible that no intelligent signals may be received. This is a conjecture, only, on the part of the author but, in light of the kind of summary withdrawal and lack of subsequent contact by the Anunnaki, it is not inconceivable that any artificial signal output has been masked. This hypothesis is based on a conclusion that one of the major reasons for their phasing off this planet was not just because they needed a ballistic rocket launch window to reach their planet when it came through the inner solar system last time but because they had come to realize that we needed to be left on our own to find our own species identity. A scan of this type should be undertaken immediately. It should be assumed that our signals have been monitored since their phase-off.

A second mode of proof or disproof is available through genetics. We will shortly have the entire human genome read out. That process and the information available as a result should afford us the opportunity to examine the entire genome for the evidence of the merging of the two species gene codes, *Homo erectus* and Anunnaki. A protocol for such a novel determination would have to be developed. A potential problem may lie in the fact that the melding took place some 250,000-200,000 years ago. A practical spin-off of the effort may be not only the identification of the two codes or, at least, the indication of the basic merging, but evidence for why we have some four thousand cataloged genetic diseases and other species on this planet hardly any at all. It is at least a reasonable speculation that imperfections, due to the complexity of the major merging of the two genomes, is the cause of those defects in the first place. We recommend that this investigation be implemented again with highest priority for the sake of proving or disproving the Sitchin paradigm.

The Negative Factors Still Operant in Human Cultures Springing from Our History as a Genetically Engineered, Subservient Race

The First Factor: Background of Conditioning to Subservience

The overwhelming evidence from the Sitchin paradigm demonstrates conclusively that we were genetically engineered by the Anunnaki, treated as slaves, and then as limited partners—but always as subservient to them. The major ramification (Neil Freer: *Breaking the Godspell*) of the Sitchin explication is that "religion," as we have known it, is the transmutation, the transmutation of the Anunnaki-human relationship of master-subject servitude, of slavery and then limited, subservient partnership. The Anunnaki phased off this planet at the latest around 1250 B.C.

Since then, we have been going through phases of a traumatic transition to species maturity and independence. The major characteristic of this process has been the transmutation in all cultures of them, in particular Enlil/Jehovah in Western culture, into a cosmic deity, commonly called "God" in the Judeo-Christian tradition. *(Is this atheism? No, not as such. It simply is a long overdue correction of some local, intra-solar system politics, relatively rather pedestrian in cosmic perspective. Garden variety atheism can now be understood as an early sign of precocious species adolescent rebellion and questioning of the authority of the obviously all too humanoid characteristics of the particular local Nefilim "god" of the Hebrew tribe and Christianity, Yahweh/Jehovah. The new paradigm, once the ancient, subservient godspell is dispelled, simply frees us to go one on one with the universe and to seek directly whatever unthinkable or thinkable ultimate principle is behind it.)* In a later phase we have mythologized them into unreal beings and then, more "sophisticatedly" into psychological archetypes. Only with cumulative evidence and restored history through modern scholarship have we now been enabled to grasp the true nature of our genetic creation, our traumatic transition, and the opportunity to emerge from species adolescence and amnesia into species maturity.

The Second Factor: The Babel Factor, the Splintering of the Human Race into Hostile Religions

And then they phased off the colony planet. Pretty much just left without closing the laboratory door, apparently beginning around 1250 B.C.. The foreman-kings are suddenly depicted in the stone carvings, standing where they used to stand when listening to instructions from the master, pointing to the master's now empty chair in utter dismay. The laments are still engraved in the clay tablets: "What do I do when my master is no longer here to instruct me? ...What shall I tell the people?" We went into grief, despair, denial. We blamed ourselves and looked to the sky for their return. The good kings did their best, the leaders sometimes were told to go up the mountain to get some instructions, long distance from space, or make a wooden box lined with metal just so to act as a receiver. "Now hear this." Finally, we were alone and in confusion, beginning to fight over who still knew what the master really said, really meant, what we really should be doing if he did show up. Service at their table transmuted into ritual sacrifice of food; attendance at their baths turned into bathing and clothing of surrogate statues of them. Gradually, the routine services turned into cargo-cult rituals and their palaces became empty temples. And the less than good kings began to take advantage, began to swagger. Sometimes they got away with it on their own. Sometimes the people, in desperation, raised their king to a symbolic god. And the god-king and the seed of the notion of the "divine right of kings" became. And the chief servants went along with it because it was to their advantage to become known as priests, or to preserve their jobs and status. And those who had been taught, seeing that the advanced knowledge of technologies and science and the arts, learned as part of their function (writing, mathematics, astronomy, science, metallurgy, and the fine crafts in general), was being lost, set an agenda to preserve it. In the face of misunderstanding and threat, they disguised it, withdrew it, hid it. And the "occult" became.

Eventually, the situation evolved to a very macabre stage. In an effort to demonstrate our subservience, and zeal to make things right if they would just come back, we kept the rules, we maintained the routines of service but, after a long time of disappointment, we reached a point of abject, abysmal desperation where we would do anything to get them to come back—and we did. Remembering the Nefilim males' attraction to our young women, we began to cut their hearts out on top of the empty pyramidal palaces in a collective, craven, pleading shriek to the heavens—from whence they had come and gone. But that unspeakable and unappreciated horror could not last: we began to doubt, to entertain frightening cynicism, secret thoughts of independence, and "why bother?"

Slowly, a classic dissociative process developed due to separation in time, and we began to sublimate the once flesh and blood Nefilim into cosmic absolutes, and their personalities into mythic archetypes. Looking back over the history of our species, the traumatic transition we have gone through might well be characterized as the creation of the concept of a cosmic God, by us, through a series of psychological mutational phases. Eventually, we simply began to forget.

The transition from species amnesia to species maturity has been a very traumatic passage. Breaking the godspell has seen us go through the stages of abandonment to dissociation, to transmutation, to religion, to rebellion, and now to recovery. It is analogous to the dysfunctional family syndrome on a planetary scale.

So, down to our day, incredibly, we have remained still Babel-factored for good crowd control, broken into tribes each proprietarily telling the other that ours is the only accurate tradition of what some particular "god" intended, what rules to follow, what we should be doing to demonstrate we are still loyal and docile servants. Sometimes we just kill each other over it. And persecutions, Crusades, Jihads, Inquisitions, evil empires, the saved and the damned, the martyr, the infidel, the saint, the protestant, the fundamentalist, the atheist, became—and remain.

The Third Factor: A Tradition of Absolutism, Suppression and Repression

It is the nature of the historical events by which Yahweh/Jehovah became the monotheistic (single, supreme—and alien) "god" of the Hebrews, which furnishes the third key to how the UFO/Alien and the Sitchin Human History Paradigm are interrelated.

Modern scholarship, working on the foundations laid as far back as the German school, has reassessed the Old Testament. When the Mesopotamian records began to be unearthed in the 1800s, it was realized that the history revealed from 4000 B.C. forward, was the source of the history of the Old Testament. The Jews, confined to captivity by the Babylonians by their "god" Jehovah, had drawn on that history and committed forgery (Sitchin) by rewriting it to their need to establish Enlil/Jehovah as their supreme ruler. That history shows clearly that two Anunnaki brothers, Enlil and Enki, had always been at odds with each other personally and politically. Enki was the Anunnaki scientist who, together with his half-sister scientist sister, Ninhursag, had created humans and had always been favorable to them. Enlil had always had reservations about humans and dominated them with severity.

Gardner has made the case *(Bloodline of the Holy Grail; Genesis of the Grail Kings)* that when the Old Testament referred to The Lord (Adonai, Enki) it was when good things were being done to or for the Hebrews. When terrible things were being done or allowed to happen to them, the reference was always to Jehovah/Yahweh/Enlil, and it was to Enlil's dominance that they finally capitulated and worshipped in fear. Enki (The Lord, Adonai) initiated a bloodline of human leaders, further enhanced with Anunnaki genes, and taught the advanced scientific knowledge they possessed (Gardner). This royal bloodline, coming down through David and the anointed messiahs (anointed ones), was recognized but treated ambiguously by the large faction of Hebrews who paid allegiance to Enlil. The Old Testament, a collection of books from which some considered unacceptable, promulgates a religious attitude based on subservience and the "fear of God." It is this attitude, an extension of the ancient master-slave relationship, which is at root of Western culture and the pervasive looking to the holders of power and dominance as ultimate and often absolute authority.

The scenario replayed itself when the strain of Judaism that eventually became known as Judeo-Christian allied itself with Rome and became the Roman Church. It perpetuated the Enlil-type fear of God tradition and, in its turn, suppressed, persecuted and brutalized the human-centered strain of Christianity springing from the tradition fostered by Enki.

It was this powerful religion of the Bishops and the Inquisition which could torture, main and kill to dominate and control, that also controlled and dictated to the early Universities. Our schools of higher "learning" still parade the trappings of the Medieval university on ceremonial occasions and, all too often, in their limitation of discussion to approved subjects.

This policy and position of dominant absolute authority on the part of the Roman Church extended itself gradually in the modality of the Roman political and military way and controlled and formed governments and government policies through kings and queens whose crowns were bestowed by the Church. Its policies unchanged, the Inquisition exists under the title of the Sacred Congregation. The latter day solution to the religious mayhem, always just under the surface, developed in the U. S. Constitution, still saw it necessary to give deference to the fearful God of the Judeo-Christian tradition, Yahweh/Jehovah-Enlil the Anunnaki, alien "god."

Strong Similarities and Critical Interrelationships Between the UFOA and Sitchin HH Paradigm

The focus of the control and suppression of information turns out to be identical between: 1) The existence and presence, action and interaction of an **alien**, *intra*-solar system civilization in the past and possibly contemporaneously (HH); and 2) the existence and presence, action and interaction of an **alien**, *extra*-solar system civilization in the past and contemporaneously (UFOA).

The type of authority and their agenda in enacting the control and suppression are similar: the dominant power players in the Judeo and Christian contexts working to patronizingly consolidate a proprietary religio-political regime in self-interest and corrupted from the original ideal; the dominant power players in our society working, probably sincerely at first but, subsequently, patronizingly, to consolidate a political regime in self-interest and corrupted from the Democratic ideal.

The methodology of the use of suppression of information, manipulation of the pertinent history, deception, the use of threat, intimidation, and force is similar and sometimes identical: the billy-club slapped across the palm to emphasize the threat of death to the daughter of a witness at Roswell echoes the Inquisitional threats and execution of "heretics;" the Project Blue Book agenda mirrors the Egyptian Exploration Fund's suppression and expunging of Petrie's publication of his find of the Annunaki gold processing plant at Mt. Horeb (Gardner: *Genesis Of the Grail Kings*).

It is not surprising, therefore, in light of our half-alien but subservient slave background, that we have tolerated the patronizing forgeries and abuses of authority that have been exercised by those who have controlled the UFO/Alien situation since at least the 1940's.

It is not surprising that so many react, almost reflexively, to the possibility of another race coming here from the stars or a tenth planet in our own solar system by immediately assuming their superiority and benevolence, or their power to control. If we have been looking to the sky for some three thousand years for "Daddy" to return from where the Anunnaki went when phasing off the planet, waiting for their return to make everything right and tell us what to do, we put ourselves in the dangerous and highly vulnerable position of being taken over by anything that happens to show up here—even if they are androids. We must break this godspell to become fully conscious, effective, and independent.

It is not surprising that even those who recognize the reality of the alien presence now and the half-alien nature of our own genetic background can still be taken in by demands for subservience. Some New Age lecturers would lead people up the mountain where they expect the space ship to land and the rescued to be incorporated into some alien sub-culture. Some would claim that we should allow ourselves to become GI-Joes in some alien conflict between purported light and dark forces so that we can be rewarded by the victorious light leader and given advanced technology at the victory picnic.

Consider even the U.S. Constitution in the godspell perspective: it was constructed to create a society where a religiously pluralistic population could coexist with the minimum of inter-denominational mayhem. A result of this enforced acceptance of Babel-factored plurality has been an uncomfortable protocol of avoidance of discussion and an attitude that any criticism is automatically partisan prejudice. This makes extremely difficult any impartial reexamination and evaluation of the history of the race because it is, in effect, inescapably, some denomination's "religious" history.

The religious background and belief systems of UFO investigators, politicians, and scientists cause internal conflicts that often enervate their efforts. The degree of evolvement of the consciousness of the scientist, the scholar, the politician, the philosopher, the UFO investigator, determines the level of effectiveness of their actions. The most expert of UFO investigators who is still looking for some superior being to show up to help us out, "save" us, instruct us, is looking through an outmoded and restrictive, even submissive, filter. The scientist who ignores or denies the evidence for the alien presence, present and past, due to peer, grant, government or religious pressures, is just as limited. The denial or ignoring of the evidence of alien presence by SETI, present and past, and directly connected with our own origins, is analogous to the denial or ignoring of the archaeological evidence for the presence and role of the Anunnaki in our past by the sciences and religions of the world.

The attitudes we have exhibited, the ways in which we have acted, and the way in which we have let ourselves be manipulated by the controlling powers with regard to UFO/Alien presence and our own species' history, and the postures we continue to exhibit, clearly are the direct offshoot of our ancient subservient godspell background and history.

Integration of the Two Parts of the Alien Paradigm Can Move Us to a New Plateau of Species Existence

It is the conviction of this author that, unless and until we restore our true history, attain a generic, consensual definition and understanding of what a human being is, and thereby step out of species adolescence, we shall not resolve the current UFO/alien questions fully because we will not have the species' maturity and planetary unity to be able to interact gracefully with a strange species, knowing easily what is acceptable and unacceptable for both of us. This is simply another facet of the reasoning by those who, in the past, felt desperately compelled, militarily and diplomatically, to deal with the incoming alien greys in ways to keep the matter as secret as possible.

Restoration of our true half-alien history, however, will free us to attain the unassailable species integrity to enable us to demand and present credentials, determine intent, agenda, and negotiate confidently so that we are accepted into stellar society with full dignity. It will enable us to have the individual and species self-confidence and perspective that will prevent us from being manipulated, intimidated, or conquered by whomever is here, or shows up here, in the future. Only this kind of integration will allow us to gain explanations and understanding of many details of both the HH and UFOA scenarios.

Practical Advantages Derived From the Integration of the UFOA and HH Paradigms

The elucidation of the Anunnaki alien presence in the past explains the presence of ooparts, the puzzles concerning "sudden" civilizations, our non-standard evolutionary progress, our unique gene code, and resolves the Creationist-Evolutionary conflict. The understanding of our bicameral racial heritages, *Homo erectus* and Anunnaki, and our genetic creation for pragmatic Anunnaki purposes, may explain why we have four thousand plus genetic diseases due to imperfections in the genetic synthesis, while other species on this planet have few or none.

A more precise and complete overview of our past enables us to differentiate between myth, mythic beings, and aliens of whatever type have manifest or come here in the past and present, and will aid us in differentiating and dealing with aliens in the future. That we are literally half-alien, genetically, throws the entire question of the alien reality into a far different perspective.

Some Possible Scenarios Opened Up by the Recognition of the Annunaki

There are several possible reasonable scenarios presented by the expansion of the alien paradigm. They are simply listed here, without weighted evaluation, for the consideration of the reader.

A preliminary note: Not long ago, one could be in very serious trouble with religious authorities by expressing belief that there could be other races from other places—much less other dimensions (Giordano Bruno, a monk who claimed this, was burnt at the stake by the Church only a few years before the founding of Harvard University). The notion of dimensions beyond our comfortable three is relatively novel and still partially speculative; physicists still holding for various actual counts. It is understandable, therefore, that an aura of mystery and awe, sometimes almost transcendentally religious, is projected on "dimensionality." The added precision of differentiation afforded by this expansion of perspective removes the mystical halo from the concept of "interdimensional" applied to some aliens. It may well be true, quite probably is true, that some aliens and their technologies and, therefore, their relative consciousness, involve modalities which use or operate in dimensions other than the three that we are accustomed to perceive. Physics, human or alien, however, is still physics—whether of this sub-universe or another. It will be easier to deal with whatever physics manifests or is discovered, as the subliminal mystical elements are dismissed from our thinking and the knee-jerk—or, perhaps, knee-bending—subservient godspell reflex is eliminated.

If Nibiru, the Anunnaki home planet and tenth in our solar system, still exists in orbit in our solar system (not having been involved in some destructive catastrophic or ejection event), there is reasonable expectation that the Anunnaki still exist. The evidence gathered by the investigation using the IRAS in 1983-84 for that planet still existing in our solar system was enough to convince Harrington of the Naval Observatory. The "Nordic" alien type many have reported corresponds in physical appearance most closely to the Annunaki. It is easily conceivable that they could, at this stage of their technological development, come here, either as monitors or even as tourists any time they wish (although, in earlier times, apparently possessing only ballistic, rocket technology, they were limited to certain orbital constraints).

Some greys and other types may be found to be robots and androids of the Annunaki, used as remote probes or perhaps routine monitoring of this planet, as cautiously used envoys, perhaps sacrificed in crashes as a safe, sterile and non-threatening introductory manifestation (Roswell). The correlation with the recorded prophecies in the Mayan Codex of the appearance of many videotaped UFOs over Mexico at the time of the 1991 eclipse of the Sun and subsequently, because of the association of the Anunnaki with the Central American early civilizations, may point to these (upgraded) saucers being Anunnaki.

Some similar greys and other types may be from extra-stellar societies and fully humanoid, or android, and to be differentiated from Anunnaki-associated androids. Some extra-solar system types may be known or unknown to the Anunnaki, friendly with or antagonistic to them, or have some kind of active relationship with them.

It may be that there is, as has been alleged or claimed by some, direct cooperation/collusion with an alien species on the part of some humans of socio-economic international influence, for the purpose of controlling the population and, perhaps, even the planet. In the cases where those aliens turn out to be Annunaki, the two parts of the paradigm will merge completely.

Representations of some creatures in the Annunaki time period in the Middle East bear striking resemblance to the descriptions and depictions of the grey-type aliens known in modern times. Sitchin's interpretations of some of these images, along with their detailed descriptions, are that they were robots and androids developed and used by the Annunaki.

It is this author's opinion that the alien presence matter is simply old and, at the present stage of our collective understanding and reaction to it, is becoming rather boring. The progress we are making with these artificial problems is far behind the leading edge of our evolution, and we suffer from the artificial retardation imposed on us.

It is evident that those who found themselves with the responsibility for handling the UFOA phenomenon from at least the time of Roswell, conspired to conceal it for the purpose of learning the technology for weapons and defense, but equally because of the concern that the general population would be devastatingly disrupted. Restoring our true half-alien history will remove the naive, parochial and religious handicaps and afford a species maturity, cosmic perspective, and independence that may reassure those charged with dealing with the UFOA matter that the disruptions and chaos in the general public anticipated on revelation will definitely not take place. That they have been acting in a patronizing way toward the citizens of this country is, in a real sense, a reflection of their own limitations, a product of their military-type approach, which, as Philip Corso said, existed on a simple "friend or foe" basis. They need an opportunity to inform the public in a way that will save enough face for them, and this could be the item that affords it. They will advance the argument that the public had and has no concept of the dangers and threats from the aliens, no concept of the strangeness of their science, their society, their intentions, and the degree of advancement of their evolution over ours. This level of species consciousness and independence disengages the individual from subservience to, and reliance on, this kind of patronizing authority and they will no longer be needed. We will see the inevitable struggle to preserve their power on the part of the least evolved of them—a graceful recognition of the requisite species maturation and resultant resignation of that power on the part of the more evolved of them.

It is not as if they have possessed exclusive knowledge of the situation all along. The UFOA phenomenon has always held an element of direct contact with the general public through physical manifestations of craft, abduction, and direct communication of information, quite clearly on a gradual, planned and orchestrated basis—at least on the part of some species. Perhaps if those who control realize that we will simply go on without them, they will understand that it is no longer either necessary to patronize the general public, or continue to "protect" the classic fiction (that nothing is going on) from the "ordinary person."

The Next Step

The evaluations of the information contained herein, and decisions whether to currently consider and incorporate it into the agendas of the various organizations addressed, ironically and paradoxically, will be influenced by the same factors elucidated herein as counterproductive and suppressive.

Some will look to academia or establishment science as a criterion and reject the information for fear of loosing contact with those worlds that survive on government grants.

Some will deem it too difficult because the UFOA matter is already so controversial that to incorporate it will, in their minds, complexify the situation to the point of being unwieldy—or too politically incorrect.

Some will reject it simply because they feel it will offend religious groups and alienate those who might otherwise give support or at least be open to influence. It is a thing of great mystification and awe to witness a champion of the UFOA cause, who is ready to take on any governmental authority, cower before some "religious" institutional authority.

Some in the UFOA community will reject it, most ironically, because it contradicts their personal religious, metaphysical, philosophical, or New Age belief system without a serious consideration of the facts.

There are, however, a growing number of those who have freed themselves from the imprints and conditioning of their cultures and their religions sufficiently enough to integrate both halves of the alien paradigm into their thinking and worldview. They have reached the genetic enlightenment afforded by the restoration of our true history and it has enabled them to expand to integrate the UFOA phase. This expansion has empowered them to think and decide for themselves concerning the overwhelming mass of evidence for both the UFOA presence and the HH Sitchin worldview, and to move beyond both governmental and religious obfuscation and obstructions. For them, the Paradigm Clock has struck twelve long ago, and they are now about the business of becoming their own evolutionary artists, preparing to meet the aliens, and prepared to restore relations with the Anunnaki. They have already experienced and passed beyond the profound paradigm shift anticipated and predicted by so many. In a real sense, they are the paradigm shift: they are finished with this phase of investigation, speculation, the forcing of revelation. The current UFOA situation is like an old 1940's movie: the resistance to the HH Sitchin phase plays out like an academic soap opera in the faculty room. Those beyond it are free to answer the question, "What does it all mean?" with "Whatever we wish to make it" because they are free to experience the universe as a plenum of radical freedom in which interaction with other species is only another significant activity.

If the aliens choose those with whom they will make first overt, public contact it will most likely be from this group. They are their own persons with an unassailable integrity, self-knowledge, confidence, and sensitivity that will allow them to interact easily and intelligently without fear, subservience, or cramping preconceptions.

It is from within this group that the clarity of vision for the next phase will come, is already manifesting: the simple, logical, gathering and implementation of contact-ready teams. They know who they are and they easily recognize their kind. They know that they must be beyond the archaic divisions of parochial, social, national, and political turf borders. They know they cannot be without a common human history, cannot be at odds with each other in their basic conception of what a human being is, cannot be separated on the basis of religious belief. They know they cannot wait for the masses of the bell curve because they are the vanguard and they know their genetic evolutionary role well.

It is this expanded, radically free, self-confident and fully independent consciousness that is the key to the next step: direct, overt, contact, communication and species interchange with whomever chooses to initiate it first in that mode. It may be a species from outside our solar system; it may be a species from inside our solar system and, in that case, most probably the Anunnaki. It will make little difference to these futant humans because they will have the information and perspective to comprehend, evaluate and interact.

The first project of these new humans will be the development of a universal translator modality based on the principle of self-reference. The general principles and practical applications have already been established. The author intends this to be the subject of a second paper. [Ed. Note: See Appendix II)

Selected Reading

Freer, Neil; *Breaking the Godspell* (New Falcon, 1987; The Book Tree, 2000); *God Games: What Do You Do Forever?* (The Book Tree, 1998); *Sapiens Rising: The View from 2100* (The Book Tree, 2015).

Sitchin, Zecharia; *The Twelfth Planet*; *The Stairway to Heaven*; *The Wars of Gods and Men*; *The Lost Realms*; *Genesis Revisited*, *When Time Began*; *The Cosmic Code*; *The End of Days: Armageddon and Prophecies of the Return*; *The Earth Chronicles Handbook: A Comprehensive Guide to the Seven Books of the Earth Chronicles*; *There Were Giants Upon the Earth: Gods, Demigods, and Human Ancestry—The Evidence of Alien DNA*. (Bear & Co. HC or Avon paperbacks)

Gardner, Sir Laurence; *Bloodline of the Holy Grail* (Element Books, 1996); *Genesis of the Grail Kings* (Bantam Press, 1999).

APPENDIX II

SAVING SAPIENS
A White Paper to Leaders of the World

A BRIEFING FOR ALL HEADS OF STATE OF PLANET EARTH

THE ESSENTIAL SURVIVAL OPERATIONS NECESSARY TO PRESERVE OUR SPECIES' EXISTENCE

This briefing is intended to furnish you and your staff with a planetary overview. It is designed to enable you, in cooperation with the other Heads of State and world leaders in every area, to envision and develop a cooperative planetary system of adjustment and upgrade. This system will overcome the plague of problems facing our species and work toward an entirely new generic human society commensurate with the consciousness of the new human level of our species' development. We consider ourselves primarily planetary citizens and our focus and agenda is cosmic.

All peoples of the Earth recognize and are affected by the threatening planetary problems we face. They are a complex host of political, economic, social and physical issues viewed through the lens of diverse cultures at differing levels of economic and technological development.

Thoughtful and concerned individuals and social, political and scientific groups, advance solutions with the best of intentions but without the comprehensive quality of life results.

Some, with less than magnanimous agendas, manipulate and take selfish advantage of the misfortunes confronting us and many are hurt.

Recognizing the Problems and Solutions

Our 140 years of combined study, research, experience and analysis show us, however, that there are little recognized, potentially fatal, flaws in the conceptualizations of the nature and scope of the problems and the resolutions offered. The solutions advanced are generally from within the contexts which have become the source of the problems. It is no longer possible to solve or resolve the problems of our time within the framework of our previous context. The context itself and its parameters must be redefined. It is no longer adequate to "think outside the box"—the "box" itself must be reevaluated and redefined.

We are not working from the largest, broadest, overall planetary view.

We blame "the other" for the problems when the cause is, in essence, the lack of recognition and the denial of our unique evolutionary trajectory and progress.

We allow the powers-that-be to continue suppression of information, historical, exopolitical and scientific, vital to our survival and to maintain the Babel Factor separations that keep us divided and in conflict through political, sociological and economic ideologies, religious doctrines and absolutes, propaganda and manipulation.

Untold millions are being deprived, injured and killed. Generations of our children are being sacrificed. We are close to committing species suicide. We are at an unavoidable tipping point of planetary scale with little time left to remedy the situation. We are not powerless; far from it! *We have accumulated a vast body of factual and scientific knowledge that has the robust potential to resolve our dangerous problems and provide the basis for elucidating and realizing the essential world vision—beyond all second hand "New World Order" schemes contrived within the old context by the elite for the benefit of the elite.* It would be culpable to only hope the populaces, already preoccupied with survival, will stumble randomly into the light. The dimensions of the world vision are novel enough that it will take the wisdom and skill of enlightened Heads of State, acting as true servants of the people, to lead, educate, unify, direct, facilitate and inspire.

The Status Quo: The Broadest Planetary Overview

We are being offered a place in stellar society. There is absolutely no ambiguity about the reality of extraterrestrial contact and interaction with our world. Its ancient roots are documented by hard archaeological evidence. We have been made aware of the rules for entrance into cosmic society: you matriculate as a unified, peaceful species—not tribe, country, or civilization, but as a species—or you are not allowed in. For sixty years, a counterintelligence program has successfully been run against the United States public to misinform and mystify the alien subject. Other countries have unfortunately followed suite. Only recently have several countries begun to independently acknowledge and disclose. Included in the cover-up are advanced technologies such as free energy and antigravity. Powerful money interests and energy industries do not want to be replaced by these technologies.

The Essential Challenge to any Head of State

Our extended studies and analysis show clearly that the emergent challenge to the sociopolitical skill and creativity of any Head of State is a radically new worldview of profound import forming in the common consciousness. Certainly the immediate practical problems of poverty, inequality, social unrest, conflict and injustice are recognized but, in a real sense, they are subsumed by this overarching, new planetary paradigm that knows no borders. Whether one happens to subscribe to it as an individual or Head of State is irrelevant. Because it touches the quick of our traditional definitions of the human and cuts across the boundaries of cultures, science, and religion with a volume of information very difficult to refute, it is unavoidable. This brief is meant to inform and prepare the Head of State to intelligently comprehend and deal with this evolving consciousness.

The Essence of this Developing World View

Sourced in the archaeological, historical and linguistic information and data accumulated over the last one hundred and fifty years, particularly from the Middle East as well as the rest of the world, the new paradigm says that the transcultural "gods" known to all the ancient civilizations were not mythological. Unequivocally they were real flesh and blood humanoids, and alien. Physically, the Anunnaki (Sumerian: "those who came down," meaning from the "heavens," from space) were/are taller and huskier than we are—male and female, with the males bearded. The reasons, previously advanced, that the "gods" were mythological because of the seemingly fantastic powers and deeds attributed to them—hurling bolts of "lightning," creating humans, flying in the atmosphere and space, etc.—have been rendered invalid by our advanced sciences of lasers, atomic weapons, genetics, space flight. The Anunnaki taught us that their home planet is Nibiru (Planet X, tenth member of our solar system) and they had colonized Earth 500,000 years ago. They were here for the abundant gold on Earth, and genetically created us as a slave race by combining their genes with those of *Homo erectus* to work their gold mines, some of which have been rediscovered in East Central Africa and dated to at least 100,000 years old. We progressed from being their slave animals to limited partnership and, since they phased back and off Earth, we are now moving out of a 3000-year traumatic transition into racial independence, a rapid metamorphic process moving far faster than standard evolution, under the imperative of our advanced Anunnaki genetic component.

Central to the history of the Anunnaki's occupation of the planet was the interaction between two brothers, Enlil and Enki. Enki and Enlil shared the direction of their colony here on Earth and were melded together in the Book of Genesis as a single entity—Elohim, a plural used as a singular. Enki was/is Adonai the Lord. Enlil was/is Jehovah/Yahweh. Enki was their chief scientist who was responsible, with his sister Ninhursag (their chief medical officer), for the genetic creation of our species. Enki was sympathetic towards humans and promoted our interests. Enlil, eventually known as Jehovah/YHWH of the Old Testament, maintained the position that humans were to remain slaves, totally subservient to the Anunnaki and him, especially. The Book of Genesis is a theopolitically skewed rewrite of the three thousand year older, original, precise Sumerian historical texts. The Anunnaki are known in the Old Testament of the Bible as Anakeim, Nefilim.

The Anunnaki phased off this planet at the latest around 1250 B.C. For some three thousand years, subsequently, we humans have been going through a very traumatic transition to racial independence. If this history is indeed true, then the major ramification that demands our consideration is that the "God-fearing" religions are extensions, sublimations of the original master-slave relationship we were created under and we are only now stepping out of species adolescence. Those who promulgate this disconcerting paradigm, however, put down the caveat that *this is not atheism. It has nothing to do with whether there is a thinkable or unthinkable supracosmic entity which/ who is responsible for all that is and could create an infinite number of universes simply by thinking of them. It is simply the restoration of our true natural sociological beginnings and history and status quo. The attribution of supernatural powers and infinite nature to the Elohim came only gradually, after the fact. It is obvious that the God-fearing religions will not want to accept these historical facts when they become better known, and will resist. But, if true, these mainstream faiths have a responsibility to rethink their future in terms of service to save the species.*

Scientific evidence advanced in support of these ancient claims comes from modern astronomy. The home planet of the Anunnaki is Nibiru (Sumerian: Planet of the Crossing). It is the tenth planet in our solar system, Planet X. Similar to Uranus in size, it is traversing an extremely elongated, elliptical orbit of about 3600 years once around our Sun. Its orbit is tipped below the ecliptic plane of the other planets by about 40 degrees. It is a planet, not a failed dwarf star. The Pioneer spacecrafts in 1976 had already returned data that showed definitively that there was no binary star companion to our Sun, although there was solid evidence of a large planetary body. The IRAS, Infrared orbiting telescope, NASA-Dutch project search for Planet X, discovered it in 1983 and six announcements were made in the mainstream press. The sixth announcement by Ray Reynolds of JPL and the IRAS astronomer team, in the *New York Times*, Jan 11, 1983, stated: "Astronomers are so sure of the tenth planet that they think there is nothing left but to name it."

At that point, suppression of the information was put into place. The suppression has the astronomers thoroughly intimidated. But X/Nibiru is incoming. Its narrow elliptical orbit is bringing it up from below, south of the ecliptic to slingshot around the Sun at perigee between Mars and Jupiter. The gravitational and electromagnetic effects of this Uranus-sized planet are already causing increasingly evident climate and earth changes on our planet. Not all Passings of Nibiru cause catastrophic effects on the Earth. Depending on the relative positions of the Earth, Sun and other planets at Passing, the effects can be cataclysmic and the existence of our species can literally be threatened.

The account of the Flood in the Old Testament is an almost children's story rewrite of the precise and detailed history of the event in the three thousand year older Sumerian records. Whereas the Flood is presented as a kind of tsunami that washed over the Middle East and then subsided in the OT, the reality was that it was a worldwide cataclysmic event. It emptied seas, pushed up mountain ranges, leveled others, flooded vast areas, and left perhaps only a thousand humans alive over the entire planet. The global warming-global cooling, CO_2 increase reasoning, and other similar arguments are misdirection: they are symptoms, not causes. The powers-that-be do not want this information released even though it means potential catastrophic damage to the species because they can do little about it, except (as it can be shown) to build underground, provisioned cities or other bunkered areas for their own survival.

Three forms of suppression are currently taking place that are preventing us from moving forward in the understanding of who we are, where we came from, and where we may be going. Eventually, we may be allowed into stellar society should we mature as a planet and species.

1) The continuance of suppression of alien contact frustrates our most fundamental cosmically oriented evolutionary trajectory. The suppression of acquired alien and/or human developed advanced technology is criminal and based upon power and profit motives. Denial of environmentally benign free energy and antigravity technology forces the prolongation of polluting primitive energy sources which threaten our species' health and safety.

2) The denial and suppression of our real history as a part alien species keeps us in ignorance of our real nature, allows the continuance of the godspell slave code religions and fosters the conflicts and often wars based around religious absolutes and thereby thwarts our rapid and intelligent evolving and achieving the planetary, peace and species unity that would qualify us for stellar society.

3) The denial and suppression of the information about Planet Nibiru incoming puts our entire species at risk. Even if this Passing turns out to be a "milder" one as some intelligence insiders have told us they have been informed, "mild" can still mean physical upheavaling, destruction, and disruption.

It is not difficult to see that these three major forms of suppression are *inextricably interrelated*. It does not matter from which topic of the three that one begins. As example: Open the topic of the existence, characteristics and potential threat of the incoming Nibiru—which correspond identically to what the Anunnaki taught us and had recorded in the ancient recovered documents on clay tablets—and immediately the subject of the Anunnaki as our creators is broached, which leads directly to the alien presence in general. The suppression is thorough: the academic communities of the world, whose major responsibility is the education and informing of the public, are simply intimidated by funding fright.

There are more than seven billion people on this planet, with eight billion projected by 2024. There is no longer space or opportunity for the competitive systems that have brought us this far. The primitive systems that produced winners and losers are no longer adequate or sufficiently human. We must move beyond competition to planetary cooperation or we shall perish as a species. It is necessary to evolve beyond money, capitalism, socialism, communism, fascism, theocracy—virtually all the forms of economic, social governance and conflict resolution we have known to this point will have to be completely reborn in creative ways or, in most cases, abandoned.

We already have at hand four major technologies that, combined, afford us the powerful means to achieve the material peaceful revolution required.

These four are: Artificial Intelligence, Nanotechnology, Free Energy, and Magneto-Gravitation. These technologies properly combined will make the apparent necessity to compete for limited resources an illusion. The problems of primitive polluting technologies will be eliminated. The New Humans, already being born, for whom our paranormal is becoming their norm, and whose vision of the future expects immortality, absolute knowledge, cosmic citizenship and perfect physical and genetic health, require a New Planetary Society. It is for the children, our future, that we must make it so.

We cannot use the same thinking to solve our problems as we used when we created them. —Albert Einstein

A Four-Part Strategy for the Heads of State of the World to Cooperatively Bring About the New Human Planetary Society

Project Stellar Humanity

Phase One: The Heads of State of every country consult together, if possible, outside of the U.N. system with its dysfunctional hieratical structure, to agree to cooperate in developing the details of the concept and goals of the New Human Planetary Society. The principal point is that generic humanity is beyond tribe, culture, country, or civilization. Full disclosure of all facets of the alien topic and its ramifications is made simultaneously to all leaders and shared with populations. Advanced technology, alien or human developed, is shared and released for the benefit of all. Any agreements, contracts or treaties made with alien species are revealed openly by all nations. Amnesty is granted for all previously involved in government and/or other suppression and cover-up, unless actual crime was involved.

Phase Two: The Heads of State inform their people of the necessity, nature, and benefit of the plan. They solicit input from every individual and faction, and mandate their academic and intellectual communities to do in-depth studies and white papers on the anticipated consequences of what is ahead. The essential need to evolve from primitive competition to cooperation will be emphasized. The planetary scope of the program recognizes and supports the worldwide, evolved movements for individual rights, dignity and *ubuntu* (a philosophy of compassion and universal sharing) and subsumes them all. A date is set for finalization of the plan, agreed upon by all Heads of State who have agreed to participate. If only one Head of State is amenable to the vision and the plan, she or he should pursue it for their nation as a model for the rest of the world to contemplate.

Phase Three: It can be anticipated that difficult times are ahead for millions of believers. The Heads of State of countries that share the same religious beliefs may decide that they should meet together with spiritual leaders of their faith. The enlightened efforts of H. M. King Abdullah II bin Al-Hussein of Jordan in bringing together twenty-four of the most senior religious scholars from around the world representing all the branches and schools of Islam, resulting in the issuance of the Amman Message on the 9th of November 2004, may be taken as a model approach. From what we already know about the true origins of religions and as alien contact matures, perhaps new revelations about how and why political and other influences have changed beliefs and practices, and a deep dialogue on the issues should be undertaken. Theocratic governments should be respected, as should the religious beliefs of all individuals. But this respect will have no impact and provide little relief from the consequences of technological, economic and political changes that will happen and are needed to save the species from itself. Perhaps the most powerful example of this issue will be with Islamic nations, whose economic viability is based upon carbon resources. The market for carbon-based fuels will virtually disappear. The economic and political consequences of this would be hugely destabilizing to all sectors of society, including religion, unless it had been planned for and leaders with wisdom had prepared constructively for these changes.

Phase Four: There is no longer the possibility of patching up the old primitive sociopolitical paradigm. The consciousness of even the ordinary human has outgrown it. Keeping the doors of perception (and entrance to the cosmos) closed and shuttered, blocks directly the evolutionary trajectory of our species. This radically evolved, dimensionally expanded paradigm must be introduced concomitantly with the introduction of a sociopolitical system of physical support beyond competition, money, and the illusion of limited resources.

The Heads of State cooperatively develop a cosmically oriented perspective for their nations. The entire educational systems at all levels are upgraded to transmit the most accurate information about our beginnings, nature, and current situation. The significance and ramifications of the pooled, disclosed body of information are composed of continually acquired alien and archaeological information, which is critically appraised and correlated by the Heads of State acting as a democratic executive body, but not as a governing body. It gradually develops into a body ready to represent the Earth and act as a welcoming entity in alien contact. Peace and planetary unity is gradually developed and achieved. War is abolished completely and permanently. Militaries are gradually reeducated and transformed into social services. Contact with alien species is sought. Our particular relationship to the Anunnaki, our parent, creating species, is seen as a priority for study and an agenda for implementation. Direct contact with the Anunnaki is invited by us (a now mature and independent species) for reconciliation and mutual benefit.

The Heads of State pursue a cooperative program utilizing the four major technologies (artificial intelligence; free energy; nanotechnology; magneto gravitation) to build a planetary non-competitive system matching the consciousness of the New Human. This new system supplies a basic living support to every person. Each, in turn, will contribute according to their personal talents and proclivities. A peaceful, unified species requires a totally new system of material production of goods and services. This will, in effect, create a leisure society and provide a comfortable living for every individual on the planet. It will also redirect the focus of the common consciousness on dynamic personal evolution and species evolution as stellar citizens.

Essential Reference and Bibliography

Sitchin, Zecharia; *The Twelfth Planet*; *The Stairway to Heaven*; *The Wars of Gods and Men*; *The Lost Realms*; *Genesis Revisited, When Time Began*; *The Cosmic Code*; *The End of Days: Armageddon and Prophecies of the Return*; *The Earth Chronicles Handbook: A Comprehensive Guide to the Seven Books of the Earth Chronicles*; *There Were Giants Upon the Earth: Gods, Demigods, and Human Ancestry—The Evidence of Alien DNA*.

Gardner, Sir Laurence; *Bloodline of the Holy Grail*; *Genesis of the Grail Kings*; *The Origin of God*.

Freer, Neil; *Breaking the Godspell*; *God Games: What Do You Do Forever?*; *Sapiens Rising: The View From 2100*.

ABOUT THE AUTHOR

NEIL FREER (1930-2016) was a generalist, futant, futurist, lecturer, author, poet, and advisory board member of the www.exopolitics.org institute. He has worked with C.B. Scott Jones as co-director of their think tank, Cosmic Humanity. Neil holds a BA in English and did his graduate work in Philosophy and Psychology at the New School for Social Research. He taught college courses in Philosophy and History of Religion, gave private and public seminars and lectures, and has done over three hundred radio and TV interviews.

Neil is the author of *Breaking the Godspell*, which explores the archaeological, astronomical and genetic proofs by the Sumerian scholar, Zecharia Sitchin, for our being a genetically engineered species and presents the ramifications of this new paradigm of human nature that resolves the Creationist-Evolutionary conflict.

In his second book, *God-Games: What Do You Do Forever?*, he explores the ways in which we will live when, individually and collectively, we attain the unassailable integrity afforded by the restoration of our true, part alien genetic history. He outlines the racial maturity of the new planetary civilization and describes the new human.

Neil's third book is *Sapiens Rising: The View From 2100*, which was given in digital format to Michelle and Barack Obama, M. Gorbachev, John Petersen of the Arlington Institute, the Dalai Lama, Pope Benedict, Klaus Schwab (of Davos), Presidents Clinton and Carter, Charlie Rose, and Bill Moyers, among others.

Neil was invited as keynote speaker in February 2010, at the International UFO Congress. His presentation was advertised as Sapiens Rising to Cosmic Citizenship: The Script for a Stellar Species Performance. He has presented at numerous conferences including a presentation to a Hong Kong audience of exopolitical interest via Skype, live from his study in Santa Fe.

As a philosopher, futurist, futant, contactee, and generic human, Neil says: We are already into a profound transmutation which will characterize this 21st as our species' Century of Transformation. We are being invited into stellar society and have the keys to integrate our past and present as the new humans and meet the conditions for acceptance: firm status as a peaceful, unified species. Let us reclaim our planetary identity and dignity, our part-alien cosmic credentials, and prepare to matriculate into the heavens, into stellar society as, finally, *Sapiens sapiens*, the truly doubly wise. There are dangers, but let us face them together. I stand to speak for all of us, a young but wise species, to urge us all to make it so for our children.

Website: http://www.neilfreer.com

www.ingramcontent.com/pod-product-compliance
Lightning Source LLC
Chambersburg PA
CBHW061304110426
42742CB00012BA/2045